THE INTERNATIONAL
WINE AND FOOD SOCIETY'S GUIDE TO

BAKERY

CAKES AND SIMPLE
CONFECTIONERY

THE INTERNATIONAL
WINE AND FOOD SOCIETY'S GUIDE TO

BAKERY

CAKES AND SIMPLE
CONFECTIONERY

MARIA FLORIS

with color photographs by
Kenneth Swain
and drawings by
Leslie Thompson

The International
Wine and Food Society

Bonanza Books
NEW YORK

A Publication of
The International Wine and Food Society Limited

Bonanza Books,
a division of Crown Publishers Inc.,
419 Park Avenue South, New York, N.Y. 10016

Library of Congress Catalog Number 67–21385

This book was designed and produced by
Rainbird Reference Books Limited
Marble Arch House
44 Edgware Road, London W2

Phototypeset in Monophoto Imprint by
Oliver Burridge Filmsetting Limited, Crawley, Sussex
Printed and bound in Yugoslavia

Index : Dorothy Frame

First published, 1968
Second printing, 1970
Revised, second edition, 1971

CONTENTS

American measures are given, where necessary, in brackets.

COLOR PLATES

ILLUSTRATIONS

ACKNOWLEDGMENTS

I would like to thank some of those who so kindly helped me; first, my editors, John Hoare, who encouraged and bullied me alternately, and Mrs Rosemary Joekes. I am grateful to Miss Elizabeth Werner, who typed the manuscript and whose knowledge of cookery was a great help to me. I must mention my sons: George, who typed many drafts and helped in my researches, and Christopher, who did likewise and kept up my spirits besides. I would like to express my thanks to my manager, Mr Ivor Dyer, for his help in testing recipes and for the loan of books. Many of my staff also gave me their time and help in testing recipes. I am grateful to them all.

INTRODUCTION

After writing my first book, and this surprised me that it was a success, I began writing again, but my husband, my partner, my friend, died and I lost heart and nerve. I know time and work are most wonderful healers and the next best thing perhaps is vanity. I had to look right; I had to keep up my home, my household, just as I had done before. When, later, the Editor to the Wine and Food Society wrote that he and Monsieur André Simon would interest themselves in my writing a book again, I was rather interested, more excited and a little bit frightened. My new Editor issued a challenge to me just very casually, that I write a book – only 70,000 words – about bread, buns, rolls, any yeast pastry or cake, cakes, petits fours, *mignons*, gâteaux – anything to do with flour confectionery, and of course, if I would, some easily-made sweets. But the book should be written in such a way that even the greatest simpleton like him could understand. How easy it is to say a few sentences like these. Nobody on earth would believe how very difficult it is to explain sometimes, for me at least, the simplest things, and I am sure I am not quite clever enough to write a book which simpletons could understand. Take a very simple thing, such as *Strudel* – I don't think anything is so easy, but you have to know how to make it. It is very easy to explain, very difficult to do, but I promise you I shall try to do my best and a little more.

Now my Editor wants me to tell you about bread – all kinds of bread, to explain, for instance, what I mean when I say 'use a sour dough'. A sour dough is an ordinary piece of dough which you may keep 3 or 4 days. Everything depends on the temperature. In a warm room it goes sour more quickly, and in a cold room it goes sour less quickly. How much sour dough should you put in with so much flour? Yes, you can weigh the flour, you can weigh the sour dough; this is all true, but how does it come out just right? I experiment twenty times before I can tell you this exactly.

He wants me to tell you all about cakes. How many kinds of cakes – Madeira, Christmas cake, birthday cake, seed cake, oh, so many kinds of cakes. All right, I will give you all the recipes but don't blame me if it does not come out exactly as you wish. Fingertip feeling must play its part. For instance, I know a little story about a wonderful blacksmith who for years and years removed cataracts. Not only did the people from his own village come to him, but from miles and miles around. He would just finish shoeing a horse and not even bother to wash his hands, but would sit the patient down and in 5 minutes remove the cataract and be paid just a shilling or two and the person would go happily home. He did this for years, but once a University professor in Budapest I knew heard about this and decided he would go and see this man. He went and watched him and said to him, 'Now I have seen you, I would like you to come and see how we do it in my hospital'. The blacksmith was very proud and happy and promised next time when he went to Budapest he would visit him. When he did, the professor made him take off his coat and waistcoat and put on a white sterilised coat; and made him wash his hands very thoroughly even though he had nothing to do with the operation. He went into the operating theatre, but only to watch. The professor, his assistant and two nurses prepared the patient and the operation was performed. He was deeply impressed, but very shocked, and went home and never, never again in his life touched eyes – he was just terrified. Now, that is how I feel. I can do all these professional things without thinking and without fear of the outcome, and the outcome must be good. I am a good cook, but I wonder will I ever be able to write down all these things for you. Never mind, I will try and I hope I will succeed.

Now I have to start writing the book. I am foremost a pastrycook, but a lover of bread and of cooking in general. The first subject should be bread. I do this with love because my most loved food is bread; nothing interests me more than bread or rolls. I feel bread is a very important food in our lives. We sit down three times a day to eat and each time we have bread, rolls or buns. Bread is important in many other ways too; it is the food of all the hard-working people and hard-working people are the most important in this world. So bread has to be good, very good.

Because bread is the basic food, therefore, it ought to be made very carefully. You never can, or never should, have short-cuts if you prepare any food. But bread more than anything has to be made very well. There is now a new school which amazes but does not delight me: to mix the flour and other ingredients very lightly and bake it even more lightly. I just don't like it, and don't approve of it. I tell my bakers to

Hungarian oven

knead the bread but with all the ingredients so long and so well until it comes up to the brim, then bake it very carefully, and definitely very well. I like a good crust which for my liking has to be crisp. But I am afraid it is very difficult to prepare a really good bread at home unless you live in the country and have a proper bread oven which could very easily be built at little expense; it is worthwhile. A household oven will never bake as well.

BREAD

We eat bread at least three times a day and I wonder whether anybody ever thinks how bread comes into being. Most of us only know so much as to go or send to the local baker's shop and buy bread and rolls.

A few years ago even that was not necessary, because the local baker would bring to the door the famous 'baker's dozen', – rolls or anything else. But now life is more difficult, so we have to fetch our bread or rolls from the baker's shop.

But now, I like to tell you about bread and as my job is to make cakes, bread and rolls for you, I know a little more than you. You, all of you, take bread for granted, I want now to explain what bread is made of.

We seldom think what an enormous amount of work, together with much knowledge, research and ingenuity, was needed to turn tiny cereal germs into the ultimate refinement of flour. I don't know how it was achieved in the dark ages when hand grinding was in use before mills developed. As a mill could not use untreated corn, the grains were cleaned and separated from the little white wheat seeds, then washed very carefully; after the washing they had to be dried. So development came gradually until we arrive at the very modern methods of scientific and mechanised milling with push-button systems. I personally don't like this but I have to move with the times, because time will not stand still for my benefit. Bread, which is made of flour – wheat or rye – gives, of course, a lot of work and thought. Poor bakers are not appreciated enough for the very hard work they still do to provide us with good bread. I read in one of the papers that a baker in this country was fined heavily for selling short-weight bread in his shop or shops. Next day in my research reading I happened to note that gluten and flour, and so naturally bread too, lose weight. Before I bore you with technical expressions I want to find out how much the average housewife knows about bread.

I have, in my shop, four intelligent girls – one or two of them above average. I asked them, 'Do you know, what is gluten?' One, the most knowledgeable, said: 'I've never heard this word'. The other asked, 'Who?' (meaning 'who is gluten?). The other two simply admitted of having never heard about it. I don't think that it would be right, if I were to say much more than tell you that gluten is a part of the flour and gluten's behaviour in baking and confectionery is a very important factor. Gluten expands, gluten stretches, gluten has a breaking point, gluten can play havoc with cakes and with bread.

Why is it that a cake may sink in the middle, why does the fruit in it sink to the bottom? These are all very difficult questions and all of them are handled very scientifically. Can I explain all this to you? I can just give a few helpful hints and show you a glimpse of how the making of bread has evolved over the centuries.

The Stone Age housewife baked a kind of bread – but from what? I read a story that wheat was sown by ants and that the people learned from them how to grow it. It is true that it was believed that wheat came from Heaven. The first recorded bread was made by the Egyptians, the Jews and the Chinese. Millet and buckwheat are among the earliest known cereals. The grain was crushed between stones and then pounded by hand. I have been told by an Indian friend of my son that in some parts of India the peasants make a form of bread to this day in ways not unlike those used in biblical and even pre-biblical times. In one method a flour and water dough is prepared – the flour is, of course, whole flour and will contain salt if they are wealthy. This dough is then moulded into discs between $\frac{1}{4}$ in. and $\frac{1}{2}$ in. thick and covered over with fat, normally sheep fat. While this is being prepared a small pit has been dug in the sand and a fire is lit in this pit. When the fire has died down to the embers, the pit is cleared of the ashes, the dough discs are put into the pit and covered with hot sand and left there for an hour or more. When the baked bread is removed from the pit it is brushed over with sheep fat to prevent the sand from penetrating the dough. An alternative way in which this dough is baked is again by preparing a fire in a pit and then placing stones, as nearly spherical as can be found, in the fire. When these stones have become hot, they are removed. The dough is wrapped round the stones and left out for the heat of the stones to bake the bread.

While I would not like to say how authentic this story is, it is interesting; and it is especially so to note that this last method is noteworthy as a prototype of a new type of oven in which the bread is cooked from the inside out. It is interesting that this revolutionary new method is only 3,000 years old!

Unleavened bread influenced the lives of the Israelites, Jews and Christians alike. We know much about early unleavened bread from the Old Testament and in particular from the Book of Exodus. This describes the sad fate of the Israelites when Moses led them out of Egypt and they had no time to think or prepare for their long and perilous journey. In their terrible haste they forgot to take with them the vital ingredients for making bread. In those times the method of making dough rise with sour dough was not known. This is simply to keep a small piece of dough for three or four days. It will then ferment and help the bread to rise. So the Israelites had to make their bread without any yeast. Orthodox Jews preserve the memory of the privations of their historic past by fasting eight days before the Passover. This fast was called *pesach*. During this time only unleavened bread is eaten. As far as I am aware, there is no proper recipe for this, but one way to make it at home is this. Mix some sieved white wheat flour into a very soft dough with salted water. Roll out about $\frac{1}{4}$ in. thick and cut into 6 in. squares. Put these on baking sheets, prick very thoroughly and bake in a very low oven. They are dried out rather than baked. The Egyptians baked the first leavened bread, and also were the first to use ovens.

The first leavened bread came about by accident as have so many famous recipes and discoveries. A young Egyptian, perhaps in love, left some bread dough out in the warm sun so that it fermented. This produced the first sour dough. The story is that the young Egyptian's accidental discovery led to beer and yeast being discovered. Breadbaking was learnt from the Egyptians by the Romans; from them the Greeks learned it and then they became the world's greatest bakers in their time. The discovery of sour dough and yeast was revolutionary. Not so long ago Spanish ladies, famous for their beauty, used sour dough with great success as a beauty treatment for their faces. I find sour dough or any cream or mud useful – if you believe in it.

I find the history of bakers most interesting and at the same time, I feel the treatment of bakers has been unjust. The regulations imposed on them were absolutely cruel. The 'baker's dozen' originated in the Middle Ages when the bakers who didn't abide by their oaths, or bake enough bread for each day – or gave short-weight bread were beheaded in England; in Germany they were 'ducked' in public. Even now I find it unjust that every price is going up – travel, cigarettes, beer; nearly everything – no mourners about it. Bakers' wages, very rightly, have to go up as well; good luck to them, they deserve this rise, as baking really is very hard work. But if the price of bread goes up a penny a loaf, there are big headlines in all the papers and politicians make speeches about it in Parliament. The price of bread should go up in England, as it is cheaper than anywhere else. If the price went up, the bread would also be better, much better in quality.

In 1948 Parliament passed an act which prohibited bakers from working more than 26 weeks in any one year on night work. This was a great blow to the smaller bakers who previously had always baked bread on night shift. Three choices faced them. They could either bake half their bread on the day shift, and the rest at night, or they could bake in advance and deep freeze the bread. Or the dough could be made by day, placed in a *retarde* (a kind of cold chamber) and then proved and baked by night. The first way was not satisfactory for the bread was sometimes 18 hours old before it reached the customer, and bread, such as Vienna bread and French bread, is only good when it is fresh out of the oven.

Bread can be placed in a deep freeze and kept for several days, but I am sure that any cooked article loses a lot of its natural flavour when it is frozen. Also the crust of frozen bread becomes very brittle and is liable to break away and fall off, thus spoiling the whole appearance of the bread.

If space is available, retardation is by far superior to freezing, for in this way bakers can ensure that their customers have oven-fresh bread at all times. To do this the loaves are first moulded and placed in tins and on baking sheets; then instead of leaving them in a warm prover as is customary, they are placed in a cold cabinet with a temperature of 45–50°F. (6–10°C.). This reduces the fermentation to a minimum and bread can be kept sweet, i.e. without turning sour, up to a period of 12–16 hours. The bread can then be taken from the cold cabinet and the proving finished in a warmer temperature; it is then baked at the required time. After all, what is better than oven-fresh bread?

Much of the bread in England is made in automatic plant bakeries and requires very little baking skill or attention. Of course, there are various opinions about this 'automation' bread and many people do not like it, and it is often referred to as 'cotton wool' bread. However, it is nicely sliced and wrapped in wax paper and the public (whether they like it or not) buy it, for it is convenient and keeps well. In warm humid weather this bread will easily develop a mould; this is prevented by the addition of a little acid. This kind of bread is not baked in the usual way and often has a clammy feel to its texture.

Oven-bottom bread is baked on the floor of the oven and steam is injected into it. This steam gelatinises the gluten on the surface of the bread and when it has finished baking gives a biscuit crust to the bread. This bread is by far the most appetising of all and is very popular with those who are real connoisseurs.

I think that the bread baked today does not contain enough salt: this makes the taste dull and insipid. I firmly believe that all bread should contain 1 oz. salt to every 3 lb. flour, which is practically 3 lb. salt to every bag of flour (140 lb.).

Yeast and salt are not very good friends and I may go so far as to say that they

Granary French bread; wheatsheaf loaf; white caraway bread; granary loaf;
'Loaves and Fishes' Harvest Festival bread; black Polish rye bread

don't like one another at all. Therefore, in breadmaking they must be added as far away in time as possible from each other. Generally, the salt is added at the first stage with the fat, sugar and water and when the dough is half mixed the yeast (dissolved in a little more water) should then be added. Sometimes in a way that is known as the 'salt delayed action', the salt is added (dissolved in a little water) 1 hour after the first mixing.

Salt does two things in bread. First it gives it flavour and brings out the natural flavour of the wheat and also retards the fermentation slightly. Therefore, the more salt you use the more yeast you must use. Many years ago a very eminent heart specialist often sent his patients to me for salt-free bread and I wondered why. Later he told me that salt hardens the arteries and any person liable to suffer this way should go on a salt-free diet for 3 weeks each year.

Although bread is so very much taken for granted its manufacture is most interesting. Every kind of flour contains a small percentage of natural sugar; the yeast and this sugar start the fermentation in which a gas (carbon dioxide) is formed. While this is going on the other enzymes convert the starch in the flour into maltose and give the yeast more sugar to act upon. With the liberation of this gas the dough becomes full of gas and this is why it rises in the bowl. To ensure that no pockets of gas are left in any one spot the dough is 'knocked back' that is, as much of the gas in the dough is forced out as is possible and then fermentation starts again. The dough is ready for 'moulding' when it has risen for the second time. The dough is divided into pieces of the required weight and then 'moulded' into the required shape.

Breadmaking has not altered much since the old days. Naturally the enormous 'plant' bread factories use different methods, but we are not concerned with them. We try to make bread as it was made by our mothers and their mothers. Breadmaking was – I would love to know whether it will ever be again – sacred and romantic. When we knew that it was the day of the week for breadbaking, it was a very special day, a gay and happy day. We children all rushed home from school, because all of us got one tiny loaf, each received a little, oddly-shaped loaf. It was better than any pastry or cake and we never tired of looking forward to this great treat.

Most housewives find that baking bread at home is very difficult but if they would only follow a few simple rules they would find it very easy and what tastes better than home-made bread? What better than the joyful and proud moment when you watch your family and friends demolish your bread! Home-made bread is 'healthy and honest'.

Breadmaking is simple but as with everything else it has to be precise. Short-cuts in the end make double work or give a bad result. I think there is no truer proverb than 'what is worth doing is worth doing well'.

Austrian rye bread;
White cob loaf; double plait loaf; cob wholemeal loaf

I will tell you the general rules or methods for breadmaking and then give you very many breadbaking recipes. But you should always try to experiment. My mother used to tell us that whatever we did, as long as we made the dough properly, it would bake itself all right. I say that everything takes just so much time. If you overcome the difficulty of starting, whether it be cooking, baking or breadmaking, you will master it after a while, and then you will experiment and goodness only knows what masterpieces will come of your trying. You just go on trying.

There are two important operations or methods of preparing bread dough for baking:

The Long Method. The yeast with liquid, milk or water, sugar, flour and a few other ingredients is left overnight before being mixed with the rest of the dough. Kneading and rising follow.

The Straight Dough Method. All the ingredients are mixed in the order above before the kneading and rising period which follows immediately afterwards.

Mix vigorously and confidently in preparing the dough. To help the distribution of the ingredients and yeast cells a prolonging of the flour blending helps, and dissolving the yeast in the liquid before adding to the flour is also beneficial. Work the dough energetically by hand or with a wooden spoon. I prefer the hand, it is exercising and relaxing, pleasant and satisfying, in a primitive way. The slushing sound; the forward clumping; the hand against the board, all relieve frustrations and inhibitions. Maybe the modern woman will naturally prefer to use an electric mixer. That I do not mind as long as she mixes the dough very thoroughly until it is smooth and silky like satin. It is, some believe, better to knead it lightly and then let it rest. I don't believe in short-cuts in anything and definitely not in cooking or baking. The kneading stretches the gluten into a minute elastic network and thoroughly blends the ingredients. Then use a slightly-floured board. If the dough becomes very sticky, don't panic but sprinkle the working surface with a little flour. The dough will become a little heavier and will rise more slowly and it will make a coarser-textured bread. If it is very coarse a little oil on the hand will help. Knead until the dough becomes smooth and elastic, and you can see small bubbles under the dough. Let it rest for 10 or 15 minutes, then roll the dough into a ball, cover it with a clean cloth and leave to rise in a spot free from draughts, not too cool and not too warm, about 80-90°F. (25-30°C.), a kind of damp-proof box is ideal. We did not make much fuss at home, were not in the least bit scientific, but the result was beautiful

A selection of loaves (reading from top to bottom)
French bread; English bread; cottage loaf; granary loaf

bread. The Hungarian peasant woman who used to make the best bread put the
bread dough, rolled into a ball and covered, to rise in her bed. You can do almost
anything also. Put the dough in a bowl over a pan of hot water, or on the water
heater, or the radiator. You can even put your bread ball on the television set while
you watch your favourite programme. It will add flavour to the bread and maybe
your programme will be improved! Lucky people who live in a sunny climate can
put the dough in the hot sun and let it prove there. To know when the dough has
risen enough, press two fingers or knuckles deeply into the dough and if the dents
remain and the bubbles shyly present themselves and pop, then you can start
shaping or moulding the bread. Cut the dough into equal portions and roll them
into balls. Well-worked dough will obey and will shape to your will. It is best to use
your hand but you can use a rolling pin. Flatten the dough and press out all the

bubbles. Shape the dough into a loaf, sealing and tucking under the inner edges. Place in a greased tin with the seam side at the bottom. For a softer crust, brush the top of the loaf with shortening or butter after baking. For a glossy, crispy crust, brush the top of the loaf with a mixture of egg white and water before baking. Baking stops the rising process. A well-baked loaf should look golden yellow or light brown on the top and bottom. I like my bread crusty and I like a thick crust. A good bread test; if you press a slice of bread together it should regain its original shape immediately. A good loaf has to have holes, but not big ones and not too small.

The loaf should tumble from the tin and should be cooled on a wire rack. Now comes the hardest job of all. Keep the bread from the family until it is cool! Our cook at home could never do this! If you have to cut hot bread, use a saw-edged knife; it helps if the knife is a little warm. Cool loaves completely before putting them into a bread bin or tin, plastic bag or foil. All of these keep bread moist and fresh. Bread will keep in a refrigerator if wrapped in moisture-proof plastic or foil. The smell or aroma of fresh bread should be good, very good, nothing is better than a good bread smell. For me nothing gives more appetite than the smell of fresh bread. Brown bread again depends on taste; it is definitely tastier; it keeps fresh longer and moist, but most people prefer snow-white bread; it is still a status symbol. When I went to America immediately after the Second World War the hotel where I stayed was sorry for me coming from poverty-stricken England and showed me, proudly, snow-white bread which tasted like cotton wool!

Bread with potato in it again not only keeps much better fresh but tastes better; but very few people in this country will touch such bread.

Sometimes customers bring back to my shop a loaf of bread that they bought a few days before, saying that they have just bought it and it is mouldy. They forget that they may have a bread tin containing spores from mould in it already because there are mould spores in countless millions in the atmosphere. The only solution is to sterilise a bread tin; it is not enough merely to wash it. This applies also to keeping Christmas pudding. If you make Christmas pudding at home and the basin is not filled with pudding mixture the water will penetrate the cover and mould soon forms.

But to return to breadmaking. First, you should have a large wooden bowl. I think that is the best. I find it so because we had a huge oblong wooden bowl at home. Put in some warm and sieved flour, make a well in the middle; dissolve the yeast in warm water; put this in the middle of the flour; mix a little, sprinkle it with a little flour on the top and cover it with a linen cloth and let it rise for about 2 hours. When this so-called 'little' dough is risen add the remainder of the flour and if necessary warm water and salt. All of us have different tastes; I find bread made with yeast and sour dough tastier than without sour dough. I love caraway seed in

Breadmaking techniques: kneading bread; knocking back; shaping or 'scaling' bread dough

my bread; very many, especially English people can't stand caraway seed. There are different schools of thought for making bread; some of the health enthusiasts don't believe in kneading, just mix the flour and water and let it rise; mould and bake. I like it very well kneaded till it is silky and produces bubbles; I love the taste of a little maize flour and I like to sprinkle cornflour on the top of the already moulded bread. I like it washed over first with a little milk and sprinkled with cornflour afterwards, but you can do it just as well with water or sprinkle it with wheat or rice flour. It is always better to use warm water. If you like you can grease the tin with lard, oil, or butter; I love butter but not for this purpose. To bake bread in steam produces a very good bread, but to do this at home is complicated, but just before you put your bread in the oven you can sprinkle the whole oven with a little water; this will give a little steam.

But no more red herrings. Here is my first recipe and method, it is very simple and should be easy to follow.

In the following recipes, fresh compressed baker's yeast is recommended as it is easier to work with. Many bakers will sell such yeast and it is generally available at health food stores. Failing fresh compressed yeast, dry yeast can be used and is perfectly satisfactory for most breads. When using dry yeast, use half the recommended quantity. It has a strong, often beery flavour and is therefore not recommended for recipes which contain a high proportion of yeast to flour. Dried yeast takes a little time to dissolve in warm water and is not quite as easy to cream as fresh yeast. Fresh yeast will keep in good condition for two weeks in a refrigerator, well away from the freezing compartment. It should be stored wrapped in greaseproof paper or in a covered bowl.

Ovens should always be preheated before baking as normally it is best to start baking in a hot oven.

BREAD DOUGH (1)

3 lb. (12 cups) plain flour	3 cups (3¾) warm water
1 oz. (1½ cakes) yeast	1 tablespoon (1¼) salt
1 tablespoon (1¼) sugar	1 oz. (2 tablespoons) butter or lard

If using dry yeast, follow the directions on the package. If fresh yeast, cream the yeast and sugar together and add the liquid. Mix the flour and salt together. Add the yeast with its liquid and mix to a firm dough. Soften the butter and add it to the mixture. Knead, adding more flour if required until the dough is smooth and elastic. Put the dough into a warm bowl, cover with a cloth and leave about 1 hour or until it has doubled its bulk. Take it from the bowl, punch it down and knead it until all the air is expelled. Return the dough to the bowl, again cover and let it rise a second time until it has almost doubled its bulk. When the bread has risen, divide the dough into half. Mould the dough into shapes which are higher and rounder in the centres. Put these into well-greased loaf pans. Cover and leave until the dough has risen to the top of the pan. Preheat the oven to 450°F. (233°C.) Mark 8. Put the bread on the lowest shelf and bake for 15 minutes. Lower the heat to 400°F. (205°C.) Mark 6, and continue baking another 35–40 minutes. When the loaves are brown and shrinking slightly at the sides, tumble them out of the pans on to a rack to cool. Tap the bread on the bottom and if it sounds hollow it is a sign the bread is done.

BREAD DOUGH (2)

3 lb. (12 cups) plain flour	1 teaspoon (1¼) sugar
1 tablespoon (1¼) salt	3 cups (3¾) warm water
1 oz. (1½ cakes) yeast	1 tablespoon (1¼) corn oil

Put 2 lb. of the flour into a large bowl, preferably wooden, and add the salt (a little more or less depending on taste – I like it tasty). Mix the yeast and the sugar to a smooth paste. Add the warm water and gradually add a little of the reserved flour until it becomes a thick batter. Lightly sprinkle the top with flour. Make a well in the centre of the flour in the bowl and pour the batter into this. Cover the batter with a cloth and leave the dough in a warm place until it doubles its bulk. Add the remaining flour and knead the dough until it becomes silky and elastic. Knead for 10 – 15 minutes or until the dough leaves the side of the bowl clean. Rub the top of the dough with the oil, cover it with a slightly damp cloth and let the dough rise for 1 hour to again double its bulk. Turn the dough on to a well-floured board and divide into three pieces. Knead each piece again for a few minutes and make into compact shapes to two-thirds fill your loaf pans. Grease the pans with a little oil, add the shaped loaves (the top slightly raised and rounded), cover again and leave the dough in a warm place to rise to the top of the pans. Bake in a preheated oven at 450°F. (233°C.) Mark 8, for 15 minutes, then lower the heat to 400°F. (205°C.) Mark 6, and continue cooking for 35–40 minutes or until the loaves are well browned and shrink slightly from the sides of the pan. Turn the loaves from the pans, tap the bottoms and if they sound hollow the bread is done. Cool on a rack.

BREAD DOUGH (3)

3 lb. (12 cups) plain flour   **2 oz. (3 cakes) yeast**
1 oz. (2 tablespoons) cooking fat   **3 cups (3¾) warm water**
1 tablespoon (1¼) salt

Sieve the flour into a bowl and rub in the fat. Sprinkle in the salt. Dissolve the yeast in the water. Mix this into the flour and make a firm dough. If there is too much liquid, add a little more flour. Proceed as with the previous recipes for kneading, proving etc.

COBS

Use any of the previous doughs. Break off pieces of the required size and shape into rounds. Leave to rest for 1 hour. After 30 minutes mark the tops with four criss-cross slits and then finish proving. When the loaves have doubled their size, place them on well-greased baking sheets and bake at 450°F. (233°C.) Mark 8, middle shelf for 15–20 minutes, lower the heat to 400°F. (205°C.) Mark 6, and continue cooking until the loaves are brown. This method of cooking the bread gives a thick crust.

COTTAGE LOAF

Use any of the bread doughs. Divide into two pieces, one twice as large as the other. Shape into balls. Place both balls of dough on a well-floured baking sheet at least 2 in. apart. Brush lightly with oil. Cover with a cloth and leave to rise and double in bulk. Carefully lift the smaller ball of dough and place on top of the larger one. Make a hole in the top using the thumb and forefinger, and reaching right down to the bottom ball. Notch the sides of both balls of dough with kitchen scissors. Bake on the middle shelf of the oven at 450°F. (233°C.) Mark 8, for 20 minutes. Lower the heat to 400°F. (205°C.) Mark 6, and continue baking until the loaves are brown and done.

ENGLISH BREAD

English bread was mostly used on the Continent as a very special bread. They used it for canapés, special hors d'oeuvre or toasted for tea. English bread can be made in any shape and even in a loaf pan. With the right kind of oven you can make a bottom-baked oven bread out of the mixture.

5 lb. (20 cups) plain flour	**2 oz. (3 cakes) yeast**
1½ tablespoons (2) salt	**warm water**

Sift the flour and salt into a bowl, rub in the yeast, if using fresh (otherwise follow the directions on the package). Add enough warm water to make a soft dough. Cover and leave in a warm place to rise to double its bulk. Turn out the dough and knead it for 10 – 15 minutes or until it is smooth and bubbling. Cover again and leave to rise for another 1½–2 hours. Put the risen dough on to a floured board and cut into 8 or 10 pieces. Shape these into any favourite designs. Place on floured baking (cookie) sheets, cover and leave again to rise until double in size and bake on the top shelf of the oven at 425°F.(216°C.) Mark 7, for 20 – 30 minutes or until golden brown and firm. Test by tapping the bottom of each loaf – if it sounds hollow it is done. Take from the oven and brush with softened butter.

FRENCH BREAD

We hear much about how wonderful French food is. Of course, I appreciate French cooking as much as anybody else, but my greatest joy in France is the bread. In my bakery we make thirty-seven kinds of bread, but there is not one I like so much as real French bread. I think that it never tastes so good as in Paris in the Café de la

Paix, sitting outside in the street, having a glass of wine, with a long, very long sandwich made with wonderful French butter and ham.

I could eat twice as much, if I had not been ashamed before the waiter.

French bread is made from a very special flour, which is not obtainable in Britain. A kind friend of mine took the trouble to obtain for me a recipe from his local baker and sent it to me with a friend who himself brought a few pounds of the flour as well. Even from this French flour my copy of the French bread did not taste the same as the one I ate in the Café de la Paix. Maybe it is the water, as we used to say in Budapest when we got tea from England and tea made from it was still not as good as a cup of tea in England.

I make French bread here with English or Canadian flour, but I mix in a little brown flour. But for me it is still not the same. I give the recipe:

¾ lb. (3 cups) plain flour	1 cup (1¼) warm water
¼ lb. (1 cup) brown flour	1 oz. (2 tablespoons) butter
½ oz. (¾ cake) yeast	pinch of salt
¼ teaspoon (⅓) sugar	corn oil

Cream the yeast and sugar and add the water. Gradually add the flours, then the butter and salt. Mix thoroughly. Knead until the mixture is smooth and silky, cover with a cloth and leave for 90 – 95 minutes in a warm room or until the dough has risen to double its bulk. Knock it back and leave it to rise again. This will take about 35 minutes but much depends on the warmth of the room. (We, in my bakery, prove out bread in a heated prover.) When the bread has sufficiently risen turn it out on a floured board and roll it about ¼ in. thick and then roll it into a long stick shape. It should be between 12 and 14 in. in length. Shape it well with your hands and press down at both ends. Rub a baking (cookie) sheet with corn oil, put the bread on to it, shape it again with your hands, then score it with a sharp knife four or six times about ¼ in. deep. Brush the top of the loaf with cold water and let it rest again for 30 minutes. Bake in the middle shelf of the oven at 425°F. (216°C.) Mark 7, for 15 minutes, lower the heat to 400°F. (205°C.) Mark 6, and bake until firm and brown. Take out and tap the bottom of the loaf to test. If it sounds hollow it is done.

FRENCH LOAVES (Small)

Make a dough as in previous recipe and roll into a similar long stick shape. Cut off pieces to any desired size. With the hands shape these into sticks and point the ends. With a sharp knife score shallow slits over the top. Place on a floured baking (cookie) sheet and leave to rise until they double their size. Put into the oven at 440°F.

(228°C.) Mark 7–8, and bake for 25–30 minutes or until brown and firm. Test as in previous recipe.

FLORIS BREAD

1 lb. (4 cups) plain flour   **1 cup (1¼) mashed potato**
2 teaspoons (2½) salt   **1 oz. (1½ cakes) yeast**
½ tablespoon (⅔) corn oil   **1 cup (1¼) warm water**

Sift the flour with the salt, mix with the oil and potatoes. Dissolve the yeast in the water and pour this into the flour-potato mixture. Mix to a firm dough and leave to rest for 1 hour. Knock it back and then shape into a round. Cut a cross in the top. Place it on a greased baking (cookie) sheet, let it rise to double its bulk and bake in the oven at 450°F. (233°C.) Mark 8, for about 15 minutes. Lower the heat to 400°F. (205°C.) Mark 6, and continue cooking until the bread is brown and firm. Take from the oven, tap the bottom, if it sounds hollow, it is done.

GRANARY BREAD

2 lb. (7 cups) stone-ground flour **1 oz. (1½ cakes) yeast**
1 dessertspoon (1 tablespoon) salt **1 tablespoon (1¼) malt**
corn oil   **2 cups (2½) warm water**

Rub two loaf pans (medium size) with oil. Keep them warm. Mix the flour and salt in a large bowl and warm in a very low oven. Crumble the yeast into a large bowl, add the malt and ½ cup (⅔) warm water. Leave for 10 minutes or until it froths up. Pour this mixture into the flour, add the rest of the water and stir the whole (with a wooden spoon) until the flour is evenly moistened. The dough must be so wet that it is positively slippery. Divide the wet dough into two warmed loaf pans and put them in a warm oven to rise, i.e. 375°F. (191°C.) Mark 5, cover with a cloth and leave for approximately 20 minutes. The dough will rise by about one-third. Remove the cloth. Reheat the oven to 400°F. (205°C.) Mark 6, and bake the loaves for 45–60 minutes. It is important to use a relatively warm oven, otherwise the malt will burn and the loaf will be over-coloured and undercooked. For variety, raisins or chopped and stoned dates may be added to the dough.

HONEY BRAN BREAD

2 lb. (7 cups) wholemeal flour
1 tablespoon (1¼) malt
2 oz. (3 cakes) yeast
2 pints (5 cups) warm water

1 lb. (12 cups) bran
6 oz. (¾ cup) honey
1 tablespoon (1¼) salt

Put half the wholemeal flour with the malt in a bowl. Dissolve ¼ of the yeast in half the water, add this to the flour. Leave for 24 hours in a warm place. Next day, when it will be slightly sour, add the remaining flour, the bran, honey and salt and mix this all together. Dissolve the rest of the yeast in the second half of water. Add this to the flour mixture and mix thoroughly. When completely blended divide into two. Grease two loaf pans and three-quarters fill each with dough. Cover and leave until the dough doubles its size. Bake on the middle shelf of the oven at 425°F. (216°C.) Mark 7, for 16–20 minutes, then lower the oven to 400°F. (205°C.) Mark 6, until the bread is brown and, when taken from the pan, the bottom sounds hollow when tapped. This is an unusual type of bread with a distinctive flavour of its own and contains all the roughage needed in a modern diet.

OAT BREAD

1 cup (1¼) scalded milk
1 cup (1¼) water
1 cup (1¼) golden syrup
1 teaspoon (1¼) salt
1 oz. (1½ cakes) yeast

1½ lb. (6 cups) plain flour
8 oz. (3 cups) rolled oats
fat for greasing
melted butter

This bread should be started early in the day. Cool the milk to about 80°F. (27°C.) and heat the water to the same temperature. Pour both into a bowl and add the syrup and the salt. Crumble and add the yeast and stir until the yeast is dissolved. Add 1 lb. (4 cups) flour and beat until the mixture is smooth. Leave in a warm place until the dough is double its size. Mix in the oats and the remainder of the flour. Knead this until the dough is smooth and elastic. Grease a large bowl, add the kneaded dough and turn it round and round until it is coated lightly all over with fat. Cover and leave until the dough doubles its size. Punch it down thoroughly and again leave it to double its size. Cut the dough into two pieces and put them into well-greased loaf pans. Brush lightly with melted butter and leave until they have risen to the top of the pans. Bake in the middle of the oven at 375°F. (191°C.) Mark 5, for 20 minutes, lower the temperature to 350°F. (175°C.) Mark 4, and continue baking for another 40 – 45 minutes or until the loaves are a lovely brown. This bread is somewhat sweet and is best eaten at tea-time with plenty of butter.

MILK BREAD (1)

2 lb. (8 cups) plain flour
2 oz. (3 cakes) yeast
2 cups (2½) warm milk

1 tablespoon (1¼) corn oil
1 teaspoon (1¼) salt

Dissolve the yeast in the milk. Sift the flour, oil and salt into a warm bowl, add the milk and stir well. Mix to a firm dough. Cover and leave until the dough rises to double its bulk. Divide into two portions and place these on a well-greased baking (cookie) sheet. Cover each piece of dough with a loaf-shaped pan and leave until the dough has risen (peek from time to time to see what is happening under those pans). Bake on the middle shelf of the oven at 420°F. (216°C.) Mark 7 for 35–40 minutes.

MILK BREAD (2)

I have eaten this good milk bread in the Palace Hotel at St Moritz. All the food in the hotel was very good. I got this recipe from the manager of the confectionery department of the hotel kitchen under whose management everything had to be perfect. Now I give you her recipe:

2 lb. (8 cups) plain flour
1 oz. (1½ cakes) yeast
1 cup (1¼) warm milk
1 tablespoon (1¼) salt
1 tablespoon (1¼) granulated
  sugar

2 eggs, lightly beaten
1 oz. diamalt powder (optional)
4 oz. (½ cup) butter
extra milk

Sift the flour into a warm bowl and keep it warm. Make a well in the centre. Dilute the yeast with a little milk and pour this into the well. Add the salt and sugar, mix well, then add the rest of the milk – the dough must be firm but not hard. If necessary add a little more milk. Beat in the eggs and the *diamalt* (if using), mix thoroughly, add the butter slowly, little by little. Work the dough until it is smooth and silky and let it rest for 1½ hours. Grease 2 oblong loaf pans – each 1 lb. size – and three-quarters fill each with the dough. Leave to rise until the dough reaches the top of the pans; brush lightly with milk and bake in the top shelf of the oven at 400°F. (205°C.) Mark 6, for 30 – 40 minutes. N.B. *Diamalt* is a German product used in bread mixtures for added flavour. It can be omitted from this recipe without harm.

NEWBARNS FRUIT LOAF

½ lb. (1 cup) butter
½ lb. (1 cup) caster sugar
1 lb. (4 cups) plain flour
2 teaspoons (2½) baking powder
2 eggs, beaten
½ lb. (1⅓ cups) currants

½ lb. (1⅓ cups) sultanas (white raisins)
2 oz. (⅓ cup) almonds, blanched and chopped
1½ cups (2) warm milk

Cream the butter with the sugar. Sift the flour with the baking powder and add this with the eggs, a little at a time, beating well after each addition. Lightly stir in the fruit and almonds and enough milk to make a firm dough. Mix lightly until all the ingredients are blended. Turn into a well-greased loaf pan and bake in the oven at 350°F. (175°C.) Mark 4 for 2½ – 3 hours or until the mixture is dry when tested with a skewer.

PLAIN CURRANT BREAD

2 lb. (8 cups) plain flour
1 oz. (1½ cakes) yeast
1 teaspoon (1¼) caster sugar
¾ pint (scant 2 cups) warm water (approx.)

2 teaspoons (2½) salt
¾ lb. (2 cups) currants
milk

Sift the flour into a warmed bowl. Make a well in the centre. Cream the yeast with the sugar, add 1 cup (1¼) warm water. Stir well, then pour this into the well. Mix to make a thick batter, sprinkle the salt over the top. Cover and stand in a warm place for about 30 minutes to set the sponge. Stir in the remainder of the flour, knead well, add the currants, knead again until the dough is smooth and leave to rise again for about 1 hour until it doubles its bulk. Divide into 2 or 3 pieces and knead into smooth balls. Press lightly into greased and floured loaf pans, filling them just over half-full. Cover and leave in a warm place to rise until the bread has reached the rim of the pans. Brush the tops lightly with milk. Bake in an oven at 450°F. (233°C.) Mark 8 for 15 minutes, lower the heat to 375°F. (191°C.) Mark 5 for between ¾ hour or until the bottoms sound hollow when tapped. Cool on a wire tray.

PLAITED LOAF (SWEET)

1 oz. (1½ cakes) yeast

1 cup (1¼) warm milk

4 oz. (½ cup) sugar

1 lb. (4 cups) plain flour

5 egg yolks

2 tablespoons (2½) grated almonds

1 tablespoon (1¼) sweetened milk

Mix the yeast with a little milk and very little sugar. Leave it to rise for 15 minutes. Sift the flour into a warm bowl, make a well in the centre, add the risen yeast; add 4 egg yolks and the rest of the ingredients (except the remaining egg yolk and sweetened milk), and knead until the dough is smooth and very silky. It should have plenty of bubbles. Leave it to rise to double its size. Turn out on to a floured board, break it into 3 equal-sized pieces and roll these into balls. Roll out each ball into rolls 12–14 in. long and with these make a plait. Make the ends neat. Place on a floured baking (cookie) sheet. Beat the remaining egg yolk with the sweetened milk. Brush the plaited dough with this, let it dry, brush it again and then let the dough rise again to double its size. (If it does not completely double its size the bread will burst while baking.) Bake in the oven at 375 °F. (191 °C.) Mark 5 for 30 – 35 minutes or until golden brown and when lifted it feels light. Test with a skewer, if it comes out dry the bread is ready.

RYE BREAD

There are many different types of rye bread and nearly all continental countries have their own rye bread speciality. Rye is normally milled in three grades: fine, light rye, medium rye or coarse. To make a true rye loaf it is important to produce a sour dough.

1 lb. (2 cups) medium rye flour

1 oz. (1½ cakes) yeast

1 tablespoon (1¼) sugar

3 cups (3¾) warm water

1 lb. (4 cups) fine rye flour

½ lb. (2 cups) white flour

1 tablespoon (1¼) salt

caraway seeds to taste (optional)

milk

Put the medium rye flour into a large bowl. Dissolve half the yeast and sugar in 2 cups (2½) water. Stir this into the rye flour, cover and place in a warm place for 24 hours or until the dough ferments and becomes sour. Add the two remaining flours, the salt and the caraway seeds. Dissolve the remaining yeast in 1 cup (1¼) warm water. Mix this into the flours and work it all to a firm dough. Leave it to rest for 20 minutes and then punch it down. Divide into pieces each about 1 lb. in weight and pat them into rounds. Shape these into cylinders roughly as long as they are broad and taper the ends. Leave to rise until double their size. Bake in a hot oven at 400°F. (205°C.) Mark 6 for 30 minutes. Turn the loaves round and lightly brush with milk. Lower the heat to 350°F. (175°C.) Mark 4 and continue baking for another 1½ hours.

N.B. To obtain a crusty loaf, put a small pan of hot water in the bottom of the oven This creates steam and is important for rye breads.

RYE BREAD (Austria)

1½ lb. (6 cups) plain white flour	3 tablespoons (3¾) salt
2½ lb. (10 cups) fine rye flour	4 tablespoons (5) caraway seeds,
3 cups (3¾) warm water	pounded
2 tablespoons (2½) sugar	1 oz. (1½ cakes) yeast

Put ½ lb. (2 cups) white flour and ½ lb. (2 cups) rye flour into a large warmed bowl. Mix well, add the water and the sugar and leave in a warm place for 24 hours. It should be sour by this time. Add the remaining white and rye flours, salt, caraway seeds and yeast and enough warm water to make a smooth firm dough. This type of bread dough should be moulded in small well-greased baskets and then allowed to rise in the usual manner, i.e., until it has doubled its bulk. Turn out the risen loaves and place carefully on to greased baking (cookie) sheets. Bake in the oven at 375°F. (191°C.) Mark 5 until they are well baked – baking must be slow and thorough with rye bread.

RYE BREAD (Denmark)

1½ lb. (5¼ cups) coarse rye flour	4 cups (5) warm water
½ oz. (¾ cake) yeast	½ lb. (2 cups) plain white flour
2 oz. (¼ cup) sugar	1 tablespoon (1¼) salt

Sift 1 lb. (3½ cups) rye flour into a large bowl with the yeast, sugar and water and leave in a warm place for 24 hours to get sour. Add the remaining flours and salt and knead to a firm dough. Shape these into pieces approximately 1 lb. each and half fill into loaf baking pans. Leave to rise until the bread comes to the top of the pans, always remembering that sour dough mixtures take much longer both to prove and to bake. Bake in the oven at 375°F. (191°C.) Mark 5. Continue baking the bread at this heat for another 1½ hours, turning them round in the oven about half-way.

RYE BREAD (Poland)

4 lb. (15 cups) medium rye flour	caraway seeds to taste
1 tablespoon (1¼) sugar	1 tablespoon (1¼) salt
3 pints (7½ cups) warm water	1 oz. (1½ cakes) yeast
1 lb. (4 cups) plain white flour	

Sift half the rye flour into a large warm bowl, add the sugar and 2 pints (5 cups) of the water. Leave it in a warm place for 48 hours by which time it will have fermented and become sour. Sift the remaining rye and white flours into another bowl, add caraway seeds, salt and the sour dough. Dissolve the yeast in the remaining water (make sure it is warm but not hot), and work to a fairly firm dough. Leave it to rise until double its bulk, and the time this takes varies considerably as rye flour also varies. Break off 1 lb. weight pieces and shape into long loaves, rather flatly rounded at each end. Let them rise on a floured baking (cookie) sheet until they double their bulk, wash lightly with water and bake in the oven at 400°F. (205°C.) Mark 6 for 30 minutes, lower the heat to 350°F. (175°C.) Mark 4 and continue baking until the loaves are firm. Tap the bottom to test for doneness.

SODA BREAD

1 lb. (4 cups) plain flour	2 teaspoons (2½) bicarbonate of
1 teaspoon (1¼) salt	soda
2 teaspoons (2½) cream of tartar	1 cup (1¼) sour milk or buttermilk

Sift the first four ingredients into a warm bowl. Mix thoroughly. Make a well in the centre and add enough sour milk to make a spongy dough which should be soft but not sticky. Turn the dough on to a lightly floured board and shape into a round cake about 2 in. high. Work quickly and carefully. Place on a floured baking (cookie) sheet and cut across the bread about ½ in. deep. Bake on the top shelf of the oven at 450°F. (233°C.) Mark 8 for approximately 30 − 45 minutes, it depends upon the thickness of the dough. Wrap the bread in the folds of a clean napkin to cool; this keeps the bread soft. To make brown soda bread, use wholemeal (graham) flour; and for a fruit bread of the same type, add cleaned dried fruit such as currants or raisins and finely chopped candied peel. These breads are made in the same way.

VERY SWEET BREAD

Whenever life is not as you like it, if you are bitter about anything or anybody, don't

Rolls (reading from top to bottom): knots; granary rolls; brioches;
Vienna rolls; Kaiser rolls; fancy rolls

despair. I give you a recipe of a very sweet bread which will make you feel better. You just make the following recipe.

6 eggs
1 lb. (2¼ cups) caster sugar
2 tablespoons (2¼) curaçao

2 lb. (8 cups) plain flour
10 oz. (1¼ cups) butter
1 egg, well beaten

Beat the 6 eggs with the sugar until the mixture is thick. Add the curaçao and about ⅓ of the flour, enough to make a firm dough. Sift the remaining flour into a warm bowl, add the dough. Slightly warm the butter and thoroughly work it into the mixture. When the dough is smooth and pliable, shape into a roundish loaf. Brush the top with beaten egg and bake on the middle shelf of the oven at 370°F. (189°C.) Mark 5 for 30 minutes. Test with a knife; if, when inserted, it comes out clean the bread is ready.

VIENNA BREAD

2½ lb. (10 cups) plain flour
1 tablespoon (1¼) salt
1 oz. (1½ cakes) yeast

4 oz. (½ cup) butter
2 cups (2½) warm milk

Sift the flour into a warm bowl and make a well in the centre. Sprinkle salt round the edge. Cream the yeast with a little warm water and pour it into the well. Warm the butter until melted but not too hot (too much heat kills the yeast). Pour this into the well. Gradually add the milk and mix lightly but thoroughly. Work through the dough with fingers and thumbs and turn it on to a floured board and knead for 15 minutes to get a smooth springy consistency. Return the dough to the bowl, cover with a cloth and leave in a warm place to double its bulk. Break off 4 pieces and shape longish ovals with tapering ends. Score the tops with short diagonal cuts and place the loaves on greased baking (cookie) sheets. Bake at 450°F. (233°C.) Mark 8 for the first 15 minutes, lower the heat to 400°F. (205°C.) Mark 6. During the first 5 minutes have a pan of hot water at the bottom of the oven but remove 5 minutes after the bread has been in the oven. Half-way through cooking time the loaves should be turned and painted with a little rich milk.

VIENNA ROLLS

Use the same dough as for Vienna Bread but break off small pieces and shape these into balls. Let the dough rise etc., and bake as in previous recipe.

Wedding cake

WHITE BREAD

I give you here another recipe for white bread which you may like.

1 lb. (4 cups) plain flour
1 oz. (2 tablespoons) butter
1 teaspoon (1¼) salt
1 teaspoon (1¼) sugar

½ oz. (¾ cake) yeast
1 cup (1¼) warm milk
1 egg, beaten

Rub the butter into the flour and add the rest of the ingredients. Mix well to a dough, turn out on to a board and knead until your hands are free of dough. Leave to rise and double in bulk. Knock it back and let it rise again for another 30 minutes. Put the dough on to the board and shape it into a loaf, like a French loaf but shorter and much wider. Put it on a greased and floured baking (cookie) sheet, wash over with a little milk and score it with three slits on the top. Bake in the oven at 425°F. (216°C.) Mark 7 for 15 minutes, reduce the heat to 400°F. (205°C.) Mark 6 and continue baking for a further 40 – 45 minutes until the colour is golden and the crust seems crisp.

WHOLEMEAL BREAD

1 lb. (4 cups) plain flour
2 lb. (7 cups) wholemeal flour
2 teaspoons (2½) salt
1 oz. (2 tablespoons) butter

2 oz. (3 cakes) yeast
1 tablespoon (1¼) sugar
3 cups (3¾) warm water

The quantity of water will vary according to the absorbency of the flours used. Sift both the flours and salt into a large bowl and rub in the butter. Cream the yeast with the sugar, add the water and mix well. Make a well in the flour and pour the yeast liquid into it. Mix thoroughly to form a smooth dough and working quickly to keep the dough warm turn on to a floured board and knead until the fingers come clean from the dough. Cover the dough and leave in a warm place until it doubles its bulk. Knock back and cut into 4 and shape these into round or oblong loaves. Return the loaves to the board and let them remain, covered and warm, until they double their size. Bake at 450°F. (233°C.) Mark 8 for 15 minutes, lower the heat to 400°F. (205°C.) Mark 6 and continue cooking for 30 – 35 minutes. Cool on a wire rack.

POTATO BREAD

I experimented with making bread with potato during the war, when there was a cry everywhere: 'Save flour, eat more potatoes'. The experiment resulted in very good bread, so I thought, 'Save flour and eat very good bread!' Here is the result of my experiment:

1 lb. mashed potatoes   **warm water as required**
4 oz. (6 cakes) yeast   **1 tablespoon (1¼) salt**
3 lb. (12 cups) plain flour   **caraway seeds (optional)**

Mix the yeast with a little flour and enough water to make a 'little' dough. Mix the potatoes with salt, 2 tablespoons (2½) warm water, the remaining flour and leave overnight. Mix the two doughs together and work to a smooth dough – you may have to add extra water as the potatoes take up quite a lot. Knead the dough in the usual manner until your hands come clean from the bowl. Add caraway if liked and to taste (I like it and add plenty). Cover the kneaded dough with a warm cloth and let it rest 1 hour or until it has risen to double its bulk. Break off pieces of the bread, as many as you like and shape these into loaves. Place each loaf on a piece of floured cloth and drop into a little basket. Leave to rise for at least another hour to rise well. Bake in the oven at 375°F. (191°C.) Mark 5 for about 1 hour. Instead of making several loaves, the mixture can be made into 1 or 2, in which case baking time will have to be increased. Take out and tap the bottom. If it sounds hollow, the bread is ready. Cool on a wire tray.

DIABETIC BREAD

I have always been very concerned about diabetics and their diet. Being a professional concerned with food, naturally it was very close to me. I cannot answer the natural question – why diabetes and not one of the hundreds of other illnesses? Of course, all the illness and trouble of the world concerns me, as it does everybody else. I suppose I am particularly interested because I had an uncle, whom I liked more than the others, who died comparatively young. He was a character and a very interesting one! He was straightforward and, I could say, uncomfortably honest. As a child he was sent to a boarding school, having parents who lived in the country where no day school existed. The first holiday, his parents sent a coach to collect him, and when the time came for him to arrive, the whole family went out and waited by the gate for his arrival. When my uncle noticed the gathering, the big family reception, he started to shout from far away, 'I failed in my exam!' He just could not face the nice reception with the knowledge that he had disappointed his people, especially his mother, whom he adored. He had quite a lot of difficulty in his schooldays, but in the end he became an excellent engineer. He married in due course, and his wife was just as uncomfortably honest as he was. Unluckily for him, they had no children. This was a bitter disappointment for him; he adored children, but it was no help; he had to find other children to love. He lived a very quiet, hard-working life; if you like you can call it happy; no worry, but no joy either. Suddenly, somehow, he noticed that he was over-tired and always thirsty and his wife urged him to see a doctor, who diagnosed diabetes. My uncle asked what the remedy was. I suppose at this time insulin did not exist. The doctor prescribed a very strict diet. He gave my uncle a sheet on which were all the things he could eat; all very strict measurements. My uncle looked at it very seriously, folded the paper nicely and asked what would happen if he did not keep to the diet. The doctor answered his straight question with a straight answer: 'You will die in a very short time.' My uncle replied that was O.K. by him and never kept to the diet and in due course he died. Since then diabetes and diabetic people have been my concern.

Several times in Hungary people asked me if I would make diabetic pastries, petits fours and chocolates. I flatly refused. I dared not; I could not play with people's lives. I could not take such a responsibility. My workrooms, my business have never been big enough to have proper dieticians or proper laboratories, with chemists who could assure me that what we would make would be harmless.

NIGERIAN BREAD

During one of my holidays recently I read in the American magazine *Time* an article about Nigerian millionaires. One of them was a baker. I thought that perhaps he could help me and as a colleague I wrote to him and asked if he could send me some local or any African specialities; any bread, pastries, cakes or such like. I got back a friendly and cordial letter. He would like very much to help me but all that he knows and makes originated from this country or the United States. However, he wrote, we have one national cake. If I remember well it was a soya flour affair; I never got this recipe either. Then I got a letter from his son saying that his father, the baker from Nigeria, was ill and in a London hospital and he would like to visit me. He came and had lunch with me; he told me all about his business. Two of his 6 children are already in the business and his wife is very active, too. It seems to be that they have a very large enterprise with very many kinds of interests, 5 shops, restaurants, coffee bars, everything. He found our production wonderful; I sent him over to our chocolate factory and bakery. He was delighted with everything and in our long discussion he mentioned that in Nigeria they have a lot of difficulty with raw materials; they have to import everything. I asked him whether they grew potatoes and he said yes, plenty of potatoes, so I told him I would give him a recipe and I make for you white bread with 40 or even 50 per cent of potato. He got terribly excited and he said 'Oh, now I can take something home from here to please my wife', and I answered that I hoped it would be a success and would make him further millions. This is just my luck – I ask somebody for help and it turns out that I have to do something for them instead. But I suppose it is so because I like it this way. I now very much hope that I will get in exchange for my good deed another one, that is, the soya bread or cake.

ARAB BREAD

I search everywhere for the origin of bread, all kinds of bread, everywhere I go or have any connections from whom I could get information. Perhaps I don't tackle my job properly, or I am just unlucky in finding the right people to enlighten me about the subject. From one friend who means very well I got a recipe – if you can call it that – the title of the recipe is 'Arab Bread'. Before the recipe it says: 'Arabic, Mediterranean countries, particularly Syria, Lebanon, Iraq, use this very simple way of breadmaking.' Use flour, water, salt and sour dough. How much salt? That is always individual. How much water? Depends on the flour you make the bread from. That is simple as that.

But I have to tell you that our bread, in my country, a very much of a bread-loving population, the bread was made from a recipe like this. The imaginative housewife or baker would elaborate on the recipe. And I can assure you that these 4 ingredients – flour, water, salt and sour dough – can make a very enjoyable bread. The most important, of course, is the flour.

This form of bread baked in the Arab countries of the Middle East, particularly Syria, Lebanon and Iraq and was very popular, although in the towns less is now being baked with the introduction of modern bakeries. These bakeries produce 'Western'-type bread. The usual recipe for Arab Bread is:

8 lb. (32 cups) flour   **2 pints (2½ pints) water**
½ oz. (2 teaspoonfuls) salt   **a little 'old' dough**

This is all mixed together, together with a piece of old dough, i.e. a piece from the previous days' dough or some flour and water mixed together and left for a few days to catch wild yeasts and commence fermentation. In recent years some bakeries have been using dried yeast.

This dough is left an hour, weighed off in approximately 1 lb. pieces and then placed into an oven with top heat and left for about 8–10 minutes, normally the time required to bake the top row. The lower rows will take proportionately longer. Pieces are placed in the oven on a long, thin piece of board, similar to our peels. The bread, when put in the oven, expands rapidly like a football and then collapses while being brought out.

DAMPER BREAD (Australia)

8 oz. (2 cups) plain flour   **½ teaspoon (⅔) salt**
4 teaspoons (5) baking powder   **¾ cup (1) milk**

Sieve the dry ingredients together in a bowl and add the milk to make a soft, moist almost scone-like dough. Place between 2 enamel plates and bake for 30 minutes in a camp oven. A camp oven took the form of a hole in the ground packed with red-hot coals and topped with mud for insulation. Due to its low fat content, this was an inexpensive bread but it staled quickly. An interesting recipe but not for daily use.

LANGOS

I am a terrible worrier. I have worried my life away ever since I was a little school girl. At first about the friendship of my school mates, the likes and dislikes of my school teachers. Then I was worried whether they loved me. I worried over little things; I worried over important things; I worried over things that would never happen. The silliest thing with me is that I know the basic wisdom of life and that worrying could not help me or change matters; and meanwhile I am always outwardly cheerful and most of the time nobody notices my worrying. Another wisdom I know, but do not practice, is that the simplest things in life are the most enjoyable. I do always the most complicated and difficult and expensive things. Yesterday I learned again how enjoyable and very simple the cheapest food can be; how much pleasure you can give to people with something that needs very little to do and costs hardly anything. Take *langos* as an example. The great passion of our childhood was *langos* – we always had this when bread was made. We looked forward to it, not only my own family but I could say this about nearly everybody in my country.

Langos is made from bread dough, usually white bread dough. It is made with flour, yeast, lukewarm water, as for ordinary bread. The cook would put away from a batch of bread about 1 lb. of dough and we had *langos* mostly for breakfast. The bread dough, I say about 1 lb., is rolled out with a rolling pin ¼ in. thick and cut into rounds like a pancake. Prick with a fork and bake for 15–18 minutes in a big bread oven or the ordinary kitchen oven. We used to eat them warm with butter. I would tell stories of my childhood to my elder son in his all too frequent illnesses. My stories,

I noticed, helped him to recover more than medicine. Suddenly in middle age he asked me could I make him *langos*. Naturally I made it for him and I couldn't have given a greater treat for tea, but not only for him but several of my friends, than hot *langos* with butter.

My husband always accused me of 'knighting' my dishes. He meant that I refined them. Sometimes he did not approve of my variation of our *langos*. I make small bars, roll out finger-thin and then fry in hot oil with great, great success.

BREADFRUIT

In my search to find you something new, something old, something historical in our bread line I came across an interesting tree which has very unusual-shaped fruit. It looks like an overgrown acorn. The botanical name of breadfruit is *Artocarpus incisus*, or *Artocarpus communis*, as it is known in the U.S.A. It is supposed to be a beautiful tree, according to my book of reference. It is a native of the tropical regions of Asia and of the South Sea islands. It is cultivated in the islands of the Asiatic archipelago and the Pacific near to the equatorial region. These breadfruit trees were the main reason for Captain Bligh's long, terrifying journey; he wanted to bring this very useful tree with the wonder fruit to the West Indies in 1789, the time of the French revolution. The tree is about 50–65 feet tall. It has a milky sap, thick and viscous, which made into a kind of glue used for various purposes. The timber is also very useful for building huts for the natives. The leaves are enormously big and are used as roofing. They are also used as a very valuable wrapping for food. The fruit, which is my greatest concern, is large and spherical. The colour is green, really greenish-yellow and it is the most basic food for very many islanders. When it is ripe it has a short life, as it rots quickly. Before it is fully ripe, the right time for gathering, the flesh is firm and white and very floury and starchy and has nearly the same nutritive value as wheat bread. Cut in slices it is baked or toasted on hot coals; the fruit can be also baked whole in the oven until the outside skin becomes dark brown. In this way it is a very valuable and nourishing food. It tastes like fresh bread with a slight flavour of artichoke. Two or three of these trees produce enough fruit to feed one man for a whole year. The seeds of this fruit are also edible roasted in cinders or boiled like chestnuts; the taste is also a little like chestnuts.

ROLLS

Every day I eat 1 or 2 rolls for breakfast, and in my bakery we make thousands and thousands every day. Eating and seeing them and endlessly criticising them has never brought back the painful nostalgia that writing about them now does. Rolls, lovely, crisp, happy, cheerful-looking rolls. The baker's shop – clean, pleasant and with a delightful smell which you cannot find anywhere except in a baker's shop. The girls also, fresh, healthy, good-humoured, the rolls many kinds, in big baskets, always in baskets. Which I like the best it is difficult to tell. You choose the rolls according to your mood and your mood turns good when you enter a baker's shop. Friendly faces always ready for a few jokes and gossip. In Hungary, the people have always been full of jokes. The darkest Nazi era, and the terrible repressions of Stalin and Kruschev could not kill their sense of humour.

In Hungary you choose your rolls according to the food you eat them with. For coffee – plain and very crisp rolls with no butter. For tea you eat the soft or crisp rolls with butter, and that is how fresh butter came to be called tea-butter in Hungary. For elevenses you choose the so-called water or Kaiser rolls. Cut the rolls, spread very lightly with butter, and sandwich with 1 or 2 thin slices of salami. There was such a variety of salami, that you could put in a different type each time. We did not call it all salami because there were so many varieties, but some was called *wurst*. It is difficult to explain how it looked. Even more difficult to tell how it tasted, but you have to believe me it tasted heavenly. Perhaps you will call them sausage, because in England, you call everything like this sausage – and it is sacrilege. What we called sausage you sometimes call liver sausage or garlic sausage, but who am I to break your old traditions? I have to go back to my rolls – I am always inclined to wander. The large water rolls, which get their name from the recipe, are slightly sour, but very tasty.

The Kaiser roll was the most popular, and deservedly so. It got its name because the Austro-Hungarian Kaiser liked it so much. As far as I know, he was not a gourmet, in fact, he was rather frugal with little or no good taste, but the Kaiser roll was delightful, made with butter and a little milk. The next best was the plainer, crisp little Vienna roll. I could go on talking about rolls endlessly, but I have to leave you alone for a while. I must, though, tell you about *brioches* and *croissants*, which are really the best in the world.

The origin of *croissants* dates back to the seventeenth century in the year 1686, when the Turks were besieging Budapest. They had dug tunnels under the city, but a surprise attack was foiled by some bakers working at night who heard the noises made by the Turks and raised the alarm. The bakers were subsequently rewarded by the granting of the privilege of making a special pastry. This was to be crescent shaped – the crescent being the emblem borne on the Turkish flag and so symbolizing the defeat of the Ottomans.

There were three very popular *croissants* – one was very slim, very crisp, quite large with crystallized salt or caraway seeds sprinkled on the top which you could pick off and eat separately. Once you started, *it* was very difficult to stop. These *croissants* were mostly eaten with elevenses, with the Vienna sausages which here you call Frankfurters. Crisp plain *croissants* are eaten without butter.

BRIOCHES

Once upon a time, when life was easy and leisurely – at least for some people – *brioches* were a luxury, not so much because they were expensive, but because they have elegance and standing; they ought to be eaten in a salon, put only on a thin China plate, and eaten with drinking chocolate in delicate, thin, china cups. Nobody who did not belong to the upper classes would think of buying or ordering *brioches* in Hungary. *Brioche* is a favourite roll in France, Austria and Hungary. It is an elegant roll and it is comparatively expensive. If you make it at home, of course, it is cheaper than if you buy it, and, I suppose, better. It is served mostly with a good, rich cup of chocolate. *Brioches* are more suitable than French *croissants* for drinking with chocolate because they are lighter; a French *croissant*, as we know it, is made with a lot of butter and, therefore, it is a little bit heavier. I love drinking chocolate, but I can never have it for breakfast. In the afternoon however, I know nothing better. It is a pity that it went out of fashion; afternoon tea on the continent is at 5 o'clock. It is much more usual for young people to prefer savouries and sandwiches for tea.

BRIOCHE (1)

12 oz. (3 cups) plain flour
1 teaspoon (1¼) salt
3 eggs
2 oz. (3 cakes) yeast

1 tablespoon (1¼) sugar
1 tablespoon (1¼) cream or milk
8 oz. (1 cup) softened butter

Sift the flour and salt into a bowl, make a well in the centre, add the eggs and mix well. Dissolve the yeast with the sugar and cream. Add the butter to the flour, work it well into the dough. Add the yeast and continue to work the mixture until the yeast is completely incorporated. Cover and leave in the refrigerator overnight. Next day knead the mixture thoroughly until smooth and divide it into 2 balls one much larger than the other, like making a cottage loaf. Grease a *brioche* mould (these are deep round fluted moulds) and place the large ball in the mould. Make a deep hole in the middle and put the smaller ball of dough into the hole. Leave to rise in a warm place for 15–20 minutes. Bake in the oven at 400°F. (205°C.) Mark 6 for 45–60 minutes. Before being baked the mixture can be lightly brushed with the yolk of an egg mixed with just a pinch of sugar if liked. Or it can be turned into a greased loaf pan and, after it has risen, sliced candied fruits arranged on top. Or, after baking and while still warm, the *brioche* can be brushed with soft icing (frosting).

BRIOCHE (2)

1 lb. (4 cups) plain flour
½ oz. (¾ cake) yeast
warm milk
8 eggs

1 tablespoon (1¼) caster sugar
1 teaspoon (1¼) salt
8 oz. (1 cup) softened butter
1 egg yolk

Take about 1 tablespoonful (1¼) of the flour and mix it with the yeast and a little milk. Mix to a dough and put it in a warm place to rise. Sift the rest of the flour into a bowl, make a well in the centre, break in 6 of the eggs, add the sugar and salt. Work the whole to a fairly stiff dough. Then work in the remaining 2 eggs and the butter. When all the ingredients are well incorporated in the mixture add the first dough. Mix well, cover with a cloth and leave in a cool place, i.e. the larder or refrigerator, overnight. In the morning add a little warm milk, as much as is needed to make an unctuous smooth and silky dough. Knead it well. Leave to rise again. When the dough has doubled its bulk, break off a quarter of it. Divide the remainder of the dough into equal-sized pieces and shape these into balls. Put them into buttered fluted *brioche* or castle pudding pans. With the remaining dough make an equal number of small balls. Make a well in the middle of each *brioche* and put a ball of dough into each. Leave them to rest for about 1 hour and then brush each one with beaten egg. Bake in an oven at 425°F. (216°C.) Mark 7 for about 15–20 minutes.

FRENCH CROISSANTS

Brioche and French *croissants* are among the most elegant and perhaps the most sophisticated of foods to eat with tea, coffee or chocolate. If well made with the right ingredients they are really very attractive to look at and just as good to eat. There are very many ways to make *croissants*. In Paris they are made quite differently than in the French provinces; the Swiss make a different one and we here make our own variety.

CROISSANTS (1)

10 oz. (2½ cups) plain flour
1 oz. (2 tablespoons) lard
1 teaspoon (1¼) salt
1 tablespoon (1¼) sugar
½ cup (⅔) warm milk

1 oz. (1½ cakes) yeast
4 oz. (½ cup) butter
1 egg yolk, beaten with a little
   milk

Put the lard, salt and sugar into a warm bowl. Add the milk, it must be hot enough to melt the lard. Mix well, then leave until cool. Dissolve the yeast in a little warm water, add this to the bowl and stir. Add the flour gradually and knead everything to a smooth soft dough. Cover the bowl with a floured cloth and leave to rise until the dough has doubled its size. Punch the dough down and put in the refrigerator to thoroughly chill. Wash the butter in a bowl of cold water squeezing it between the fingers until it becomes spreadable. When the dough is chilled take it from the refrigerator and roll it out on a floured board into a rectangle three times as long as wide. Spread with the softened butter and fold in the ends to make a square. Roll the dough out again into another rectangle the same size as before and again fold over the ends to make a square. Put back into the refrigerator and leave for 30 minutes. Repeat this rolling and folding twice more, putting the dough into the refrigerator between each rolling. After the final rolling and folding, the dough can be left in the refrigerator for an hour or so or overnight.

   To shape the *croissants*, roll the dough on a floured board to ¼ in. thickness. Cut it out into squares and then each square into halves to make two triangles. Roll up each triangle beginning at the long side and then curve or shape them into crescent forms. Place them on lightly floured baking (cookie) sheets. Leave to rest in a warm place for 15–20 minutes. Brush lightly with the egg yolk mixed with a little milk and,

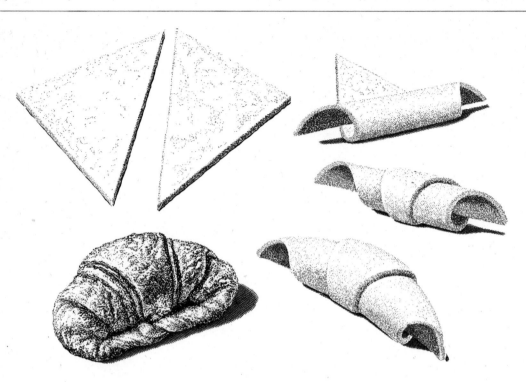

if liked, a little sugar. Bake in the oven at 425°F. (216°C.) Mark 7 for the first 5 minutes, reduce the heat to 375°F. (191°C.) Mark 5 and continue baking for 10 – 15 minutes or until the *croissants* are a golden brown.

CROISSANTS (2)

1 lb. (4 cups) plain flour	**1 oz. (2 tablespoons) softened**
1 tablespoon (1¼) sugar	**butter**
1 cup (1¼) warm milk	**2 teaspoons (2½) salt**
1 oz. (1½ cakes) yeast	**1 egg yolk**

Mix the sugar with a quarter of the milk in a bowl, add the yeast, stir well, add the butter, stir this until it has been incorporated into the milk, then add the flour and salt. Stir and leave until the yeast has risen. Add enough of the remaining milk to make a soft dough. Cover the bowl and leave in a warm place to rise to double the volume. Turn the dough out on to a floured pastry board and break off 6 or 8 pieces. Roll these into balls, cover with a cloth and leave for 15–20 minutes to rise again. Roll out the balls until thin trying to keep them square. Cut each square in half crossways to make triangles. Roll these into crescents as in the first *croissant* recipe and place them on a greased baking (cookie) sheet. Beat the egg yolk with a little milk or water and brush the tops of the crescents. Leave to rise. Bake in the oven at 425°F. (216°C.) Mark 7 for 5 minutes, reduce the heat to 375°F. (191°C.) Mark 5 and continue cooking for 15 minutes or until the *croissants* are nicely browned.

BAPS

1 lb. (4 cups) plain flour
1 teaspoon (1¼) salt
2 oz. (¼ cup) lard or butter
1 oz. (1½ cakes) yeast

1 teaspoon (1¼) sugar
1 cup (1¼) mixed warm milk and
water

Sieve the flour and salt into a warm bowl. Rub in the fat. Mix the yeast and sugar and stir until creamed. Add the liquid and pour it all into the middle of the flour. Mix to a soft dough. Cover and stand in a warm place until its bulk is doubled. Knead lightly and divide into small squarish pieces. Place these on a greased baking sheet and dust with flour. Leave again to rise until they have doubled in bulk, about 15 minutes. Bake in the oven at 425°F. (216°C.) Mark 7 for about 5 minutes, lower the heat to 400°F. (205°C.) Mark 6 and continue baking for a further 10 minutes. When they are ready the baps will be pale brown in colour and should be served hot.

BRIDGE ROLLS

Vienna bread dough (page 37)
1 egg white

1 egg yolk
a little sugar

Make the Vienna bread dough and let it rise once. Knead well and break off small pieces, how large depends on the size of the rolls required. If to be used at tea-time, they should be between 2 and 3 in. long; for cocktails only half this size. Roll out the pieces into fingers, pointed at both ends a little thicker in the middle. Put them on to a greased baking (cookie) sheet in neat rows, not too close to each other so they do not stick together. Slightly beat the egg white and brush this over the rolls, then beat the egg yolk with a pinch of sugar and with this brush again over the rolls. Leave to rise. When the rolls have doubled their size, put them into the oven at 400°F. (205°C.) Mark 6 and bake for 5 minutes. Reduce the heat to 350°F. (175°C.) Mark 4 and continue baking for another 10 minutes or until brown. If you like the rolls very glossy, brush them over again with the egg yolk and sugar mixture and return them to the oven for a minute or so to dry.

FINGER ROLLS

There are many ways of making these rolls. I think the following recipe is a good method which makes appetizing rolls filled with ham or frankfurter-type sausages.

1 lb. (4 cups) plain flour   **1 tablespoon (1¼) sugar**
½ oz. (¾ cake) yeast   **1 teaspoon (1¼) salt**
1 cup (1¼) warm milk   **fresh cream**
2 oz. (¼ cup) butter

Sieve ⅓ of the flour into a bowl. Mix the yeast with the milk, let it dissolve and then pour it into the middle of the flour. Mix to make a 'little' dough. Let this rest. In the meantime sift the remaining flour into a bowl, make a well in the middle, add the 'little' dough and leave for 1 hour. Soften the butter, add this to the dough with the sugar, salt and about 1 tablespoon (1¼) cream. Knead the dough very firmly until it is smooth and silky. Sprinkle the top with flour, cover with a cloth and leave in a warm place to double its size. Turn out the dough on to a floured board and break off small pieces – the size is a matter of personal choice. Roll them with the hand in long shapes. Place on a greased baking (cookie) sheet and leave, covered, to rise until they have doubled in bulk. Bake in the oven at 450°F. (233°C.) Mark 8 for 5 minutes, lower the heat to 400°F. (205°C.) Mark 6 and continue baking for another 10 minutes or until golden brown.

HAMBURGER ROLLS

Prepare the dough as for finger rolls. Break off small pieces and shape these into balls. Roll these nearly flat. Place on a greased baking (cookie) sheet and leave to rise until they almost double their size. Bake in the oven at 450°F. (233°C.) Mark 8 for 5 minutes, lower the heat to 400°F. (205°C.) Mark 6 and continue for 7–10 minutes or until a golden brown.

JEWISH CHOLA OR PLAITED BREAD

1 lb. (4 cups) plain flour   **1 cup (1¼) hot milk**
2 teaspoons (2½) salt   **1 oz. (1½ cakes) yeast**
2 teaspoons (2½) sugar   **1 large egg**
2 oz. (¼ cup) butter or shortening

Sift the flour and salt in a bowl. Make a well in the middle. Mix the sugar and fat with the hot milk (water may be used instead). When the fat is incorporated with the milk, let the mixture cool. Dissolve the yeast in a little of the cooled liquid. Stir the yeast into the flour, cover the bowl and leave until the yeast makes a sponge in the centre. Lightly beat the egg, add this to the spongy mixture. Add the remaining liquid and stir to make a dough. Turn out on to a floured board and knead firmly until the dough is smooth and elastic. Return the dough to the mixing bowl, sprinkle it lightly with flour, cover the bowl and leave in a cool place to rise and double its bulk. Take the risen dough from the bowl and knead again for 10 minutes. Divide the dough into 3 pieces. Roll each piece out into a 'sausage' $1\frac{1}{2}$ – 2 in. in diameter. Rub a baking (cookie) sheet with oil. Plait the three pieces of dough loosely together. Place the plait on the baking sheet – make sure the ends are neat. Leave again to rise. Bake in the oven at 450°F. (233°C.) Mark 8 for 10 minutes, lower the heat and continue cooking for 45 minutes at 350°F. (175°C.) Mark 4. Makes 1 plaited loaf.

WATER SEMMEL or ROLLS (Austria)

$2\frac{1}{2}$ lb. (10 cups) strong flour	1 tablespoon ($1\frac{1}{4}$) salt
$\frac{1}{2}$ oz. (1 tablespoon) butter	2 cups ($2\frac{1}{2}$) warm water
1 tablespoon ($1\frac{1}{4}$) sugar	1 oz. ($1\frac{1}{2}$ cakes) yeast

Sieve the flour into a mixing bowl, rub in the butter, add the sugar and salt. Mix well; add half the water. Mix to a dough. Dissolve the yeast in the remaining water and mix it into the flour to make a firm dough – a little extra water may be required, it depends on the absorbency of the flour. Work the dough until it is smooth and leave in a warm place, covered, for 3 hours. Turn it out on to a floured board and knead thoroughly. Break off pieces of the usual size for a substantial roll, shape into rounds, place on a greased baking (cookie) sheet and leave to prove for a full 30 minutes. Preheat the oven to 460°F. (238°C.) Mark 8 and place a pan of boiling water at the bottom of the oven – the oven should be full of steam. Bake the *semmel* in the oven, without reducing the heat for 15–20 minutes or until they are a light brown.

SCONES AND BUNS

SCONES

Scones are still very popular for tea, toasted, split and buttered, or heated in the oven or under the grill. In Hungary, we had something very similar which we called butter *pogacsa*. We used to have them for breakfast, freshly made the same morning by the long-suffering cook who had to get up at 4 o'clock in the morning to have them ready for breakfast. You cannot imagine how very good these breakfasts used to be. Here you have baps and soft rolls instead. I would like your scones better, however, if they were made with less baking powder and more butter. But perhaps it is just a matter of acquired taste, and one day I may prefer scones as you make them.

The art of making scones is a very simple one. Scones are cheap, quick and appetizing. They are extravagant only in that they should be eaten absolutely fresh, and are only eatable the day after baking, if they are toasted. The secret of making good scones is that the dough or paste should be as wet as is consistent with handling. The mixing should be done as quickly as possible and there should be the minimum of handling. The raising agents may be buttermilk, sour milk or cream, eggs, cream of tartar, bicarbonate of soda or baking powder. Oven scones should be baked very quickly in a very hot oven and should be wrapped at once in a soft cloth. Griddle scones, oatcakes, drop scones or pancakes should be cooked on a flat greased hot plate, heavy pan or griddle (girdle in Scotland) and should be turned over once during cooking.

BROWN FARMHOUSE SCONES

2 oz. (½ cup) plain flour	**2 oz. (¼ cup) butter**
good pinch of salt	**6 oz. (1½ cups) wholemeal flour**
2 oz. (¼ cup) caster sugar	**¼ pint (full ½ cup) milk**
3 teaspoons (3¾) baking powder	

Sieve the plain flour into a mixing bowl with the salt, sugar and baking powder. Rub in the butter, mix well, add the wholemeal flour. Mix thoroughly. Add the milk – enough to make a soft dough, so add it bit by bit. Knead the dough lightly into a flat round. Place this on an ungreased baking (cookie) sheet and divide it into 6 triangles with the back of a floured knife. Bake in the oven at 450°F. (233°C.) Mark 8 for 15 minutes. Serve as hot as possible, separated and split, with plenty of butter inside them.

BUTTERSCOTCH SCONES

8 oz. (2 cups) plain flour	**pinch of salt**
1 oz. (2 tablespoons) cornflour	**butter**
(cornstarch)	**milk to mix**
1 teaspoon (1¼) baking powder	**soft brown sugar**

Sieve the flour and cornflour with the baking powder and salt into a mixing bowl. Rub in 1 oz. (2 tablespoons) of butter and mix well, and gradually add enough milk to make a firm dough. Work this until it becomes soft and pliable. Knead it lightly on a floured board and roll out in a rectangle ¼ in. thick. Spread with butter and sprinkle liberally with sugar. Roll it up in the same way as a Swiss or jelly roll. Cut into ½ in. slices and bake flat on an ungreased baking (cookie) sheet in the oven at 475°F. (246°C.) Mark 9 for 8 – 10 minutes.

CINNAMON FARLS

8 oz. (2 cups) self-raising flour	**1½ oz. (3 tablespoons) bacon fat**
½ teaspoon (⅔) ground cinnamon	**a little sugar**
pinch of salt	**½ cup (⅔) milk and water mixed**

Sieve the flour, cinnamon and salt into a mixing bowl. Rub in the fat, add the sugar and enough of the liquid to make a soft but still firm dough. Turn this out on to a lightly floured board and shape into a round. Roll out, still in the round, to the thickness of ½ in. Cut the round into traingles. Place these a little apart on a greased baking (cookie) sheet and bake at 425°F. (216°C.) Mark 7 for about 10 minutes or until dry and light in colour.

CREAM SCONES (U.S.A.)

These scones rise very well and taste as good as they look.

8 oz. (2 cups) plain flour
4 teaspoons (5) baking powder
2 teaspoons (2½) sugar
2 oz. (¼ cup) butter
2 eggs, well beaten

¼ pint (full ½ cup) cream
pinch of salt
1 egg white or yolk
fine sugar

Sieve the flour, baking powder and sugar into a bowl. Rub in the butter, add the eggs, cream and salt and mix thoroughly. Put the dough on to a floured board, work it a little more and then roll it out to a thickness of ¼ in. and cut out wedges, about ½ in. in thickness. Let them rest for a short while, then wash over with egg white or yolk. Sprinkle the top lightly with fine sugar and bake for 15 minutes at 450°F. (233°C.) Mark 8. Serve hot with butter and jam. There is a surprising quantity of baking powder in the recipe making the scones very light. Therefore, do not on any account take the scones from the oven until they are fully baked and, if inspecting them, avoid causing a draught as you open the oven door. Makes 14–15 4 in. scones.

CREAM SCONES

Make a scone dough as for sultana scones (see page 56) but omit the fruit. Roll out the dough and cut into rounds or triangles with a cutter. Place them on an ungreased baking (cookie) sheet and leave for 20 minutes. Bake on the middle shelf of the oven at 425°F. (216°C.) Mark 7 until they are lightly browned underneath. Turn them over and lightly brown the top. The time for baking each side is 6–8 minutes. After baking, cool the scones, split and fill them with jam and whipped cream.

DROP SCONES

8 oz. (2 cups) plain flour
1 oz. (2 tablespoons) caster sugar
½ teaspoon (⅔) each bicarbonate of
   soda and cream of tartar

1 egg, beaten
1 cup (1¼) buttermilk
suet for greasing

Heat a griddle or heavy large frying pan (skillet) over a moderate heat. Sift all the dry ingredients together in a mixing bowl. Add the egg and half the buttermilk. Stir until the mixture is smooth, then thin with the remainder of the buttermilk until the mixture has the consistency of thick cream. Beat it well, preferably with a wooden spoon. Pour the mixture into a jug. Rub the griddle or pan with a piece of suet and pour the mixture into rounds of about 3 in. in diameter. Cook until bubbles form on the tops and the undersides are a golden brown. Lift with a palette knife, turn and cook on the other side. Serve at once with butter, honey or jam, or with butter and brown sugar. If not wanted immediately, place the scones between the folds of a clean warm towel until required.

DROP BANNOCKS

1 egg, well beaten
½ pint (1¼ cups) milk
pinch bicarbonate of soda

salt to taste
oatmeal and flour
suet for greasing

Heat the griddle over a moderate heat. Beat the egg into the milk. Add soda and salt and equal quantities of oatmeal and flour (mixed) to make a 'dropable' batter. Rub the griddle with a piece of suet. Pour on the batter in small rounds, as for drop scones. Cook over a moderate heat until bubbles form on top, lift with a palette knife, turn the bannocks and cook them on the other side until a golden brown.

JAM SCONE ROUNDS

Prepare a dough as for sultana scones (see page 56) but omit the fruit. Divide the dough into 4 pieces and shape each piece into a round ball. Flatten each one to ¼ in. thickness and place on a greased baking (cookie) sheet. Brush the edge with beaten egg and spread a little jam, preferably raspberry, in the centre of each round. Cover 2 rounds of dough with the remaining 2 and lightly press down to ensure adhesion. To help keep their shape, flan rings could be used. Lightly brush the top with egg and mark each round into 8 equal portions. Rest the scones for 20 minutes and then bake at 400°F. (205°C.) Mark 6 for 15–20 minutes.

POTATO SCONES

1 lb. cold cooked potatoes   **pinch of salt**
1 oz. (2 tablespoons) melted butter   **4 oz. (1 cup) plain flour**

Heat the griddle over a moderate heat. Mash the potatoes working in the butter at the same time. Add salt and the flour and mix to a firm dough – a little more or less flour may be required, it depends upon the absorbency of the potatoes. Roll out the dough thinly and cut into rounds. Grease the griddle. Place the potato scones on the hot griddle or in a hot plate or a heavy frying pan (skillet) and prick all over with a fork. Cook for 3 minutes on each side. Serve at once with butter and brown sugar or jam or apple purée or place in the folds of a clean napkin if not required immediately. They can also be served with the breakfast fried bacon.

SULTANA SCONES

1 lb. (4 cups) plain flour   **4 oz. (½ cup) caster sugar**
¼ teaspoon (⅓) salt   **4 oz. (⅔ cup) sultanas (white raisins)**
½ oz. (1 tablespoon) baking powder   **1 cup (1¼) milk**
4 oz. (½ cup) butter

Sieve the flour, salt and baking powder together on the top of the table or on to a pastry board. Rub in the butter – but let the texture remain somewhat sandy. Add the sugar and sultanas and make a well in the middle. Gradually add the milk to make a softish dough. This can be either rolled flat and cut with a small round cutter or rolled into a thick 'sausage' and cut into rounds with a knife. Place on an ungreased baking (cookie) sheet, brush each scone with egg wash (see page 58) and sprinkle with granulated sugar. Let the scones rest for 20 minutes and then bake for 15–20 minutes in the oven at 460°F. (238°C.) Mark 8.

SODA SCONES

1 lb. (4 cups) plain flour   **1 teaspoon (1¼) bicarbonate of soda**
salt to taste   **1 cup (1¼) buttermilk**
1 teaspoon (1¼) cream of tartar

Heat the griddle over a moderate heat. Sieve the flour and salt into a mixing bowl, mix with the remaining dry ingredients. Add the buttermilk and mix to a light elastic dough. Roll out ⅔ in. thick on a floured board. Divide into 4 pieces. Bake on a fairly hot griddle, allowing 3–4 minutes for each side. Cool in the folds of a clean napkin.

SOUR MILK SCONES

8 oz. (2 cups) plain flour
I teaspoon (1¼) baking powder
½ teaspoon (⅔) baking soda
pinch of salt

2 oz. (¼ cup) butter
¾ cup (1) thick sour milk
a little beaten egg

Sieve the flour, baking powder and soda with the salt together in a bowl. Rub in the butter. Add the sour milk and mix to a soft pliable dough. Use a knife to mix and toss the mixture as you work it. Roll out on a lightly floured board to ½ in. Cut with a floured cutter into rounds, place these on a greased baking (cookie) sheet. Brush each scone lightly with egg and bake for 7–10 minutes at 450°F. (233°C.) Mark 8.

TREACLE GRIDDLE SCONES

½ lb. (2 cups) plain flour
½ teaspoon (⅔) bicarbonate of soda
½ teaspoon (⅔) cream of tartar
salt to taste

½ oz (1 tablespoon) butter
1 tablespoon (1¼) black treacle or molasses
buttermilk as required

Heat the griddle over a moderate heat. Sieve the flour with the soda, cream of tartar and salt. Melt the butter and treacle together adding 2 or 3 tablespoonfuls of buttermilk. Stir this into the flour, adding enough extra buttermilk to make a firm but soft dough. Turn this on to a floured board, knead lightly and divide into 2 pieces. Roll out each piece into a round about ½ in. thick. Divide these into 4. Flour the griddle lightly and cook the scones over a moderate heat until dry and lightly browned underneath – about 5 – 6 minutes. Lift with a palette knife, turn and cook on the other side. Serve hot with butter.

BUNS

BASIC BUN DOUGH

Buns should be made from a mixture containing yeast. They are similar in texture to bread but contain sweetening, usually fat, and frequently dried fruit and spices.

1 lb. (4 cups) plain flour
2 tablespoons (2½) sugar
pinch of salt
3 oz. (6 tablespoons) fat

1 egg, beaten
1 oz. (1½ cakes) yeast
1 cup (1¼) warm water

Sieve the flour with the sugar and salt into a bowl. Rub in the fat and add the egg. Cream the yeast with a little of the water, then add the rest of the water. Mix this into the flour and work to a fairly soft dough. This is the basic bun dough and is used for Hot Cross buns, Chelsea buns, Danish buns etc.

BUN WASH

Bun wash keeps well so if frequently making buns the following recipe can be used as it is. For those who seldom make buns, halve or quarter the quantities.

2 cups (2½) water

1 lb. (2 cups) sugar

Combine the water and sugar and cook slowly until the sugar is dissolved, then bring to the boil and boil for 1 minute.

EGG WASH

Beat together 1 egg with 1 or 2 tablespoonfuls of water.

BATH BUNS

1 lb. bun dough (page 57)
4 oz. (⅔ cup) sultanas (white raisins)
2 oz. (½ cup) chopped candied peel

grated rind 1 lemon
4 oz. (½ cup) caster sugar
1 egg beaten with a little milk
sugar nibs

Prepare the basic bun dough, cover and let it rise for about 1 hour or until it has doubled its bulk. Mix the sultanas, peel, lemon rind and sugar together and slightly warm. Turn the dough on to a floured board and mix the fruit roughly into it – do not knead the dough, if you do the result will not be correct. Divide the dough into 12 or 14 pieces, they can be roughly shaped, and placed them on an ungreased baking (cookie) sheet. Let them rise for 15 minutes, then brush with beaten egg and milk, sprinkle with sugar nibs or, failing this, crushed loaf sugar. Bake at 425°F. (216°C.) Mark 7 for about 20 minutes.

A selection of buns: 1. jam doughnut; 2. Danish pastry; 3. Chelsea bun; 4. Bath bun; 5. knotted bun; 6. Swiss bun

CHELSEA BUNS

1 lb. basic bun dough
melted butter
2 oz. (⅓ cup) currants
good pinch mixed spices

1 beaten egg, mixed with a little water
bun wash (page 58)

Make the basic bun dough (see page 57), put it into a bowl, cover and leave until the dough doubles in bulk. Punch it down, pull back the sides to the centre, return it to the bowl and leave to rise again. Turn the dough on to a floured board and roll it out into a rectangle 10 × 16 in. and brush this with melted butter. Sprinkle with the currants and the mixed spice. Brush the four edges with beaten egg and roll the dough into a fairly tight cylinder and cut into 16 slices, but before separating them brush with melted butter. Place the slices flat down on a lightly greased baking sheet fairly close together. Brush the tops with beaten egg, cover with a damp cloth and leave in a warm place for 30 minutes. Bake at 425°F. (216°C.) Mark 7 for 20 – 30 minutes. Immediately you take the buns from the oven wash them with bun wash (see page 58).

DANISH BUNS

Make a basic bun dough (see page 57), put it into a bowl, cover and leave to rise until it doubles its bulk. Punch back the dough, pull down the sides to the centre and return the dough to the bowl. Let it rise again for 30 minutes. Roll out the dough into a rectangle 9 × 16 in. and mark it into 3 strips lengthwise. Spread the centre strip with raspberry jam and brush one of the remaining strips with beaten egg. Fold the plain strip over the jammed strip, and then fold the egg-washed strip over to seal the other strips. Turn the bun over and divide into 16 equal portions. Place these on a lightly greased baking (cookie) sheet and brush with egg beaten with a little milk. Cover with a slightly damp cloth and leave to prove for 30 minutes. Bake at 450°F. (233°C.) Mark 8 for 15–20 minutes. As soon as the buns are taken from the oven, brush them with bun wash (see page 58).

HOT CROSS BUNS

1 lb. (4 cups) plain flour	2 eggs, well beaten
salt	3 oz. (6 tablespoons) melted butter
½ teaspoon (⅔) ground cinnamon	1 oz. (1½ cakes) yeast
½ teaspoon (⅔) ground nutmeg	1 egg yolk, milk and sugar to glaze
4 oz. (⅔ cup) sultanas (white raisins)	2 oz. (¼ cup) sugar
1½ oz. (⅓ cup) chopped candied peel	1 cup (1¼) milk
mixed spice	

Cream the yeast with a little of the milk. Sieve the flour into a warm bowl. Add the salt, cinnamon, nutmeg, sultanas, peel and mixed spice. Mix well and make a well in the centre. Pour the beaten eggs and the butter into the well and gradually add the yeast and the rest of the milk. With the hands mix to a dough, it will be a rather soft and sticky one. Beat it thoroughly, still using your hands, for 5 minutes. Cover and leave in a warm place to rise for about 2 hours or until the dough doubles its bulk. Punch it down thoroughly and then let the dough rise again for another 30 minutes. Put it on a floured board, break off small pieces, shape these into balls and place in neat rows (not too close together for they have to rise) on a greased baking (cookie) sheet. Flatten them down slightly and on each make a cross. Cover and put aside for the buns to rise. Mix the egg yolk with a little sugar and milk, brush the buns with this and again mark the cross on top – it must be a fairly deep indentation. Bake at 425°F. (216°C.) Mark 7 for 15–20 minutes, turning them round as necessary. When they come from the oven brush them again with the egg and milk glaze.

JAM BUNS

Make and prepare 1 lb. basic bun dough as for Chelsea buns (see page 59) to the point of turning the dough out on to a floured board. Divide the dough into 16 equal pieces and mould into balls. Place them on a lightly greased baking (cookie) sheet and allow them to half-prove. At this stage make a fairly deep hollow in the centre of each bun, wash with beaten egg and fill the hollows with raspberry jam. Leave them to finish rising, then bake at 425°F. (216°C.) Mark 7 for 15–20 minutes. As soon as they come from the oven, brush with bun wash (see page 58).

KNOTTED BUNS

Prepare a basic bun dough as for Chelsea buns to the point of proving it (see page 59). Work about ½ cup (⅔) of currants into the dough, then divide it into 16 pieces. Shape each piece into a ball and flatten each ball with a rolling pin until it is some 6 in. across. Place on lightly greased baking (cookie) sheets. With a sharp knife cut 8 slits in the surface of the dough, cover with a floured cloth and leave to rise until they have doubled their bulk. Bake at 450°F. (233°C.) Mark 8 for 10 – 15 minutes. As soon as the buns are taken from the oven, brush with an egg wash (see page 58).

CURRANT BUNS

basic bun dough (page 57)   **1 egg, beaten**
4 oz. (⅔ cup) currants   **bun wash (page 58)**
mixed spice (optional)

Prepare the basic bun dough as for Chelsea buns (see page 59) to the point of adding the currants and spice. Divide the dough into 16 pieces, shape each piece into a ball and place on a lightly greased baking (cookie) sheet, not too close together. Brush with egg and leave them covered to rise until they double their bulk. Bake at 450°F. (233°C.) Mark 8 for 10 – 15 minutes or until they are a golden brown. Immediately they are taken from the oven, brush them with bun wash (see page 58).

ORANGE BUNS

These are made in the same way as currant buns except that instead of currants, coarsely chopped candied orange peel is used, about 4 oz. (1 cup). After shaping the buns, garnish each one with a strip of orange peel. After the buns are taken from the oven and brushed with bun wash (see page 58), they should be brushed with an orange-flavoured water icing (frosting).

RICE BUNS

2 oz. (½ cup) self-raising flour	**2 eggs**
2 oz. (¼ cup) butter	**3 oz. (½ cup) ground rice**
3 oz. (full ⅓ cup) sugar	**grated rind 1 lemon**

Cream the butter and sugar together. Beat in 1 egg then the ground rice and lemon rind. Beat well, add the second egg and the flour, beating the mixture thoroughly. Put the mixture into greased patty-pans (muffin pans) and bake at 350°F. (175°C.) Mark 4 for 20 minutes.

SWISS BUNS

Make a basic bun dough and treat it as in Chelsea buns (see page 59) to the point of proving the dough. Divide it into 16 pieces and shape each into a ball. Leave to rest for 10 minutes then roll into sticks about 3½ in. long with blunted ends. Place on a greased baking (cookie) sheet, brush with egg wash (see page 58) and leave to rise in a warm place until they double their bulk. Bake for 10 – 15 minutes in the oven at 450°F. (233°C.) Mark 8. Immediately the buns are taken from the oven, brush them with water icing (frosting).

POTATO CAKES

Very many years ago, during the war, that most wonderful woman, Constance Spry, invited me with my husband for a weekend at her nice house in Orpington. They had very good food in spite of the severe rationing. We found their fellow guests interesting and pleasant people. Her house was pretty, large, spotlessly kept and furnished in excellent taste and she had some beautiful and valuable antiques. Her only help in the large house was a little 14-year-old girl. Her table was most beautifully laid with lovely china and glass, and the food, I think, was the best I ever tasted in England. For breakfast we all went into her kitchen where she cooked on a large cooker for all of us; on the table was a large jug of coffee, another jug with hot milk and a big pot of tea and then she cooked eggs and 1 slice of bacon for everybody. Then she made potato cakes which were so good freshly made that I would happily have eaten nothing else. She gave me the recipe, so I pass it on to you.

1½ lb. freshly boiled floury potatoes   6 oz. (1½ cups) plain flour, sifted
pinch of salt   milk

Crush the potatoes until they are smooth and without lumps. Put on to a floured board, add the salt and gradually work in the flour. Knead the mixture lightly and quickly, adding just enough milk to make a stiff dough. Roll out the paste as thinly as possible and cut into rounds about 6 in. in diameter. Bake on a hot griddle for 5 minutes, turning them once.

CRUMPETS

I give you another completely English recipe – crumpets. I am afraid I am not such a friend of crumpets as I am of muffins because when for the first time in my life I met the English crumpet it was a sad disappointment and you know that if we are once disappointed we can never feel the same again. When I first saw a crumpet I was delighted and I thought this is a lovely something made of potato and that it would taste like the potato pancakes which belong to my childhood memories. I tasted the first crumpets cold; oh, how I disliked them. Later on I tasted them nice and hot and buttered so I feel that they deserve to be written about, and therefore I give you the recipe:

1 lb. (4 cups) plain flour   1 teaspoon (1¼) salt
2 cups (2½) warm milk   pinch bicarbonate of soda
½ oz. (¾ cake) yeast

Heat the milk to lukewarm and dissolve the yeast in a little of it. Sift the flour into a warm bowl, make a well in the middle, pour in the yeast-milk mixture and stir. Gradually add the rest of the milk, stirring all the time to a batter of a thick cream consistency. Cover the bowl and leave in a warm place for 1 hour. Dissolve the salt and soda in a little water, beat this into the spongy batter and leave it for another hour. Grease the crumpet rings and heat the griddle over a moderate heat. Set the rings on the griddle. Pour in enough batter to fill the rings by ½ in. and bake over slow to moderate heat. When the bottoms of the crumpets are a light brown (they must not get too brown as they are to be toasted), remove the rings, turn the crumpets and bake on the other side for about 3–4 minutes or until they are thoroughly dry. To serve, toast the crumpets first on the smooth side to a good brown and then somewhat less brown on holey side. Butter the crumpets generously.

MUFFINS

'How English can you get?' I wonder whether any of you who will read my book are interested in making this very nice, very ordinary and very traditional English tea bun. Can you call a muffin a tea bun? I hope the muffin will not be offended! I like muffins and I feel very English when I eat one. So I give you the recipe:

1½ lb. (6 cups) plain flour   **2 cups (2½) warm water or milk**
1 oz. (1½ cakes) yeast   **1 teaspoon (1¼) salt**

Dissolve the yeast in the water. Sieve the salt and flour together and gradually mix this into the yeast liquid. Beat thoroughly for at least 15 minutes – this is important. The dough should be soft and smooth, not like a crumpet batter. Cover the bowl and leave in a warm place between 2 and 5 hours (recipes vary) but the dough must double its bulk. Punch it down, knead it well and leave again for 30 minutes. Divide the mixture into 20 – 24 pieces on a floured board and pat these into shapes to fit the crumpet rings, but just a little smaller to allow for rising. Let them prove for 20 minutes. In the meantime heat the griddle over a moderate heat and grease the crumpet rings. Set these on the griddle. Carefully drop the muffins into the rings and place them on the hot griddle and bake for 5 minutes. Turn the muffins over and bake 5 minutes on the other side. Remove the rings and press the sides of the muffins to see whether they are done. Toast the muffins on both sides, split and spread with butter. Put them in a warm oven to allow the butter to melt before serving.

A selection of scones: 1. sultana scone; 2. scone round; 3. muffins; 4. drop scones.

MUFFINS (U.S.A.)

The Americans make muffins of many kinds, using a number of interesting combinations. American muffins are baked in the oven in muffin pans similar to English patty-pans.

8 oz. (2 cups) enriched flour	**1 egg, beaten**
2 oz. (¼ cup) sugar	**½ cup (⅔) milk**
4 teaspoons (5) baking powder	**2 oz. (¼ cup) butter or shortening**
a good pinch salt	

Sift the dry ingredients together. Beat the egg, milk and fat together. Add the egg mixture to the flour, stirring just enough to dampen it. If the batter is lumpy, this is correct. Fill greased muffin pans ¾ full and bake at 400°F. (205°C.) Mark 6 for 25 minutes. Makes 12–15 muffins. It is important not to over-mix the batter and to have the oven preheated to the right temperature to get muffins of the right texture. These muffins can be served with butter and jam. Blueberries, cheese, cranberries, dried fruits, nuts, chopped cherries and pineapple are but a few additions to the basic mixture for variety.

OATCAKES (Scottish)

8 oz. (1⅓ cups) fine or medium oatmeal	**1 tablespoon (1¼) melted bacon fat or dripping**
½ teaspoon (⅔) salt	**about ¼ – ½ cup (⅓ – ⅔) hot water**
pinch bicarbonate of soda	

Heat the griddle over a slow heat. Mix the oatmeal with salt and bicarbonate of soda. Make a well in the centre and pour in the melted fat. Mix in enough hot water to make a stiffish dough. Place this on a board, floured with oatmeal. Knead it well. Divide it into 2 pieces, work these into 2 balls, then roll into rounds of a thickness of ⅛ – ¼ in. Cut out neatly with a saucepan lid into rounds, and cut into squares or triangles. Or, if preferred, simply cut the dough with a plain cutter. With a spatula, slip the oatcakes on to the hot griddle, smooth side uppermost, and bake over a moderate heat until the edges of the cakes begin to curl. Remove carefully on to a board. Sprinkle the smooth side with oatmeal. The oatcakes can be cooled and stored in a tin – handle them carefully as they are brittle. Toast under a grill until crisp and slightly brown and serve with butter.

CAKES

Nothing worries me more than to make, bake or cook very English food, cakes, pastry, crumpets or muffins, things that I have not seen before I came to this country. Of course, this was long ago; that was the time when I made the birthday cakes of the greatest Englishman, according to me the greatest man in the world. I made birthday cakes for Sir Winston Churchill for many, many years; a very special mixture about which I will tell you. But from the first one to the last one, they were all great successes and I got the most beautiful letters of appreciation from this great man. Of course, this helped enormously and gave me confidence and daring. I miss this wonderful job I did for so many years. I planned the design of his cake the whole year and this gave me more pleasure than anything else; I can't do it any more. I have a little consolation that I still have the opportunity to make Lady Churchill's birthday cake. I have done this, too, for very many years.

In Hungary we did not have birthday cakes, not traditional ones as in England. Anybody in a family had their favourite food on his or her birthday and at the end of the meal their favourite gâteau or pastry.

My favourite was – don't laugh, please – a savoury cream-cheese *gomboc* or dumpling. I still like it better than any cakes or gâteaux. When I first visited England about 40 years ago, one of my greatest interests was looking at the windows of bakers' shops. I admired some of the round and heavily decorated cakes, which had written on them 'Happy Birthday'.

I think, in my whole life nothing has given me so much pleasure as to plan and make cakes for Sir Winston Churchill. These cakes have given me the unearned reputation of being able to design just the right birthday cake for anybody. That is not true. He gave me the ideas for his own birthday cakes from his very varied activities. My favourite was a cake in the form of a spiral, decorated with 32 models of his famous hats. I suppose it is very wrong on my part to call that cake a masterpiece, that is if we can call a cake a masterpiece at all, but I do, and I do more. I called it 'Churchill's life story in hats'.

I had an amusing episode with this cake. A picture of the cake appeared in a newspaper and the next day a little man, very modest, came up to see me. My secretary guarded me like a prize pig – as friends said – and tried to find out from him what his business was. He said: 'The fact is that I am a colleague of hers and therefore I must see her in person.' Since my secretary knew that I did not like to refuse anybody who insisted on seeing me, she showed him into my office. Coming in, he greeted me very jovially: 'You know, we are colleagues. I have a fruit-stand in Covent Garden.'

I told him, I felt very honoured and asked, what I could do for him. Then he told me that he was the proud father of a six-year-old boy whose birthday it was in ten days time. So he wanted, whatever the cost, the same cake that Sir Winston Churchill had just had.

I replied to him that while I did regret it very deeply, unluckily the man who had done the actual work had gone for a fortnight's very well-deserved holiday. So, I could not make the same cake, but I could make another very nice cake. He would not hear of it – a Churchill cake or nothing. Very likely I lost a very important customer!

I worked and planned the Churchill cake from the beginning of December till the following November. I planned it, I dreamt of it and I have to admit, so did my whole family – everybody had ideas. We pooled them and we enjoyed discussing them. Now I miss the whole procedure more than I can tell. . . .

The mixing of the Churchill cake was also special, according to Lady Churchill's wish. She is a most exacting woman, always knowing what she wants. She liked only light fruit cakes with specially chosen raw materials. We used the very best fruit which was soaked in the best brandy for days. The success I had with these cakes, the most wonderful appreciation I got from his letters was so rewarding that it made worth while the many bitter, sad and nasty experiences which come your way, if you work for a long time in this kind of business.

On his 80th birthday, which was celebrated at No. 10 Downing Street, my husband and I were invited. He greeted me, took my hand between his two hands and said: 'How nice to see you, Madame Floris. You've played such a big part in my life'.

What is a knighthood or any other reward equal to this?

GENERAL INSTRUCTIONS

A few simple rules, a few common errors to avoid, will make all the difference to successful cakemaking. Once these are grasped, however, commonsense and experience are the best guides. Differences in utensils, materials, the temperament of the oven and of cooking conditions all play a part.

Utensils

There are many different types of cake tins, baking sheets and so on. Some are designed for a particular purpose, others are suitable for a variety of uses. Examples of specialized cake tins are *guglhupf*, a deep fluted tin; angel cake, a deep tin with a funnel; and *savarin* mould, a ring mould. Cake hoops or rings are useful for gâteaux, especially for those with a nut and egg base. Removable bottoms are helpful when cakes are inclined to stick to their tins. For small cakes use paper cases, patty tins, *madeleine* moulds or bun trays.

The cake tins most in use can be either round, square, or rectangular. The most common sizes are 6, 7, or 8 in. in diameter; they range from those 1 in. deep for sponges, tortes and flans, to ones 3 in. or more for large cakes. It is false economy to buy any except the best available. Tins made from poor materials are difficult to keep clean, and may warp. Also if the material is thin, the edges and bottoms of the cake may burn before the centre is cooked through. Cake tins should be quite clean and dry before use. It is often a good idea to warm the tin before greasing. It is advisable to line large tins meant for fruit cakes with greaseproof paper or tinfoil. The paper lining the bottom of the tin should be cut to fit the tin and the lining paper should be a little higher than the sides.

The quantity of the cake mixture in relation to the size of the tin may be important. Rich mixtures should fill the tin to about two-thirds of its depth. Sponge cakes and those cakes which will rise and increase their volume greatly should about half fill the tin. As a rough guide, a cake with 3–4 eggs will require a tin 7 in. in diameter; a 2 egg mixture, a tin 5 or 6 in. in diameter; while a mixture with 6 and more eggs will need a 7, 8, or 9 in. tin. This criterion obviously will depend also upon the remainder of the ingredients. In making light sponge cakes, a 2-egg mixture will require a 7 in. sandwich tin. A cake baked in a large shallow tin will cook more quickly than the same quantity in a smaller deeper tin.

Fruit cakes and rich cake tins should be greased. Some authorities say that it is advisable to use a salt-free fat, such as one of the vegetable fats now on the market, or fresh butter, to prevent sticking. Sponge cakes and gâteaux tins are usually floured after greasing. Generally speaking large cakes and fruit cakes and pastries should be left to cool in the tin, but light cakes and sponges should be turned out immediately.

Materials

It is advisable to collect all the ingredients before starting. Flour should be sifted, eggs and butter brought to room temperature; bowls, tins and trays cleaned and dried. When using dried fruits, toss them in a little flour before adding to the mixture. This will help to prevent them sinking to the bottom of the cake. The consistency of the mixture may vary according to the size of the eggs, quality of the flour and so on. The amount of liquid may be adjusted accordingly.

Methods

There are different techniques for the principal ingredients involved in cakemaking, that is, flour, eggs, sugar and butter. Let us consider them in turn. The difference in flour qualities, the raising agents, together with the method of adding them to the mixture will all influence the texture of the cake. If a close texture is desired, add the eggs and flour alternately: if an open spongy texture, lightly fold in the flour last of all. In some recipes, cake crumbs or ground nuts take the place of the flour, but the same principles apply. Eggs should be fresh, but not less than three days old, as new laid eggs do not beat or whisk so well. When the recipe calls for very stiffly beaten whites of eggs, whisk until the mixture will not start to slide out of the bowl or jug when it is inverted. When whisking yolks and sugar together, warm the bowl first or beat over a pan of hot water. A copper bowl is considered by some the ideal for whisking whites of eggs.

Creaming butter and sugar is again facilitated both by warming the bowl and making sure that the butter is at room temperature. Do not, however, heat the butter till it melts; this is fatal, except where the recipe calls specifically for melted butter, as in Genoese cakes. Cream the butter alone just a little before adding the sugar. The blessing of an electric mixer for beating and whisking in cakemaking cannot be overestimated. But remember always to cream or beat butter at a slow speed, reserving the high speed for incorporating eggs to a mixture, or for whisking yolks or whites.

The actual baking should present few difficulties providing you have an oven thermometer or thermostatic heat control. It is difficult to overcook rich cakes. The richer the cake, the lower the temperature is a useful rule. The higher the proportion of eggs, butter, etc. to the flour, the richer the cake will be. Cakes with a high proportion of fruit must cook at a low temperature for long periods. If the top browns before the cake is cooked through, cover with paper or foil. To test, pierce with a knife or skewer. When the cake is cooked, this will be clean on removal.

Cake and pastry tins: 1. *Gugelhupf* tin; 2. sponge sandwich or open tart tin; 3. *Savarin*; 4. honey cake tin; 5. petit four or tart ring tins

For light cakes, sponges, etc., there is one absolute rule. Do not open the oven door to look at your cake before the prescribed time is up. A sponge is cooked when a finger mark leaves no lasting impression on the surface of the cake. Meringue mixtures should be cooked very slowly and never touched until they are quite cold.
Caster sugar is the English equivalent of the American superfine.

ANGEL FOOD CAKE

Just before the Second World War we heard more and more of two very able American ladies working in England. They made three kinds of cakes, nothing else but these three cakes. They were most successful. I wonder now, where and how I heard of them, but I had. And then I had the opportunity to taste all the three cakes; they were threatening competitors of mine. I had to admit that the cakes were first class. They looked very well and tasted just as good.

The ladies made one very large yellow sponge cake, about 8 or 10 in. high and about 10 or 12 in. in diameter. The sponge was very plain, but the best I've ever tasted. There was also a very large angel cake, snow white and very light, and a chocolate devil cake.

I have to admit that I tried, but I could not copy them. With my very long experience I can generally copy anything, food or cakes. Most of the times I have a good idea of what are the ingredients and how to do it. But I just could not make these cakes, at least not so well as they did.

But, as luck had it, I heard that the two American ladies had left England. They did not want to be involved with our war. With the same luck I heard that two English girls who had worked with the American ladies were looking for similar jobs. Of course, I jumped at the opportunity and engaged them both. They worked for me for many years. They made in my bakery angel cakes, devil cakes and sponge cakes.

4 oz. (1 cup) cake flour
10 oz. (1¾ cups) caster sugar
½ teaspoon (⅔) salt
8 – 10 egg whites

¾ teaspoon (1) cream of tartar
½ teaspoon (⅔) vanilla essence
¼ teaspoon (⅓) almond extract

Sift the sugar twice. Sift the flour once and then twice with ½ cup (⅔) of the sifted sugar and salt. Beat the egg whites until foamy, then add the cream of tartar. Continue beating until the eggs are stiff but not dry. Gradually add remaining sugar, beating the eggs well after each addition. Add flavourings. Sift ¼ of the flour over the mixture then fold it in carefully. Pour this mixture into a large ungreased angel cake pan (a deep round tube pan), cut through the batter with a spatula to remove large air bubbles and bake at 350°F. (175°C.) Mark 4 for 45 – 60 minutes. Take the cake out of the oven and invert it, still in its pan, on to a wire rack. Leave for 1½ hours. Lift off the pan and sprinkle sifted icing (confectioner's) sugar over the top. Makes one 9-in. cake.

CHOCOLATE DEVIL'S FOOD CAKE

3 oz. (3 squares) bitter chocolate
½ cup (⅔) boiling water
9 oz. (2¼ cups) plain flour
2 teaspoons (2½) baking powder
½ teaspoon (⅔) salt
6 oz. (¾ cup) shortening or butter

½ lb. (2 cups) moist brown sugar
3 – 4 eggs
½ cup (⅔) thick sour milk
1 teaspoon (1¼) vanilla essence
butter cream filling
shredded coconut

Break the chocolate into pieces. Pour the boiling water over it and cook over a low heat until the chocolate has melted. Beat until creamy and thick. Put aside to cool. Sift the flour, baking powder and salt together twice. Cream the fat with the sugar until light and fluffy. Beat the eggs thoroughly and blend into the creamed fat, beating the mixture well. Add the flour and milk alternately in small amounts, with the vanilla, and beat well after each addition. Rub 3 layer cake (or sandwich) pans with fat. Pour the cake mixture into the greased pans and bake in the oven at 375°F. (191°C.) Mark 5 for 20 – 25 minutes. When baked, turn out on to a wire rack to cool. Spread a butter cream filling between the layers and over the top and sides of the cake and sprinkle liberally with shredded coconut.

WHITE SPONGE CAKE

12 oz. (3 cups) plain flour
2½ teaspoons (3) baking powder
pinch of salt
4 oz. (½ cup) white vegetable fat
12 oz. (1½ cups) caster sugar

½ teaspoon (⅔) vanilla essence
¼ teaspoon (⅓) almond extract
¾ pint (2 cups) milk
4 egg whites

Sieve the flour, baking powder and salt into a bowl. Cream the fat with the sugar and flavourings until fluffy. Add the sifted dry ingredients alternately with the milk, beating well after each addition. Beat the egg whites until stiff but not dry. Fold into the cake batter. Pour into greased sandwich (layer cake) pans and bake at 350°F. (175 °C.) Mark 4 for between 30–35 minutes. Take from the oven and turn out carefully on to a wire rack and cool. This type of cake is usually sandwiched together with a cream filling and lavishly decorated. See Hazelnut Gâteau.

YELLOW SPONGE CAKE

12 oz. (3 cups) plain flour
2½ teaspoons (3) baking powder
12 egg yolks
¾ teaspoon (1) salt

1½ teaspoons (2) lemon extract
1 lb. (2 cups) caster sugar
¾ cup (1) hot water

Sieve the flour with the baking powder four times. This is important. Beat the yolks until smooth, add the salt and lemon extract, and continue beating until the mixture is thick. Divide the sugar into 4 portions. Beat in one portion of the sugar with a quarter of the hot water and continue beating the mixture until it is very thick. Repeat this until all the sugar and hot water is incorporated into the egg yolks. Gradually fold in the flour, a little at a time. Pour into an ungreased large tube pan (an angel cake pan would be good) and bake in the oven at 375°F. (191°C.) Mark 5 for 1 hour. Invert the pan on a wire rack and leave the sponge to cool in the pan.

This cake makes a splendid foil against the dead-white angel cake. Now you have the three favourite cake recipes of my American ladies.

ALMOND CAKE

A useful everyday cake for tea.

10 oz. (1¼ cups) butter
4 oz. (½ cup) sugar
2 egg yolks
8 oz. (1⅓ cups) ground blanched almonds

1 whole egg
a little cherry brandy
½ lb. (2 cups) plain flour

Slightly soften the butter, mix with the sugar and beat together until creamy. Add the egg yolks, one by one, beating well after each addition. Finally add the almonds, the whole egg and beat again vigorously. Add enough cherry brandy to give flavour. Sift the flour on to a board and make a well in the middle. Pour in the creamed butter and egg mixture and work it in thoroughly until the mixture is smooth. Turn it into a greased ring mould and bake in the oven for 50 minutes at 375°–400°F. (191°–205°C.) Mark 5 – 6. Turn out on a wire rack and leave until cold.

BAUMKUCHEN (Germany)

Baumkuchen is a cake shaped like a tree which originated in Germany but has not become popular in other countries. It is very decorative and I think nearly every

German household which can afford it has one on the Christmas table.

Baumkuchen is something that a housewife cannot make. It should be a joy for us professionals that this is so, but unluckily *Baumkuchen* is not an everyday 'bread-and-butter' necessity. So we can keep our secret, but it isn't much help.

A *Baumkuchen* is very decorative. I tell you the ingredients in spite of the fact that they are of no use to you – flour, ground almonds, a lot of butter, many yolks and whites of eggs, and sugar. This is all mixed together into a thick batter, something like pancake batter but thicker.

Now comes the problem you cannot solve. To bake a *Baumkuchen* you need a big, clumsy piece of equipment which is neither a tool nor a machine. It is a big sheet of tin with many holes in the back. In the middle it has a $2\frac{1}{2}$ ft wooden tube with a little wheel at one end which one person has to turn like a spit. The gas is lit, the flames come out through the numerous holes and the batter is poured on the big wooden tube with a big spoon. This process is repeated for about an hour or two; it depends how big the tree cake will ultimately be. When it is big enough, then it is left on the wooden tube to cool. Then we take it off and you can do two things with it. Either cover it with thin white fondant or with chocolate. Either is equally good. When you cut the cake, it looks and tastes layered. The layer effect is from the baking.

BIRTHDAY CAKE

$\frac{1}{4}$ lb. ($\frac{1}{2}$ cup) vegetable fat or margarine
$\frac{1}{4}$ lb. ($\frac{1}{2}$ cup) butter
$\frac{1}{2}$ lb. (1 cup) sugar

4 large eggs
9 oz. ($2\frac{1}{4}$ cups) plain flour
$1\frac{1}{2}$ lb. (5 cups) sultanas (white raisins)
$\frac{1}{2}$ lb. ($1\frac{1}{3}$ cups) glacé cherries

Beat the vegetable fat, butter and sugar together until light and creamy. Add the eggs, one at a time, beating after each addition. Continue beating until the mixture is light and fluffy. Fold in the flour but do not over-mix at this stage. Finally add the sultanas and cherries, mixing gently but thoroughly. Fill into two 6-in. pans and bake at 350°F. (175°C.) Mark 4 for $2\frac{1}{2}$ hours or until a skewer comes out clean when inserted.

BASIC FRUIT CAKE (rich)

6 oz. (¾ cup) butter
6 oz. (¾ cup) sugar
4 eggs
9 oz. (2¼ cups) plain flour
2 oz. (⅓ cup) ground almonds
juice and rind 1 lemon

10 oz. (1⅔ cups) sultanas (white raisins)
6 oz. (1 cup) currants
3 oz. (½ cup) glacé cherries
blanched almonds
a little sweetened milk

Beat the butter and sugar together until creamy. Beat in the eggs one by one, beating well after each addition. Add the flour a little at a time, folding it in – do not over-mix at this stage. Add the ground almonds, lemon juice and rind, the fruit and cherries. Mix these ingredients well together but work gently. Grease a cake pan 8 × 3 in. Bake in the oven at 375°–400°F. (191°–205°C.) Mark 5–6 for approximately 2½ hours. After the cake has set, lower the heat a little and if the top seems to be getting too brown cover the cake with paper. About 1 hour before the cake is ready, take it half out of the oven (it can rest on the oven shelf) and scatter over the top a few blanched whole almonds. Continue baking for 40 minutes, again half remove the cake, brush it quickly with sweetened milk and return it to the oven to finish baking. This is a very good cake and will keep well if stored in a cake tin – but make sure it is absolutely cold before putting it in the tin.

CHEESECAKES

Before I went to the United States of America I had always been told that the best cheesecake is made in that country. I ate several and they were really good. Some American cheesecake tops are covered with fresh strawberries, brushed over with orange jelly. Some cheesecakes are covered with large pineapple rings and are brushed over with pineapple jelly.

I was determined to bring home a cheesecake recipe, but I did something even better. I went to classes held by an Italian pastrycook in New York. There for my five dollars fee they showed me how to make cheesecake. I spent altogether fifteen dollars – because you have to have three lessons and pay in advance.

Cheesecakes are not difficult to make and there are many recipes. What is very important is never to take the cakes from the oven while they are hot, this causes the centre to sink. Therefore the advice in every recipe which follows is to turn off the heat in the oven until the cake is quite cold, about 1 hour.

CHEESECAKE (1) (U.S.A.)

½ lb. shortcrust pastry
1 lb. Philadelphia cheese
3 oz. (6 tablespoons) butter
6 oz. (¾ cup) sugar

4 eggs, separated
½ cup (⅔) cream
2 oz. (⅓ cup) sultanas (white raisins)
2 oz. (½ cup) plain flour

Roll out the pastry and line an 8-in. cake pan, either a spring form or one with a loose bottom. Rub the cheese through a sieve. Beat the butter and sugar together until creamy. Beat in the egg yolks, the cream and the sultanas. Fold in the flour. Whip the egg whites until stiff, fold into the cheese mixture. Pour into the lined cake pan. Bake in the oven at 350°F. (175°C.) Mark 4 for 1 hour or until the centre is set. Turn off the heat, open the oven door, leave it ajar and let the cheesecake stand in the oven at least 1 hour or until it is cold.

CHEESECAKE (2) (U.S.A.)

½ lb. digestive biscuits (graham
   crackers)
1 tablespoon (1¼) caster sugar
4 oz. (½ cup) melted butter

1 lb. cream cheese
3 eggs
6 oz. (¾ cup) sugar
2 teaspoons (2½) grated lemon rind

Crush the biscuits until they look like flour. Mix with the first quantity of sugar and melted butter. With this mixture line the bottom and sides of a 9-in. cake pan, preferably with a loose bottom or spring form sides. Press it down well into the pan. Chill. Rub the cheese through a sieve. Beat the egg yolks and the whites separately. Beat the yolks, sugar and lemon rind into the cheese mixture. Fold in the egg whites and pour into the lined cake pan. Bake 1 hour in the middle of the oven at 350°F. (175°C.) Mark 4. Turn off the heat, open the oven door, leave it ajar and let the cheesecake cool in the oven.

CHEESECAKE (3) (Germany)

1¼ lb. (5 cups) plain flour
2 eggs
5 oz. (10 tablespoons) butter
2 oz. (¼ cup) sugar
pinch of salt
1 tablespoon (1¼) rum

filling:
6 eggs, separated
4 oz. (½ cup) butter
grated rind and juice 1 lemon
¾ lb. (1½ cups) cottage cheese
5 oz. (full ½ cup) caster sugar

Have everything as cold as possible and work quickly. First make the pastry. Sieve the flour on to a board and make a well in the middle; break the whole eggs into the well. Mix the flour into the eggs. Add the first quantity of butter bit by bit, rubbing it well into the flour until it is crumbly. Add the first quantity of sugar, the salt, rum and enough water to make dough. Knead the dough until smooth and silky. Cover with a cloth or bowl and let it stand for 2 hours before rolling out. Line two 9-in. cake pans – either spring form or pans with a loose bottom.

Beat the egg yolks slightly, add the butter little by little and beat until the mixture is smooth. Add the juice and the grated lemon rind. Rub the cheese through a sieve and beat the egg whites until stiff. Mix the cheese into the egg mixture, add the sugar, mix well, then fold in the egg whites. Pour the mixture into the two prepared cake pans. Bake at 350°F. (175°C.) Mark 4 for 1 hour or until the centre is set. Turn off the heat, open the oven door, leave it ajar and leave the cakes in the oven until they are cold.

CHERRY CAKE

This is one of the trickiest cakes to make. It is easy to make it too tough or else too wet and sloppy and then find that after baking all the cherries are at the bottom. Glacé cherries are usually too full of syrup, so it is essential to wash and dry them thoroughly, otherwise your cake will not be a success. If your time is limited you can wash the cherries and dust with flour which will soak up the moisture; but before using the flour must be shaken off.

4 oz. (1 cup) plain flour	**4 oz. ($\frac{1}{2}$ cup) caster sugar**
2 oz. ($\frac{1}{2}$ cup) self-raising flour	**2 eggs**
2 oz. ($\frac{1}{4}$ cup) butter	**milk to mix**
2 oz. ($\frac{1}{4}$ cup) white vegetable fat	**$\frac{1}{2}$ lb. ($1\frac{1}{3}$ cups) glacé cherries**

Sieve the two flours together into a bowl. Beat the butter and vegetable fat with the sugar until the mixture is creamy. Beat in each egg separately and continue beating until the mixture is fluffy. Gently fold in the flour, add if necessary a little milk to make a soft batter. Fold in the cherries and bake at 350°F. (175°C.) Mark 4 for about 1–1$\frac{1}{4}$ hours or until a skewer when gently inserted into the cake comes out clean.

CHOCOLATE CAKE (1)

A simple cake, easy to make, not expensive and suitable for everybody. It is not rich; it is very good for people who have delicate stomachs but like chocolate cake and want something sweet. I ate it in an English house well over 30 years ago. Everything around the house was lovely and the food was perfect. Since then I can never stay silent if people say that English food is not good and that the English can't cook. I spent a delightful weekend with these very rich people. A river ran through their beautiful garden and on the river a sizable yacht was moored. But on Sunday evenings after dinner I have seen our host take off his coat, put on an apron and with his son wash up the dinner dishes. Very naturally, smilingly, they say the staff have a day off. Mind you that was 30 years ago. They had two large Labrador dogs which I loved. The dining room was all old oak furniture, highly polished, I went on stroking the table which felt like silky velvet; I am sure it had been polished for over 400 years. Our bedrooms were perfect and had everything, even a tiny basket hung on the head-board of the bed; I suppose they were for paper handkerchiefs. I was most intrigued by the framed samplers on the walls. I don't know if that is the right name, but they are very English.

But I had better give you the recipe otherwise I can go on and on writing about this house.

I ate this cake over 30 years ago and I still remember it.

4 oz. ($\frac{1}{2}$ cup) butter	2 oz. ($\frac{1}{2}$ cup) plain flour
4 oz. ($\frac{1}{2}$ cup) sugar	1 packet vanilla powder
4 oz. (4 squares) bitter chocolate	1$\frac{1}{2}$ oz. ($\frac{1}{4}$ cup) ground almonds
4 egg yolks	4 egg whites

Beat the butter and sugar until creamy. Melt the chocolate in the top of a double boiler (a tablespoonful of rum may be added). Beat the chocolate into the creamed butter. Add the egg yolks, each one separately, beating after each addition. Add the flour, vanilla and the almonds and again beat well. Beat the egg whites until stiff and fold these into the cake mixture, making sure they are evenly mixed, otherwise the cake will be streaky. Butter 2 sandwich pans 9 × 6 in. and pour in the chocolate mixture. Bake in the oven at 400°F. (205°C.) Mark 6 for 35–40 minutes or until a knitting needle inserted into the cakes comes out clean. Cool the cakes in the pans before turning out. Avoid disturbing the cakes while in the oven as there is so little flour in them they are apt to subside in the oven. However, although the cakes may look sad when baked they have an excellent, true chocolate flavour. Cut into fingers to serve.

CHOCOLATE CAKE (2)

When I was in America, naturally I went round and round looking at bakeries and pastry shops; and the cake and pastry trolleys in restaurants. All, all looked wonderful, beautifully finished and enormously rich decorated with cream, fruit and jellies. Everything looked tempting and appetizing. There was everything from apple *strudel*, poppyseed *strudel* to large salt pretzels.

My friends all urged me to come and open a business there. My answer was 'What for? Nobody is waiting for me here, nobody needs me'. When, afterwards, I tasted these wonderful-looking and lovely cakes, I was not so sure!

As you know, America has everything of the very best quality. There fruit looks so lovely, their apples are so beautiful, you could not paint them, they are so beautiful; but they do not have the flavour of the English Cox's Orange Pippins.

I'm afraid the same applies to the pastries. They look very fine, but don't taste so good. I think, one of the troubles there is the 'Food and Drug' laws. These force the pastrymakers and chocolate manufacturers to use the tested essences instead of the real article – the fruits, cream and butter we use here.

I saw there a beautiful chocolate cake and I obtained the recipe from the owner of the restaurant and now I hand it over to you.

6 oz. (¾ cup) butter
12 oz. (3 cups) plain flour
pinch of salt
1 teaspoon (1¼) baking powder
6 oz. (¾ cup) caster sugar
4 eggs, separated
2 oz. (½ cup) cocoa
½ teaspoon (⅔) vanilla essence
milk or buttermilk

filling:
3 eggs, separated
4½ oz. (1 cup) icing (confectioner's) sugar
4 oz. (½ cup) butter
1 teaspoon (1¼) vanilla essence
4 oz. (4 squares) bitter chocolate
chocolate flakes:
3 oz. (3 squares) bitter chocolate

Rub 2 sandwich pans generously with butter. Sift the flour, salt and baking powder together. Beat the butter to a soft cream, add the caster sugar and beat until the mixture is soft and almost white. Add egg yolks, one at a time, beating well after each addition. Gradually add the flour and baking powder and the cocoa, mixing it very well. Add the vanilla and the milk. Beat the egg whites until stiff and fold these into the cake batter. Divide between the prepared pans and bake in the middle of the oven at 400°F. (205°C.) Mark 6 for 25–30 minutes or until a knitting needle inserted into the cakes comes out clean. Turn the cakes out on to a wire rack to cool.

While the cakes are cooling, prepare the filling. Put the egg whites into a bowl and sift in the icing sugar. Stand the bowl well above simmering water (it must not touch the water) and stir the egg white mixture without allowing it to boil. When the sugar has dissolved, whisk for 5–8 minutes until it becomes thick and creamy. Take the bowl from the heat but continue beating the mixture until it is almost cold. Gradually beat in the butter and finally add the egg yolks, beating hard. Add the vanilla. Break the chocolate into small pieces and melt it in the top of a double boiler over hot water. When it is smooth beat it into the icing. Put it aside and let it get quite cold.

Finally make the chocolate flakes. Break the chocolate coarsely and put into a large soup plate. Put this over a pan of hot water and stir the chocolate with a wooden spoon until it is melted. It should not be allowed to overheat. Pour the chocolate on to a marble slab or an upside-down enamel tray and spread it evenly over the surface. Leave to almost set. Scrape a knife down the chocolate strip by strip and it will form into rolls or flakes.

Spread two-thirds of the chocolate icing over the top of one of the cakes, cover with the second cake and spread the remaining chocolate over the top. Lift the flakes off the marble with a palette knife and lay them evenly and carefully on the top of the cake. Over the top sift icing sugar.

CHOCOLATE CRUNCH

As I said in my first book I have so many kinds and nationalities of pastry cooks and bakers from the whole world that we could make our own United Nations, but, as I said before, they are not always united! When I have a new man I let him loose so that he can do what he likes for a week or so. I have a young man just now who came to me from the U.S.A. but who is a Swiss by birth. He made two very interesting looking cakes. He called the first one chocolate crunch. The recipe is:

corn oil	¾ lb. packet cornflakes
6 oz. (¾ cup) butter	2 egg whites
6 oz. (1½ cups) icing (confectioner's) sugar	½ pint (1¼ cups) whipping cream
5 oz. (½ cup) golden syrup	1 large red apple
6 tablespoons (7½) cocoa	1 large green apple
	lemon juice

Grease two 6-in. rounds of greaseproof paper with corn oil. Line the bottom of one cake pan with 1 round of paper. Put the butter into a large pan and melt it over a gentle heat. Take from the heat, stir in the icing sugar and then the golden syrup. Mix well, add the cocoa and finally and very carefully the cornflakes. Try not to break these. Pour half the mixture into the cake pan. Smooth it over and cover with the second round of paper. Pour the remaining mixture over the top. Press it down carefully to level it and place in the refrigerator overnight. To take it out of the pan, run a knife round the edges of the cake, it should turn out easily. Separate the two rounds of cake. Beat the egg whites until stiff, and the cream until it begins to make peaks. Mix the two together. With a star tube pipe a little of the cream on to the centre of one layer of cake. Spread the second half with the remaining cream to make a filling. Quarter both the apples, remove the core and peel two of the quarters of both apples. Chop these quarters finely and sprinkle them over the filling. Sandwich the cakes together again. Slice the remaining apple very thinly and decorate the top of the cake with a ring of apple slices, alternating red with green. Sprinkle with lemon juice. If not using the cake immediately, use canned pineapple, well drained, as apples once peeled and cut discolour easily.

CHOCOLATE ROLL

3 oz. (3 squares) plain chocolate
1 tablespoon (1¼) black coffee
3 eggs, separated
pinch of salt
3 oz. (⅓ cup) sugar

1 oz. (3 tablespoons) ground almonds
— not blanched
sweetened whipped cream
icing (confectioner's) sugar

Line a Swiss roll pan with buttered greaseproof paper. Break the chocolate into small pieces and melt with the coffee in a pan over a low heat. Beat the egg whites with the salt until stiff and gradually add the sugar, beating all the time. Beat the egg yolks until fluffy, stir these into the melted chocolate. Add the ground almonds. Fold a quarter of the beaten egg whites into the chocolate mixture. Pour this over the remaining egg whites, work gently together. Spread the pan with the mixture. Bake in a moderate oven at 380°F. (194°C.) Mark 5 for 10 minutes, reduce the heat to 350°F. (175°C.) Mark 4 for 5 minutes or until top is firm. Take from the oven, cool in the pan. Turn out on to sugared paper, remove the paper lining. Roll up lightly over sugared paper. When cold unroll, spread with sweetened whipped cream and roll up again. Dust with icing sugar.

CHRISTMAS CAKE

I love Christmas in England. Here Christmas is jolly, gay, it is party time for children and grownups. You give the Christmas presents on Christmas day; we on Christmas Eve. Christmas Eve in Hungary was the most exciting evening of the whole year. Our biggest room, the sitting-room, suddenly was closed, shut and locked, at least 3 or 4 days before; we couldn't go near to it. When we asked why, the answer was, the angels are working and if we disturb them they will go away and there will be no Christmas tree and no Christmas presents. These days were tantalising. I still feel the excitement but the longest day was the 24th; it would not end. At last a faint, heavenly bell rang. I could never forget it; I hear it still; suddenly the big door opened and there was the miracle, from the floor to the ceiling – a huge, huge Christmas tree, decorated and snow painted, I thought there was nothing so beautiful. Hundreds and hundreds of candles, not electric, but **real** candles, gold angel hair as they called it. Little gold, silver, red and green balls, shining, sparkling, on the top a huge angel with lovely wings and a smiling beautiful face. Under the tree were parcels, beautifully packed. Each parcel was a different colour, green, yellow, red, pink tied with all kinds of coloured ribbons. Even the little cards were homemade and home-painted. Christmas wasn't commercialized then. How I would love to have just one more moment with something of the joy that we experienced then. We did not have Christmas cakes, but the tree was hung with little home-made biscuits and sweets packed in coloured paper, suspended on golden threads. Walnuts and apples too covered with gold hung on the tree, and oranges in hand-crocheted nets. Everybody, everybody had parcels. Dinner on Christmas Eve was not important; really nobody was hungry; the excitement was too much. Anyway the dinner was without meat and included nothing really sweet.

1 lb. (2⅔ cups) sultanas (white raisins)

1 lb. (2⅔ cups) raisins

3 oz. (½ cup) crystallized cherries

6 oz. (1½ cups) mixed peel

brandy or rum, optional

¾ lb. (1½ cups) butter

¾ lb. (1½ cups) soft dark sugar

3 oz. (½ cup) ground almonds

3 oz. (¾ cup) blanched almonds, roughly chopped

6 eggs, separated

¾ lb. (3 cups) plain flour

Wash, thoroughly clean and stone the fruit; cut the cherries into halves; chop the peel. (Crystallized fruit can be used instead of peel.) If feeling extravagant, soak the fruit (not the cherries or peel) overnight in brandy or rum. Drain off the liquid, it can be used to moisten the cake. Dry the fruit. Rub a 9-in. cake pan with butter; if you like the bottom can be lined with greaseproof paper but this is seldom necessary with modern cake pans. Cream the butter, add the sugar and beat well. Add the ground and chopped almonds, the fruit and the cherries. Add the egg yolks, one at a time, alternating with the flour. Beat the egg whites until stiff and fold these into the cake mixture. If the mixture seems a little too stiff, add some of the brandy or milk. Make sure all the ingredients are carefully mixed and pour the mixture into the prepared cake pan. Before putting it into the oven, hollow out the centre slightly, this helps to ensure a flat cake when baked. Bake at 300°F. (146°C.) Mark 2 for 4 – 6 hours or until a skewer inserted into the cake comes out clean. When the cake comes out of the oven and is still hot, baste it with brandy or rum.

CUMBERLAND FRUIT CAKE

1 lb. (4 cups) plain flour

¼ teaspoon (⅓) baking powder

pinch of salt

½ lb. (1 cup) lard

1 lb. (2⅔ cups) currants

4 oz. (½ cup) brown sugar

2 oz. (¼ cup) butter

Make a light short pastry. Sieve the flour, baking powder and salt into a mixing bowl. Rub in the lard. Mix with enough cold water to make a dough, not too stiff but soft enough to roll out. Divide the pastry into 2 and roll the pieces out into 2 rounds. Cover a deep fireproof plate with 1 round of pastry. Fill this with currants, add sugar and the butter, cut into slivers. Cover with the remaining pastry. Bake in the oven at 400°F. (205°C.) Mark 6 until a golden brown. If liked, the top can be brushed with egg white and sprinkled with sugar before baking. Such 'cakes' are also filled with chopped apples, blackcurrants and other fruit. Lard is the traditional fat for this recipe.

DUNDEE CAKE

1 lb. (4 cups) plain flour
1 teaspoon (1¼) baking powder
8 oz. (1⅓ cups) currants
8 oz. (1⅓ cups) sultanas (white raisins)
8 oz. (1⅓ cups) raisins
½ lb. (1 cup) butter

½ lb. (1 cup) white vegetable fat
1 lb. (2 cups) caster sugar
8 – 9 eggs
3 oz. (½ cup) ground almonds
4 oz. (1 cup) chopped candied peel
about 1 oz. (1⅓ tablespoons) almonds, blanched and split

Sieve the flour with the baking powder. Clean all the dried fruit. Beat the butter and vegetable fat with the sugar to a cream. Beat in the eggs one at a time. With the last of the eggs, begin to add the flour, taking care at this point not to over-mix. Add the ground almonds. Fold in the cleaned fruit and peel. Grease an 8-in. cake pan with butter. Turn the cake mixture into this, spread the top flat and strew with split almonds. Bake at 350°F (175°C.) Mark 4 for about 2 hours or until a skewer inserted into the cake comes out clean.

Dundee cake

GERMAN CAKE (Walnut and Coffee)

A few years back I went to Bad Wörishofen, where I stayed in a hotel in the middle of a beautiful forest. The cure kept everybody busy the whole day long. The food was not particularly good but I was told that was part of the cure, and alcohol was not allowed at all.

But one evening they served us with a cake and we all found it the best thing we ate there. In memory of this great occasion I give you the recipe:

8 eggs
½ lb. (1 cup) sugar
½ lb. (1⅓ cups) ground walnuts
4 oz. (1 cup) cake crumbs
½ oz. (2 tablespoons)
  finely ground coffee beans

filling:
8 oz. (8 squares) plain chocolate
4 oz. (½ cup) sugar
4 tablespoons (5) hot water
6 oz. (¾ cup) butter
4 egg yolks
icing (confectioner's) sugar

Beat the eggs and sugar until the mixture is creamy. Add the walnuts, cake crumbs and coffee. Mix thoroughly and turn into 2 well-greased and floured layer cake pans. Bake in the oven at 325°F. (162°C.) Mark 3 for 30 minutes. Take from the oven and turn out on to a wire rack. Leave until cold. Break the chocolate into small pieces and put into a bowl with the sugar. Add the hot water and place the bowl over a pan of hot water and stir without stopping until the mixture is creamy. Take it from the heat and stir until the mixture is cold. Beat the butter with the egg yolks and then combine with the chocolate mixture. Continue stirring until it is smooth. Spread the filling over one of the rounds of cake, cover with the remaining round and sprinkle the top lightly with chocolate powder or icing sugar.

GUGELHUPF (1) (Germany)

1 oz. (1½ cakes) yeast
4 oz. (½ cup) sugar
1 cup (1¼) milk
4 oz. (½ cup) butter
2 oz. (scant ⅓ cup) almonds,
  blanched and slivered

3 egg yolks
1 lb. (4 cups) plain flour
grated rind 1 lemon
4 oz. (1 cup) seedless raisins
vanilla sugar

Cream the yeast with ½ oz. (1 tablespoon) sugar. Warm the milk to just lukewarm, stir a little into the creamed yeast. Stand in a warm place to rise. Butter a *gugelhupf* pan (deep fluted pan with a centre tube) and sprinkle the almonds round the bottom of it. Cream the butter with the remainder of the sugar, add the egg yolks and beat thoroughly. Add a little of the flour, then the proved yeast. Add the rest of the flour, alternately with the rest of the milk. Beat the mixture well with a wooden spoon until the dough leaves the spoon and the sides of the bowl clean. Add the lemon rind and raisins, mix and then turn the dough into the pan. It should be about three-quarters filled. Leave it to rise in a warm place, covered, until the dough reaches the top of the pan. Bake at 440°F. (228°C.) Mark 7–8 for the first 6 minutes, lower the heat to 410°F. (210°C.) Mark 6–7 and continue baking for another 15 minutes, and then at 375°F. (191°C.) Mark 5 for a further 40 minutes. If the cake seems to be browning too quickly, cover the top with greaseproof paper. Turn the *gugelhupf* out on to a wire rack and let it cool. Sprinkle it generously with sifted vanilla sugar before serving.

GUGELHUPF (2) (Germany)

Gugelhupf can also be made with baking powder instead of yeast. I give you a recipe to make it in this way.

Gugelhupf

4 oz. (½ cup) butter
blanched slivered almonds
6 oz. (¾ cup) sugar
10 oz. (2½ cups) plain flour
2 teaspoons (2½) baking powder

5 eggs, well beaten
¼ cup (⅓) milk
2 teaspoons (2½) grated lemon rind
vanilla essence to taste

Grease a *gugelhupf* pan as in the previous recipe and line the bottom with blanched slivered almonds. Beat the butter and sugar until creamy. Sieve together the flour and baking powder. Add the eggs to the butter alternately with the flour and milk. Mix thoroughly, then add the lemon rind and vanilla. Bake at 400°F. (205°C.) Mark 6 for about 1 hour.

SACHER GUGELHUPF (Austria)

4 oz. (½ cup) butter
10 oz. (2½ cups) plain flour
6 oz. (¾ cup) sugar
5 eggs, well beaten
¼ cup (⅓) milk
a little rum

2 teaspoons (2½) baking powder
4 oz. (4 squares) chocolate
4 oz. (½ cup) sugar
olive oil
apricot jam

Butter a *gugelhupf* pan and sprinkle it with flour. Cream the butter and the first quantity of sugar. Add the eggs. Beat thoroughly, then add the milk, rum, flour and baking powder. Bake for 45 minutes at 375°F. (191°C.) Mark 5 or until a knitting needle run through the cake comes out dry. Turn out and allow to cool. Melt the chocolate in the top of a double boiler. Dissolve the sugar in the water and cook to the small thread stage. Cool. Stir the sugar into the melted chocolate and add 1–2 drops of olive oil. Stir the icing until it has thickened sufficiently to spread over the *gugelhupf*. Spread the *gugelhupf* lightly with apricot jam and then with the icing. Leave for the icing to set.

ISCHLER GUGELHUPF (Austria)

This is a yeast dough which in Austria and Vienna in the good olden days was never missed from a coffee table. If I remember well, it was not served with morning coffee, but in the afternoon – which was coffee time, not tea time, there.

1 oz. (1½ cakes) yeast
sweetened milk
8 oz. (1 cup) butter
4 egg yolks
1 whole egg
2½ oz. (⅓ cup) sugar

a little rum
1 lb. (4 cups) plain flour
2 oz. (⅓ cup) sultanas (white
    raisins)
icing (confectioner's) sugar

Dissolve the yeast in a little sweetened milk and leave aside for 5 minutes. Cream the butter and add it to the yeast. Then add the egg yolks, one at a time mixing well after each addition. Add the whole egg, again beat well, add the sugar, rum and finally and slowly the flour. Mix thoroughly and add the sultanas. Work all these ingredients to a smooth, silky dough. Leave to rise to double its size. Generously grease a *gugelhupf* pan and sprinkle it with flour. Put the risen dough into the pan, it should be three-quarters full, and let it rise to the top of the pan. Bake in the oven at 400°F. (205°C.) Mark 6 for about 1 hour. Turn out on to a wire rack and lightly dust with icing sugar just before serving.

JULIA SPONGE CAKE

We had a cook in my childhood home, a charming woman but very fat. She was not round, she was almost square, as broad as she was tall. She always wore a huge white apron which covered her enormous body. To us children she was very old, but now I think she could not have been more than 35 or 40 years old. She was always cross, always grumbling, but she did everything for everybody, and especially for us. I remember one occasion very vividly. My mother was very much annoyed with her. We three children smelled a very exciting aroma coming out of the kitchen and we stormed in wanting to see Julia and what she was cooking. 'Oh', she said very gruffly, 'we have guests again for lunch, guests, guests, always guests!' She grumbled but she worked quickly; nobody could have done it so beautifully in such a short time.

When we arrived in the kitchen she took out from the sizzling fat a beautifully fried, rosy chicken leg. At home the chicken leg was the important part of the chicken and one that was offered to the guest; not like the breast here. She gave each of us a big chicken leg, beautifully fried and still hot. But bad luck, at this moment my mother came into the kitchen to see how lunch was progressing. Seeing us each having a big piece of chicken, she asked Julia, annoyed, 'What will you serve to the guests?' Julia said a not very nice word, and what should happen to the guests and for me, she said, the children come first. Of course, I think secretly my mother agreed with her, but poor Julia had to go quickly and get another chicken; that meant to

Sponge sandwich cake

kill it quickly and cook it quickly but of course very well. In our yard the chickens wandered about. No great harm was done then and we all kept Julia in our memory and think of her with great love.

She always had in reserve some pastries, and biscuits in the big larder which was next to the kitchen. Her speciality was a very nice sponge cake which was layered sometimes with jam, sometimes with chocolate cream and sometimes with fresh whipped cream. My favourite was when it was layered with red currant jam or jelly. Julia's sponge sandwich recipe is a very simple one.

6 oz. (¾ cup) butter   milk
6 oz. (¾ cup) sugar   2 oz. (⅓ cup) ground almonds
3 eggs, separated   vanilla-flavoured sugar
4 oz. (1 cup) plain flour

Cream the butter and slowly add the sugar. Work this until smooth, then add the egg yolks, one by one and beating the mixture all the time until creamy. Gradually add the flour with a little milk (a little milk lightens the mixture). Add the almonds and mix well. Whip the egg whites until stiff and fold into the sponge batter. Pour into two 7-in. sponge pans and bake at 375°F. (191°C.) Mark 5 for 25–28 minutes. When cold, spread one sponge round with whipped cream, butter cream or red-currant jam. Cover with the second round and sprinkle with vanilla-flavoured sugar.

A VERY LIGHT SPONGE CAKE

fat for greasing   flavouring:
4 oz. (1 cup) plain flour   orange, lemon, vanilla or almond
3 large eggs
6 oz. (¾ cup) caster sugar

Grease and flour a cake pan 7 × 3 in. in depth. Beat the eggs in a warm bowl until they are frothy, add the sugar (lightly warmed). Continue to beat the mixture for 10 minutes, then fold in the chosen flavouring. Pour the mixture into the prepared cake pan and bake for 1 hour at 275°F. (133°C.) Mark 1. Test with a knitting needle, if it comes out clean the cake is ready. Let the cake cool in the pan, then carefully turn it out on to a wire rack. The sponge can be covered with a thin water icing or with butter cream. Or it can be split and filled with whipped cream or jam. In summer fill it with fresh strawberries and whipped cream, and dust the top with sifted icing (confectioner's) sugar.

MADEIRA CAKE

Madeira cake is light and rich yet plain. Traditionally it is always topped with two thin slices of candied peel. Unless well made, it is the dullest cake you could possibly eat.

8 oz. (1 cup) butter   ½ lb. (2 cups) plain flour
½ lb. (1 cup) caster sugar   2 thin slices candied citron peel
5 eggs

Cream the butter with the sugar. Beat the eggs and add to the mixture. Sift in the flour. Pour the mixture into a buttered 8-in. cake pan, thickly sift extra caster sugar over the top and bake for 1 hour in the oven at 375°F. (191°C.) Mark 5. Place the peel over the top of the cake as soon as it has set, but without taking the cake from the oven, and continue baking. Sprinkling sugar over the top of the cake before baking gives the cake its traditional sugary appearance. A Madeira cake used to be served with a glass of Madeira wine before lunch in days gone by.

NUT ROLL

3 eggs, separated	filling:
4 oz. (1 cup) icing (confectioner's) sugar	**cream**
	kirsch
4 oz. (⅔ cup) ground walnuts or hazelnuts	**wild strawberries**
butter for greasing	
fine cake crumbs	

Whip the egg yolks with the sugar until the mixture is pale and creamy. Stiffly beat the egg whites. Fold in the nuts alternately with the beaten egg whites. Butter a large baking sheet and sprinkle it generously with cake crumbs. Spread the hazelnut mixture over the top. Bake in the oven at 370°F. (189°C.) Mark 5 for 15 minutes. While it is cooking, get ready a sheet of greaseproof paper about the same size as the baking sheet and sprinkle it with sugar. When the cake is ready take it from the oven and turn it carefully on to the paper. Roll it over the paper and leave until it is cold. Carefully unroll the cake, add the filling – quantity is to taste – and roll it up again. This is perfectly delicious cake and the filling can be made from other similar ingredients.

ORANGE CAKE (1)

Years ago I went with my son to North Africa where we had a lot of fun mostly because we then had hardly any money. It was the time when foreign allowances for holidays were very restricted. Poverty is quite enjoyable, even a little hunger, if it is not real, but just temporary. We made a lot of silly mistakes with our travelling arrangements; we did not buy all the tickets here but used our meagre allowance on fares. We went first to Tangier, from there to Casablanca, Fez, Rabat and finally to Marrakesh. Of course we booked in the most expensive hotels, which we enjoyed enormously except for the bill; but as my holiday was a busman's holiday because I went to see and taste food, I had to go to the best places. It annoyed us very much that the beautiful hotel was surrounded with orange and lemon orchards which were heavily guarded. We had bed and breakfast in the hotel. The breakfast consisted of tea, one French *croissant*, two pieces of toast, a very small piece of butter and a very tiny portion of marmalade. Such a tiny bit of marmalade in the middle of a huge orange orchard! Lunch we had to skip but we went to all the most expensive restaurants for dinner. We could never afford a drink so we were strictly teetotal. I had and still have a very nice antique ring and I put my hand in such a position that everyone could see it and I waited for an American millionaire to fall in love with it and offer me a fantastic sum. Of course, things like that only happen in a fairy tale. It was all disastrous. In the hotel the food was outstanding; the portions elegantly small and my son, then very young, was not very satisfied with the good food, he wanted much more. It was all very amusing. Nothing tickled us more than the ridiculous portion of marmalade which we compared with any small English hotel where they serve ten times more marmalade. We stayed for tea in our hotel, which was again most elegant. They served tiny sandwiches and very nice plain cakes; one of these was an orange and the other a lemon cake.

3 eggs, separated	**rind and pulp 1 orange finely**
6 oz. (1½ cups) plain flour	**chopped**
pinch of salt	**6 oz. (¾ cup) caster sugar**
1 teaspoon (1¼) baking powder	

Whisk the yolks until thick. Sieve the flour, salt and baking powder into a bowl. Add the chopped orange and sugar. Beat these ingredients until the mixture is smooth. Add the egg yolks and beat well. Beat the egg whites until stiff, fold these gently into the mixture. Rub a rectangular cake pan generously with butter and sprinkle lightly with flour. Pour the cake mixture into the pan. Bake at 375°F. (191°C.) Mark 5 for 30–45 minutes or until the top of the cake is firm to the touch and lightly browned. Turn out of the pan carefully and cool on a wire rack. The cake can be served as it is or split and layered with a butter cream, or the top can be covered with an orange-flavoured water icing.

ORANGE CAKE (2)

As a young girl I visited an uncle who had a young wife. He was good looking and he became a very successful solicitor, and the pride of my mother's whole family.

He was the youngest of my grandmother's nine children and so naturally he was the apple of her eye. He was quite a nice man before he became successful and rich. The richer he was the harder and more heartless he grew. He started his career as a lawyer in a provincial town in Hungary, and as such he very soon married the richest girl in the town. She was tiny, plain and dull and really a poor, sad, little rich girl. She was kind to me and liked me and continually worried my parents to let me stay with her, as she was lonely when I was not there. I was about 15 years old and understood only too well what it was to be lonely. I never minded being there in my school holidays. It was a great change from my own home life. My uncle too, liked my company. I brought young girls and boys to the house. Once my uncle told me very sadly: 'You know it is very good for you to stay with us, you can learn how a marriage should not be'. It was fascinating for me to stay in this house; I could have learned a lot about life, but I suppose I did not have the inclination to learn how to be as economical as they were. I say economical because I do not want to use the nasty word, mean, but in fact they were terribly mean. The set-up of the family was amusing and could have been very pleasant. My uncle and aunt built themselves a very nice home in the most modern style of the time with a beautiful garden which an efficient gardener kept in order. In Hungary men have never known what gardening is. Next to my uncle's house lived his wife's parents. Also a brand new and then ultra-modern villa. I thought it was the most elegant house existing. Next to the villa was the old house where the old people used to live but now one of the other sons lived there with his charming wife, whom I liked very much, and who was equally astonished by the terrible economy of the whole surroundings. In the next house the other brother lived with his wife. The next house again was lived in by the very youngest brother of my aunt, again with a young wife. All of them were unbelievably petty in every way. It was really just amusing, we made jokes of it but we were sorry underneath; what is the good of being rich and living like this? I think all of them wanted to outdo the others; from saving a piece of bread to saving anything that they could save. All the lights would be switched off; it was lucky that we did not all break our necks, because stairs or no stairs, the light was switched off. Opposite my uncle's house lived my aunt's cousin who was married also to a solicitor and his delightful, gay and charming wife was madly in love with him. He lived on his wife's money, ate well and enjoyed their life; I suppose just because they could watch their relatives on the other side of the road counting the pennies day and night. I loved to go over to them and I have to admit that I went over there for the same good food that I was used to at home. There I ate for the first time an orange cake that was always in readiness. They called this Young Ladies' Cake, here we call it Orange Cake.

YOUNG LADIES' CAKE OR ORANGE CAKE

4 eggs

7 oz. (scant cup) caster sugar

4 oz. (1 cup) plain flour

2 oz. (¼ cup) cornflour (cornstarch)

7 oz. (scant cup) butter, melted

½ vanilla pod, scraped

rind and pulp 1 large orange, finely chopped

icing (confectioner's) sugar

Beat the eggs with the sugar until thick. Sieve the plain flour. Gently fold this into the beaten eggs, add the cornflour – do not beat any more after these additions. Stir in the butter – this should be warm but not hot. Add the vanilla and finally the orange. Rub a rectangular pan with butter and sprinkle it with flour. Pour the mixture into the pan and bake in the oven at 380°F. (194°C.) Mark 5 for about 45 minutes or until it is firm to the touch and a golden brown in colour. Turn out to cool on a wire rack and, when quite cold, dust with sifted icing sugar.

PINEAPPLE CAKE

6 oz. (¾ cup) butter

6 oz. (¾ cup) sugar

¼ lb. marzipan

3 eggs

3 rings canned pineapple

3 oz. (¾ cup) plain flour

3 oz. (½ cup) cornflour (cornstarch)

½ teaspoon (⅔) baking powder

apricot jam

white fondant icing (page 214)

glacé cherries

Pineapple cake

Beat the butter until soft, add the sugar and marzipan and continue until the mixture is well blended and soft. Add the eggs, one by one, beating vigorously after each addition. Drain the pineapple and chop 2 of the rings into small pieces. Add this to the creamed butter. Sift the flour, cornflour and baking powder together and fold into the batter. Turn into a well-greased small loaf pan and bake in the oven at 350°–375°F. (175°–191°C.) Mark 4–5 for 1–1½ hours or until·when tested with a skewer it comes out clean. Turn out on to a wire rack to cool. When quite cold, spread with sieved apricot jam, cover with fondant and decorate with the remaining pineapple ring, cut into two, or two glacé cherries.

PUNCH CAKE (Hungary)

Here is a very old-fashioned recipe, but very popular, especially with men. I think it is most important to please our men with our cooking; think of the lovely mink coat you would like for a Christmas present!

1 lemon	5 oz. (scant ⅔ cup) butter
½ cup (⅓) rum	5 oz. (scant ⅔ cup) sugar
6 oz. (1½ cups) plain flour	3 eggs, separated
1 teaspoon (1¼) baking powder	6 oz. (1 cup) sultanas (white raisins)

Squeeze the juice from the lemon, put this into a bowl. Remove as much pith as possible from the peel. Shred the peel finely. Add this to the juice, add the rum, stir, cover and leave overnight. Sieve the flour. Mix the baking powder with 1 tablespoon (1¼) of the sieved flour. Beat the butter with the sugar until creamy. Add the egg yolks, one by one, beating thoroughly. Add the flour, mix well but do not beat the mixture any more. Add the sultanas, fold these into the mixture, then add the rum and lemon. Beat the egg whites until stiff and fold these into the mixture. Sprinkle the baking powder over the top, again carefully stir this into the batter and pour into a large greased and floured rectangular cake pan. Bake in the oven at 375°F. (191°C.) Mark 5 for 1½ hours or until the cake is firm to the touch and golden brown in colour.

SIMNEL CAKE

The traditional Easter Simnel cake is surrounded by legends. It was originally not so much an Easter cake as a Mothering Sunday cake and one story attributed to it, is that servant girls in the large and stately homes were permitted to go home once a year on Mothering Sunday and the more progressive or liberally minded mistresses would give them the raw materials with which to make a cake to take to their mothers. This cake was usually of a rather solid consistency, perhaps because of the lack of skill on the part of the girls; perhaps because it would keep better that way and also it is said that on their sometimes lengthy walk to their homes on Mothering Sunday, they could rest on their journey by sitting on the cake.

The name of the cake is variously claimed to have derived from a husband and wife, bakers both, who developed the recipe and were called respectively 'Simon and Nelly'. It is alternatively said that it is named after Lambert Simnel who had been duped into impersonating Edward, Earl of Warwick (who was in fact a prisoner in the Tower) with a view to overthrowing Henry VII. However, Henry's armies defeated the rebels with their leader at Stoke-on-Trent on 16 June, 1518 and it is said that Lambert Simnel, the impostor, was shown mercy by the King and was given a job as a scullion in the Royal kitchens, that he progressed to become a cake baker and developed the recipe for the cake which now bears his name.

The most scientific idea about the derivation of the name is that it comes from Old French derived from a late Latin word *siminellus* – meaning fine bread, or from the Latin, *siminela* – meaning the finest wheat flour. For myself I like the story about Lambert Simnel best.

Would you take this story from me as I took it from books – a little here and a little there. It is just as good as anything else and will you please accept it.

1 lb. (4 cups) plain flour	almond paste:
good pinch of salt	**12 oz. (2 cups) ground almonds**
½ teaspoon (⅔) baking powder	**12 oz. (1½ cups) caster sugar**
1 lb. (2⅔ cups) sultanas (white raisins)	**1 egg**
	3 teaspoons (3¾) lemon juice
1 lb. (2⅔ cups) currants	
4 oz. (1 cup) chopped candied peel	
½ lb. (1 cup) butter	glazing:
½ lb. (1 cup) vegetable fat	**1 egg, well beaten**
1 lb. (2 cups) caster sugar	
8 eggs	

First make the almond paste. Mix the almonds and sugar together. Whisk the lemon juice with the egg and add to the almond-sugar mixture. Knead the mixture until it is smooth and wrap in greaseproof paper until required.

Rub a 9-in. cake pan with butter or line it with greaseproof paper. Sift the flour with the salt and baking powder. Add the dried fruit and peel. Cream the butter, vegetable fat and the sugar together thoroughly. Beat in the eggs, one by one, adding a little flour should they show signs of curdling. Add the flour etc., to the creamed mixture, mixing it well but not beating. If necessary, a little milk may be added to the batter to give it a dropping consistency. Put half the mixture into the cake pan. Smooth the surface level. Take about one-third of the almond paste and roll this into a $\frac{1}{2}$-in. thick round, exactly the same size as the cake pan. Put this on top of the cake batter, then pour the rest of the cake batter on top. Bake the cake at 325°F. (162°C.) Mark 3 for between 2 and 3 hours. The cake is done when the top feels firm and resilient to the touch, and a skewer inserted in it comes out clean. If the top seems to be getting too brown, cover with double thickness non-stick kitchen paper. Turn it out on to a wire rack and let it cool. Roll the remainder of the almond paste into rounds again about $\frac{1}{2}$-in. thick. Cut out a round from it the size of the cake and from this cut out the middle with a 3–4 in. cutter. Place the ring of almond paste neatly on top of the cake, moulding it to fit the top perfectly. Brush with beaten egg. Divide the rest of the almond paste into small egg-shaped balls, walnut-size (traditionally they number 11 to represent the 11 faithful Apostles) and place these round the edge of the cake. Brush with beaten egg and return to the oven at 450°F. (233°C.) Mark 8 and leave for 5–8 minutes or just long enough for the almond 'eggs' to brown. The cake can be decorated with a variety of small almond fruits and with the word Easter piped on it, and with a small chick nestled among the almond eggs. The cake is usually tied round with a coloured ribbon.

BISHOP'S BREAD

A fruit cake and not a bread for which there are many different recipes, agreeing only in the shape of the cake pan in which it is baked, a shallow oblong pan with a rounded bottom, deeply indented along its length and ribbed to give the bread its characteristic shape. However, the cake can be baked equally well in any shallow oblong pan. Do not fill more than three-quarters full.

4 eggs	2 oz. (2 squares) bitter chocolate
3½ oz. (scant cup) plain flour	3½ oz. (scant ½ cup) sugar
1 teaspoon (1¼) grated lemon rind	2 oz. (⅓ cup) seedless raisins
2 oz. (⅓ cup) glacé cherries	2 oz. (⅓ cup) finely chopped nuts

Rub the cake pan with butter and lightly dust with flour. Separate the egg yolks from the whites. Sift the flour, add the lemon rind. Chop the cherries, coarsely grate the chocolate. Beat the egg yolks until smooth, add half the sugar and beat until the mixture is thick and frothy. Whisk the egg whites until stiff, add the rest of the sugar and continue beating until the mixture forms peaks. Fold into the egg yolks. Add the flour, folding it carefully into the mixture. Add the fruit, nuts, chocolate and stir gently. Pour the mixture into the prepared cake pan and bake in the oven at 350°F. (175°C.) Mark 4 for 45 minutes, but check the cake after 30 minutes. Take from the oven, turn out gently on to a wire rack. Leave for one day before cutting. Instead of the recommended raisins, chocolate etc., figs, nuts, candied peel, a mixture of everything, in proportion naturally, may be used.

SATURDAY CAKE

8 egg yolks
10 oz. (1¼ cups) butter
3 strips angelica, chopped
6 glacé cherries, coarsely chopped
1 tablespoon (1¼) finely chopped
   orange peel
2 oz. (½ cup) candied peel

2 oz. (⅓ cup) coarsely chopped
   almonds
12 oz. (1½ cups) sugar
4 oz. (⅔ cup) ground rice
8 oz. (2 cups) plain flour
¼ cup (⅓) rum
4 egg whites

Rub a large cake pan with fat and line it with greaseproof paper. Beat the egg yolks with the butter until the mixture is creamy. Add the angelica, cherries, orange peel, candied peel and nuts. Stir well, add the sugar (keep back 2 tablespoons), ground rice, flour and rum. Mix thoroughly. Beat the egg whites until stiff, add the reserved sugar, continue beating until the whites form peaks, then fold into the cake mixture. Pour the mixture into the prepared cake pan and bake at 375°F. (191°C.) Mark 5 for 1½-2 hours. Test with a skewer before taking the cake from the oven. If it comes out clean, take the cake from the oven, turn out on to a cake rack and let it cool. Like bishop's bread, this cake is best left for a day before cutting.

SPICE AND SEED CAKES

ANISE (*Pimpinella anisum*). Aniseed originally came from Egypt, but it is now cultivated in Europe as well. It is the seed of the anise and is greyish-brown in colour. It contains a volatile oil, most commonly used in the preparation of cordials and in confectionery.

CARAWAY (*Carum carvi*). Caraway seed is a great friend of mine. I use it widely and find the flavour very pleasant in food, in bread, cheese, even in cakes. Caraway is native to Europe.

CINNAMON (*Cinnamomum zeylanicum*). The cinnamon is a native of Ceylon and is the bark of a tree, a member of the laurel family. The crops are gathered from May till September and two-year shoots are stripped of their bark. Cinnamon comes on the market in long, cylinder-shaped rolls, yellow-brown in colour. It is expensive, therefore cassia is sometimes added which is the bark of *cinnamon cassia* which comes from China and India. Cassia in appearance is similar to cinnamon, but coarser. It is about four times as thick and darker in colour.

CLOVES (*Eugenia aromatica*). They are the dried flower buds of an evergreen shrub, grown in Zanzibar and from the West Indies. The buds are gathered and soon turn reddish in colour, they are then spread out in the sun to dry, when the colour changes to a deep brown. Cloves possess a strong, hot flavour. Because of their strong flavour, I don't like them, despite my fancy for Zanzibar's exotic name.

GINGER (*Zingiber officinale*). This is the root of the herb, a native of India and China, but now cultivated in America, Africa and Australia. Black ginger, which I have never met before, but will search for now, is said to be the most expensive. Green or French ginger is much used in China.

NUTMEG and MACE (*Myristica fragrans*). Did you know that the two come from the same tree? They are the nut and the aril or sheath of the nutmeg tree, which grows in Malaysia and the Archipelago.

VANILLA (*Vanilla planifolia*). Vanilla is the pod of a climbing orchid, and comes from South America and the West Indies. Mexican vanilla is the most highly priced. Modern bakers and confectioners use it a great deal. The highest-priced vanilla has the smallest content of *vanillin*, this being the Mexican variety; Bourbon has more *vanillin*, while Java has nearly double. I tell you, too, that vanilla pods contain a notable amount of gum, resin and sugar, all of which contribute to the final flavour. *Vanilla planifolia* is the most common species of vanilla used today though most vanilla is artificial.

Now I promise I won't bore you any more with seeds or spices, only if I have to use them for some recipe.

GINGERBREAD

12 oz. (3 cups) plain flour

1½ teaspoons (2) ground ginger

½ teaspoon (⅔) bicarbonate of soda

2 oz. (⅓ cup) chopped candied peel

4 oz. (½ cup) butter

4 oz. (½ cup) brown sugar

½ lb. (¾ cup) treacle

2 eggs, well beaten

a little milk

Sieve the flour with the ginger and soda. Mix in the peel. Heat the butter, sugar and treacle in a small pan until the mixture is smooth. Let it cool, then add it to the flour, beat well. Add the eggs, still beating, and finally just enough milk to make a firm sticky dough. Pour the mixture into a well-greased cake pan and bake in the oven at 375°F. (191°C.) Mark 5 for 1½ hours. Flaked almonds or chopped preserved ginger may be added to the cake if liked. It is important that it bakes slowly and this is the reason why the bicarbonate, which acts slowly, is added to the cake.

GINGER CAKE

Ginger cake is very popular everywhere, so I give you a simple recipe.

4 oz. (½ cup) butter

10 oz. (1 cup) golden syrup or
    treacle

½ cup (⅔) milk

1 lb. (4 cups) plain flour

2 tablespoons (2½) baking powder

½ teaspoon (⅔) ground ginger

3 eggs

6 oz. (1½ cups) preserved ginger
    drained

½ cup (⅔) slivered almonds

Using a large pan, warm the butter and syrup (or, if preferred, a mixture of syrup and treacle). Stir until the mixture has dissolved, add the milk, stir well, then let the mixture cool. Sieve the dry ingredients into a bowl. Beat the eggs, stir these into the cooled syrup mixture and pour this gradually into the sieved flour etc. Blend carefully. Add the preserved ginger. Thoroughly grease a square or rectangular 8 – 9 in. cake pan. Sprinkle the bottom with the slivered almonds and flour, add the cake mixture, filling the pan three-quarters full. Bake at 375°F. (191°C.) Mark 5 on the middle shelf of the oven for 1½ hours or until the cake is firm to the touch. It should rise well during baking, so make sure the cake pan is not too full to allow for this.

HONEY CAKE

Honey cake in Hungary was not a 'cake', not a biscuit, not a pastry, not a food at all.

It was something romantic, something heart-warming, something heart-breaking. In Hungary, on the big markets there used to be rows of stalls full of all kinds of honey cakes. There were beautiful and very expensive ones on the bigger stands; the more modest ones were on the smaller stands. But all of them had messages to take to sweethearts.

Large heart-shaped biscuits were made from honey cake covered with pillar-box-red fondant. In the middle a little *real* mirror, underneath it a little love poem shorter or longer depending on the size of the heart.

Beautifully dressed Hungarian peasant boys in their navy-blue or black suits, with bow ties of long, black ribbon, shiny-shiny black boots reaching up to the knee, boys with round, black hats on which they had a little bouquet of flowers – these boys bought heart-shaped honey biscuits for their girls. The message, the form of the little verse on the heart, told them of the boys' feelings.

All kinds of shapes were made from honey cakes – whose manufacture was, by the way, a very big village industry – some of them were thin, the shape of plates and beautifully designed. They made from honey cake little dolls which were then coloured, and the beads which the boys bought to hang round their sweethearts' necks.

I personally used to buy the thin, flat, crisp biscuits; here is the recipe.

8 oz. (¾ cup) honey
6 oz. (¾ cup) brown sugar
4 oz. (½ cup) butter
12 oz. (3 cups) brown or rye flour
pinch each of salt, bicarbonate of soda, ground cinnamon, allspice and ground cloves

½ cup (⅔) sour milk
3 oz. (½ cup) seedless raisins
4 oz. (½ cup) chopped nuts
2 oz. (½ cup) desiccated coconut
4 oz. (1 cup) icing (confectioner's) sugar

Put all the ingredients (except the icing sugar) into a large bowl and beat thoroughly, working to a smooth firm dough. Spread it about ½ in. thick on a well-greased baking pan. Bake in the oven at 375°F. (191°C.) Mark 5 for 40 minutes. The cake is done when it springs back immediately at the touch. Take from the oven, turn out to cool and then spread with a thin layer of icing (frosting) made by mixing the icing sugar with a little water. When the icing has dried, cut the cake into squares.

SEED CAKE

This is a cake which I am afraid will not be to everybody's taste, but you can never tell and perhaps I will find a few people who will like it. It is seed cake. If you don't like it please forgive me, I do like caraway seed cake myself.

8 oz. (2 cups) plain flour
¼ teaspoon (⅓) baking powder
6 oz. (¾ cup) butter
6 oz. (¾ cup) sugar
3 eggs, separated

2 teaspoons (2½) caraway seeds
1 tablespoon (1¼) finely chopped
orange peel (optional)
¼ cup (⅓) rum

Sieve the flour and baking powder together. Cream the butter until fluffy. Add the sugar and mix well. Add the egg yolks, one by one and at the same time adding a little of the flour. Add the caraway seeds and orange peel and beat the mixture thoroughly. Beat the egg whites until stiff, fold these into the cake mixture and very slowly the rest of the flour. Add the rum and pour the cake mixture into a well-greased square cake pan. Bake in the oven at 350°F. (175°C.) Mark 4 for about 1½ hours or until when tested with a skewer it comes out clean.

SAFFRON CAKE (recipe dated 1805)

pinch of saffron
2 lb. (8 cups) plain flour
pinch of salt
1 lb. (2 cups) butter or margarine
1½ oz. (2¼ cakes) yeast

about 2 cups (2½) warm milk
4 oz. (½ cup) caster sugar
4 oz. (⅔ cup) currants
4 oz. (⅔ cup) sultanas (white
raisins)
4 oz. (1 cup) chopped candied peel

Infuse the saffron in a few tablespoonfuls of warm water for 15 minutes. Sieve the flour into a warm bowl with the salt and rub in the fat. Make a well in the middle. Cream the yeast with the warm milk. Pour this into the well. Mix thoroughly and beat to a soft dough, adding the infused saffron (with water). Cover the bowl and leave to rise in a warm place until the dough has doubled its bulk. Add the sugar, the fruit and peel and again beat well. Rub two 9-in. cake pans with butter and divide the cake mixture evenly into these. Bake in a hot oven 400°F. (205°C.) Mark 6 for 15 minutes, reduce the heat to 375°F. (191°C.) Mark 5 and bake for another 30 – 35 minutes or until the cake is risen, a golden brown, and firm underneath.

STOLLEN

The Germans have a very famous Christmas cake which is not really a cake at all but rather a very rich, very expensive and very good bun. It is oval in shape; known the world over. The most famous of these German Christmas *Stollen* were those from Dresden. It was the proud boast of the people of Dresden that Germans sent them to their friends throughout the world. I used often to be in Dresden. It was one of the most delightful of German cities, its architecture was beautiful and the atmosphere of culture was felt wherever you went. The people were very friendly, very hospitable, cultured and musical. Music making was the pastime of all. Middle-class families always had a music room with two pianos and other musical instruments, and very often held musical evenings after coming back from their shops or offices. I had a friend who had a big grocery business and who sent *Stollen* all over the world. After the Second World War, Dresden was still occupied and he started a very small bakery which has now grown large and very well known.

I give you one of his recipes which he kindly gave to me many years ago. I exchanged it for my English Christmas cake recipe!

2 oz. (3 cakes) yeast
½ cup (⅔) warm milk
2 lb. (8 cups) plain flour
4 oz. (½ cup) sugar
6 oz. (¾ cup) softened butter
1 teaspoon (1¼) salt
grated rind 2 lemons
2 oz. (½ cup) almonds

4 oz. (1 cup) chopped candied
  lemon peel
4 oz. (1 cup) chopped candied
  orange peel
6 oz. (1 cup) currants
6 oz. (1 cup) sultanas (white
  raisins)
3 eggs, well beaten

Cream the yeast with the milk; when it has dissolved, add just enough flour to make a 'little' dough. Leave this to rise. Sieve the flour into a warm bowl, make a well in the middle and pour in the risen yeast. Leave to prove. When the dough has risen well, punch it down and knead thoroughly until it no longer sticks to the sides of the bowl. Add the remaining ingredients and work the dough until it is very smooth and almost silky. Divide it into 2 or 3 portions and shape them into oval-shaped loaves. Make a dent with a rolling pin lengthways, more to one side than the other, and fold the wide sides over the dent (this gives the *stollen* their characteristic shape). Place the *stollen* on a floured baking (cookie) sheet and leave to rise again until they have almost doubled their bulk. Bake at 450°F. (233°C.) Mark 8 for 40 minutes. The oven must be hot otherwise the *stollen* might become speckly owing to the high fat content.

The *stollen* can be iced with a water icing or simply dusted with icing (confectioner's) sugar, or painted with a thick sugar glaze and garnished with candied fruits of all types. When it is cold it can be packed or stored away and will keep for months. *Stollen* do not rise like an ordinary yeast loaf as they are so heavy with fruit.

STREUSEL KUCHEN (Germany)

I feel that I have to give you this popular, very German bun. It is so popular in England that I think you should have the recipe and make it at home; it is very easy. Make it in two parts. First you make the *Kuchen* which is a light, yeast dough made as follows:

½ oz. (¾ cake) yeast
¼ pint (full ½ cup) warm milk
½ lb. (2 cups) plain flour
2 oz. (¼ cup) butter
2 oz. (¼ cup) sugar
1 egg
1 tablespoon (1¼) melted butter

Streusel:
3 oz. (6 tablespoons) butter
3 oz. (⅓ cup) sugar
6 oz. (1½ cups) plain flour
1 teaspoon (1¼) ground cinnamon

Dissolve the yeast in the warm milk, add one-third of the ½ lb. flour to make a batter. Cover and leave in a warm place to rise. Cream the first quantity of butter and sugar, add the egg and the rest of the flour. Beat it briskly, then add the yeast batter. Work to a dough and knead with the hands until the dough no longer sticks to the hands or the sides of the mixing bowl. Leave to rise. Roll the dough out thinly and spread on a greased baking (cookie) sheet. Let it rise and paint it with melted butter.

While it is rising, prepare the *Streusel*. Melt the butter and while still hot mix with the sugar, flour and cinnamon. Cut the paste with a knife and then crumble to resemble breadcrumbs. Sprinkle this over the rolled-out dough and bake at 425°F. (216°C.) Mark 7 for 35–45 minutes. Serve fresh, cut into squares. A less usual type of *Streusel* is to half-fill a largish loaf pan with the dough and let it rise until it three-quarters fills the pan and sprinkle the *Streusel* on top. Bake as above, but a little longer. Or the dough can be divided into two, one half spread with homemade jam, such as damson, sprinkled lightly with ground cinnamon and then spread with the remaining half, and finally topped with the *Streusel*. It is baked as the first *Streusel Kuchen* but a little longer time should be allowed.

SOLIMÈNE (Alsace)

½ oz. (¾ cake) yeast
2 teaspoons (2½) sugar
1 lb. (4 cups) plain flour
4 eggs

½ cup (⅔) cream
1 teaspoon (1¼) salt
2 teaspoons (2½) oil
4 oz. (½ cup) butter

Dissolve the yeast with the sugar in a little warm water, add a quarter of the flour and leave covered in a warm place to rise. Add 2 of the eggs, half the cream, the rest of the flour, salt and the oil. Work to a dough and knead thoroughly. Add the butter, little by little plus the remaining eggs and the rest of the cream. Work this all to a soft dough – if it seems too stiff add a little more cream. Rub a round deep cake pan generously with butter and half-fill it with dough. Bake at 400°F. (205°C.) Mark 6 until it is a golden brown. Take from the pan, slice horizontally and sprinkle each layer with melted salted butter. Sandwich the layers together again and serve at once, as hot as possible.

SWISS ROLL (JELLY ROLL) (1)

I am sure everybody knows how to make a Swiss roll. I am sure you know it better than I do because it is so very English. I give you the recipe because Swiss roll is such a useful standby. It keeps well; it is easy to make, it is not expensive and can be varied with a variety of fillings – jam (very many kinds of jam), chocolate or coffee cream, crème patissière, chestnut purée or whipped cream.

4 oz. (1 cup) plain flour   **4 oz. (½ cup) caster sugar**
1 teaspoon (1¼) baking powder **warm jam for filling**
3 eggs

Cut a sheet of greaseproof paper a little larger than a 9 × 11 in. Swiss roll (jelly roll) pan. Cut the paper at the corners so that it will fit neatly into the pan. Grease both the pan and the paper and fit the latter into the pan. Sieve the flour with the baking powder. Beat the eggs with sugar over a pan of hot water until the mixture is thick enough to coat the beater. Take the bowl from the heat and fold in the flour. Pour the mixture into the prepared pan, tilting it a little to spread the batter evenly over the paper. Bake at 425°F. (216°C.) Mark 7 for 8–10 minutes until the sponge is a pale golden all over and begins to shrink away from the edges of the pan. While the sponge is baking, get ready a cloth wrung out in hot water, and over this spread a sheet of greaseproof paper dredged with caster sugar. Turn the sponge cake out on to the paper and spread with jam filling. Make a small cut half-way through the sponge, about 1 in. from the end. Start rolling up the sponge at the cut end and, working quickly, roll firmly and tightly. Dredge with caster sugar and cool on a wire rack.

SWISS ROLL (JELLY ROLL) (2)

5 oz. (scant ⅔ cup) caster sugar   3 egg yolks
½ cup (⅔) cold water   4 oz. (1 cup) plain flour
2 egg whites   warm jam for filling

Prepare a Swiss roll (jelly roll) cake pan as in the previous recipe. Bring the sugar and
the water slowly to the boil, then boil hard for 5 minutes. Cool for 5 minutes. In the
meantime beat the egg whites and yolks together, add the cooled syrup and whisk for
15 minutes or until the mixture thickens. Sieve the flour and fold into the mixture as
lightly as possible. Pour into the prepared Swiss roll pan and bake in the oven at
375°F. (191°C.) Mark 5 for 10 minutes; lower the temperature to 350°F. (175°C.)
Mark 4 and continue cooking another 5 minutes or until the cake is a golden brown
and the edges begin to shrink away from the sides. Continue as in the previous recipe.

TWELFTH NIGHT CAKE

In France this cake is called the *gâteau des rois*, as Twelfth night is Epiphany, the
feast of the three kings. It used to be the last of the Christmas celebrations, and
perhaps the symbolic cake represented the gifts of the Magi to the infant Jesus.
There used to be a charming custom that this cake would be shared among the guests
and family all except for three pieces which the host would keep. These were for the
baby Jesus, his mother and the Magi. Then these pieces would be given to the poor.
A silver token was always baked in the cake and the person who found this in his or
her portion would be the king of the feast, and would have to give another party in
return.

There are, it seems, different cakes in different parts of France; in some provinces
it is a kind of flat pastry *galette*, a sort of biscuit wafer. In others it is a kind of
brioche dough shaped like a crown. You may use whichever of my *brioche* recipes you
find the most successful but you will need 1 lb. (4 cups) of flour and the other ingredients in proportion. When the dough is ready for the final shaping, make into
the form of a crown and leave it to rise in a warm place. Allow the crown to cool
and then brush over with yolk of egg and put crystallized sugar and candied slices
of lemon carefully round the crown like jewels, before baking in a medium oven.
Don't forget your silver coin or token.

WALNUT CAKE (1)

For years and years I went to Tangier for my holidays where I had friends with whom I stayed. They were a delightful couple, artistic and artists both of them. I have never met so many interesting people as I met there.

The food was good, I could say perfect, and as simple as their way of life. They had an Arab chef, who moved quietly and slowly in the kitchen. I thought he would never finish a lunch, dinner or whatever it was he was preparing, with his leisurely quiet way of working. But every meal was on time, whether we were alone, or, as was very frequently the case, there were several guests.

For tea we used to have tiny sandwiches and a very simple walnut cake which I liked very much. In memory of my lovely Tangier days I set down the recipe of that walnut cake.

1 lb. (4 cups) plain flour
¼ teaspoon (⅓) baking powder
½ cup (⅔) milk
3 oz. (⅓ cup) caster sugar
5 oz. (½ cup) golden syrup

3 oz. (½ cup) roughly chopped
walnuts
2 oz. (⅓ cup) sultanas (white
raisins)
2 eggs

Sieve the flour and baking powder together, add the milk and sugar, beat well, add the syrup and beat again. Add the walnuts and sultanas. Beat the eggs until smooth, add to the cake mixture and mix everything well together. Pour into a buttered and floured loaf-shaped cake pan, and bake at 350°F. (175°C.) Mark 4 for about 45 minutes or until when a skewer is inserted into the cake it comes out clean. Take from the oven and leave the cake in the pan until it is cool.

WALNUT CAKE (2)

8 eggs, separated
½ lb. (1 cup) caster sugar
2 tablespoons (2½) soft white
breadcrumbs
½ lb. (1⅓ cups) ground walnuts
grated rind 1 lemon
1 tablespoon (1¼) rum
coarsely chopped walnuts

filling:
3 oz. (3 squares) bitter chocolate
4 oz. (½ cup) butter
4 oz. (½ cup) sugar
1 egg

Cream the egg yolks with the caster sugar until the mixture is smooth and thick. Add the crumbs, ground walnuts, grated rind and rum and mix well. Beat the egg whites until stiff, fold into the cake mixture. Turn the mixture into 2 buttered layer cake pans and bake in the oven at 375°F. (191°C.) Mark 5 for 20–25 minutes. Do not on any account open the oven door during the first 15 minutes of cooking or the cake will collapse. When the cake is done, take it from the oven and cool on a wire rack, taking it out carefully from the pans. In the meantime prepare a filling. Melt the chocolate over hot water in a double boiler. Take it from the heat, add the butter, the whole egg and sugar and beat the mixture until it is smooth. Spread half the chocolate cream over one layer of cake, cover with the remaining layer and spread this equally with cream. Sprinkle with coarsely chopped walnuts and chill the cake before serving.

WALNUT SLICE

8 oz. (1 cup) butter
12 oz. (3 cups) plain flour
pinch of salt
1 teaspoon ($1\frac{1}{4}$) sugar
3 egg yolks

filling:
5 egg yolks
4 tablespoons (5) sugar
1 oz. ($\frac{1}{4}$ cup) chocolate powder
7 egg whites
10 oz. ($1\frac{2}{3}$ cups) chopped walnuts

Rub the butter into the flour, add the salt and sugar. Mix with the egg yolks to a stiff dough – one more egg may be required, it depends on the size also the absorption of the flour (or instead of a third egg yolk a little rum may be used). Divide the dough into two and roll each piece out on a floured board and cut into two equal-sized rounds. Bake one round at 400°F. (205°C.) Mark 6 for 5 minutes. To make the filling, whip 4 of the egg yolks with the sugar until thick and creamy. Add the chocolate powder and beat thoroughly. Beat the egg whites until stiff and fold into the mixture. Add the walnuts. Spread this on the cooked round of pastry and cover with the remaining uncooked round. Prick with the end of a fork. Mix the remaining egg yolk with a little sugar and brush this over the top of the pastry. Bake at 450°F. (233°C.) Mark 8 for 18 – 20 minutes.

WEDDING CAKES

Once upon a time I would not have believed that I would make these very strange white cakes, which resembled buildings, the reason for which I have never understood. Now as I look back at thirty years of work in this country I cannot remember how many of these strange objects I have made.

I made hundreds and hundreds, perhaps thousands, during these thirty years. I made all of them during the twenty-one years I supplied Fortnum and Mason.

Fortnum and Mason had then a very important clientele. But for many years now these people have come direct to me. One of my favourite cakes was the one which I made for the then Sir Anthony Eden's marriage to Miss Clarissa Churchill.

The reception at 10 Downing Street was very small. The cake too was small, but most elegant. Just a cake covered with white roses. Nothing could be simpler, nicer and more elegant than that wedding cake. Nothing at all like a building about that one!

I have made very many conventional wedding cakes, if the customer insisted. This mostly happened when I had nothing to do with the order. Countess Eszterhazy's mother came to me with a set idea. She wanted a wedding cake in the shape of a rabbit, because the young Countess's name – or nickname – happened to be Bunny. I just would not agree. An erect bunny would look clumsy and not at all interesting, a sitting or lying one even worse. So we agreed that I would make a very beautiful three-tier wedding cake, decorated like a forest with rabbits running round it. On the top to finish the cake, was a large erect rabbit.

I also made the Duke of Bedford's wedding cake. The cake was unbelievably beautiful. The Duke brought me a sample of a rare lily, a fresh flower which was a beautiful specimen. Only ours made of sugar looked even better.

I had, again, great pleasure and joy making the Duke's son's wedding cake which had to match the first present the young bridegroom had given his beautiful fiancée. So the cake was decorated with blue. In spite of this, it looked very beautiful, just as the bride did.

Of the many, many wedding cakes I made, I liked most the one I made for Princess Margaret. I designed it myself. Do you know where I have taken my idea from? I had just returned from Geneva where I had seen an umbrella-shaped rose tree in one of the parks. I walked there for a long time, because the park fascinated me with its unusual flower beds and those beautiful rose trees. I kept those rose trees in my memory.

When Princess Margaret became engaged, I thought that this was my opportunity to utilise my idea: the rose tree. You would not believe how badly I draw, but I do draw if I have to. So I drew a seven-tier wedding cake, covered with white rosebuds and white marguerites and on top of the cake a white umbrella of white rosebuds. Hanging from the umbrella were long sprays of white rosebuds and marguerites. When I entered my office I saw the decorations with the initials 'A' and 'M' and I put these on the top of the umbrella. It was just a dream! I gladly showed my design to everybody who came into my office. Some people became quite excited about the beauty of the cake.

If I make a wedding cake, I have to see the bride. I like to make each wedding cake

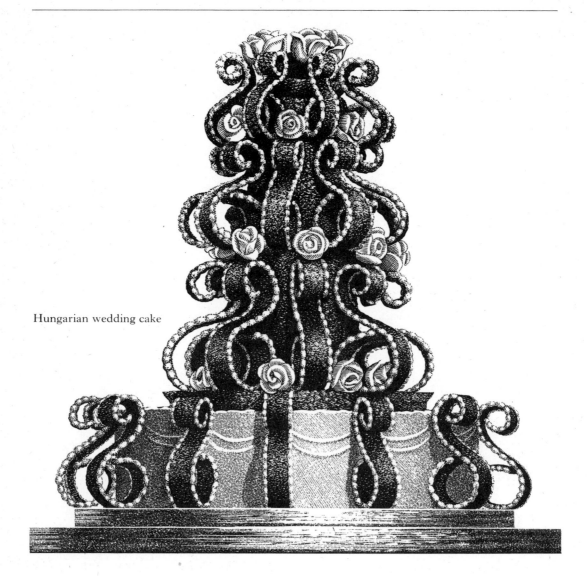

Hungarian wedding cake

just the cake for that one girl, for it will be her wedding, her day.

As I said before, we in Hungary don't have wedding cakes. The rich Hungarian peasants, however – or at least in my time – made a very big wedding gâteau, three or four feet high, covered with white icing and decorated with *crockant* (ground almonds and sugar caramelized till light brown and bent into 'S'-shaped ribbons). A four-foot column of *crockant* was erected in the middle of the cake and decorated like a tower. Orange blossoms or white roses completed the decoration.

I have also made French wedding cakes – those tall towers made of *profiteroles*, filled with *crème parisienne* and built up with caramel sugar. It is a beautiful cake, but tends to suffer if made on a very humid day.

WEDDING CAKE

4 lb. (10⅔ cups) currants
1 lb. (2⅔ cups) sultanas (white raisins)
1 egg white
½ lb. almond paste
½ lb. (1 cup) vegetable fat
½ lb. (1 cup) butter

1 lb. soft dark brown sugar
8 large eggs
1 lb. 2 oz. (4½ cups) plain flour
¼ lb. (1 cup) chopped candied peel
9 oz. (1½ cups) glacé cherries
rum or brandy
rose-water

Wash and dry the currants and sultanas. Work the egg white into the almond paste to soften it. Mix it with the vegetable fat and the butter, add the sugar and beat until the mixture is creamy. Add the eggs one at a time, beating well after each addition to avoid curdling. Lightly fold in half the flour. (At this point a tablespoonful of black treacle, burnt sugar or caramel may be added to the mixture to darken it.) Add the currants, sultanas, peel and cherries. Fold in the rest of the flour. Rub an 11-in. round cake pan or a 12-in. square pan with butter and line it with two thicknesses of greaseproof paper. Turn the mixture into the prepared cake pan. Bake in the middle of the oven and try to keep the cake from drying out; it is advisable to place the pan on the baking sheet on the oven shelf and on several sheets of newspapers. Bake at 325°F. (162°C.) Mark 3 for the first hour, lower the heat to 300°F. (146°C.) Mark 2 and continue baking another 3½-4 hours. When the cake begins to brown on top, cover it with several thicknesses of brown or greaseproof paper. Take the cake from the oven, sprinkle it with rum or brandy mixed with rose-water and cool for the first 45 minutes in the pan. Turn out on to a wire rack and let the cake cool, leaving the wrappings on until it is quite cold. Wrap in several layers of greaseproof paper and store in an airtight tin. Wedding cakes are best made about three months before being required. After six weeks, take the cake from the storage tin, pierce it with a knitting needle and sprinkle with 4 – 6 tablespoonfuls of brandy or rum. Rewrap and store as before.

It is usual in Britain to completely cover a wedding cake with an almond paste or icing. This should be done at least one week before it is coated with the usual royal icing. Although many home cooks are also good cake decorators, it is probably wiser to hand the wedding cake to a professional for icing and decorating.

ALMOND ICING (Frosting)

1 lb. ground almonds
½ lb. (1 cup) caster sugar
½ lb. (1½ cups) icing
   (confectioner's) sugar, sifted

2 eggs
1 tablespoon (1¼) brandy or rum
2 teaspoons (2½) orange-flower
   water or rose-water

Put the almonds and sugar into a bowl. Whisk the eggs with the remaining in-gredients, add this to the bowl and mix it all to a stiff paste. Another egg yolk might be required, it depends on the size of the eggs. Knead the paste with the hands until it is smooth. Before coating the cake with the almond paste, trim it if necessary and brush the top with warmed sieved apricot jam. Lightly sprinkle a pastry board with sieved icing sugar. Take somewhat less than half the paste and roll this out firmly but carefully into a round or square to fit the top of the cake. Invert the cake on the paste, trim off the edges that show beneath the cake and press it down firmly. Lift up the cake and put it aside. Roll out the remaining almond paste into two strips the same width as the sides of the cake. Brush the sides of the cake with warm sieved apricot jam. Wrap one strip round one side of the cake and then the second strip round the other. Seal the joints and roll a small rolling pin or jam pot round the sides and top of the cake to smooth it all down. Leave to dry for a week to let the oil in the almonds dry out, otherwise it will seep through the final Royal icing.

GÂTEAUX

You may well wonder what the difference is between a cake and a gâteau, why I separate them. It is hard to define sometimes, but the difference is a matter of degree rather than of kind. A gâteau is commonly richer than a cake though basically the ingredients are the same. A gâteau should be richer, more elaborate and often more expensive, I am afraid. Whipped cream, nuts, chocolate will all add to the decoration and the taste. A gâteau will not always keep well, but must be used fresh. For your dessert you would naturally think of using a gâteau, especially when you are having guests. While you might have a slice of gâteau with your coffee or tea, especially when you want to celebrate a special occasion or wish to spoil yourself, your husband or children, you would never think of offering a slice of plain cake as a dinner dessert.

In many countries I have known, the gâteau for a dinner or a party would be chosen and ordered for the event from a good pâtisserie. But it is quite possible and much nicer to make your own and I hope you will try some of the recipes.

BOHEMIAN GÂTEAU

Bohemian gâteau is a most useful and very beautiful cake. It is a great joy that it can be kept for a week or 10 days. It is very good to eat. It is not difficult to cut if you have a really sharp knife which you should first dip in hot water. The easiest method is to cut the cake in two, and then into slices. This mixture can also be made as a long rectangular cake from which you can cut slices, decorating it exactly as the round gâteau.

6 eggs, separated
7 oz. (scant cup) sugar
3 oz. ($\frac{1}{2}$ cup) ground hazelnuts
2 oz. ($\frac{1}{2}$ cup) plain flour

filling:
7 oz. (scant cup) sugar
3 oz. (3 squares) bitter chocolate
7 egg yolks
3 oz. ($\frac{1}{2}$ cup) ground hazelnuts
4 oz. ($\frac{1}{2}$ cup) butter
2 tablespoons ($2\frac{1}{2}$) whipped cream

Whisk the egg whites until stiff. Cream the sugar and the egg yolks together, add the hazelnuts and the flour. Fold the egg whites into the mixture. Spread half the mixture thinly on a buttered baking (cookie) sheet and bake at 350°F. (191°C.) Mark 5 for 10–15 minutes. Slide the cake carefully from the baking sheet on to a flat surface. Repeat this with the remaining mixture. When cool, cut each sheet of cake into four oblong pieces of equal size. Prepare the filling. Put the sugar with 2 tablespoons ($2\frac{1}{2}$) of water into a pan and stir over a low heat until the sugar has dissolved. Put aside to cool. Break the chocolate into small pieces and melt in the top of a double boiler over hot water. Put aside but keep warm. Beat the egg yolks until fluffy and whisk them into the cooled sugar. Add the hazelnuts, chocolate and butter. Return the pan to the stove and stir continuously over the boiling water to cook the mixture until it is thick. Pour into a bowl and let the mixture cool. Beat until smooth and stir in the whipped cream. Spread some of this mixture over seven of the cake slices, placing each one neatly on top of the other. Spread the top slice with a chocolate butter cream (frosting) (see page 140).

CHOCOLATE GÂTEAU (1)

This is one of the best-known and most delicious chocolate gâteaux and was the first gâteau I made in this country. The recipe is as follows:

4 oz. (4 squares) bitter chocolate
8 eggs
8 oz. (1 cup) sugar
5 oz. ($1\frac{1}{4}$ cups) plain flour

filling:
3 oz. (3 squares) bitter chocolate
3 oz. ($\frac{1}{3}$ cup) sugar
2 egg yolks
2 oz. (4 tablespoons) butter

Grease a 7-in. cake pan and line the bottom with greaseproof paper. Put the chocolate into a bowl and let it melt over hot water. In another bowl beat the eggs with the sugar until thick. Continue beating and gradually add the flour. Add the chocolate and mix everything quickly together until it is evenly blended. Pour this into the prepared cake pan. Bake at 375°F. (191°C.) Mark 5 for 30 – 40 minutes or until a knitting needle inserted into it comes out clean. Take the cake from the oven and carefully turn out on to a cake rack. Let it cool then slice into two rounds. To make the filling, put the chocolate into a bowl and over boiling water. Let it melt, then beat until it is soft. Put aside but keep warm and soft. Put the sugar into the top of a double boiler with about ¼ cup (⅓) of water and let it cook, stirring all the time until the sugar dissolves. Continue to let it boil until it threads or is thick and syrupy. Add the egg yolks, one by one, beating well each time until the mixture is very thick. It should look like a mousse. Beat the butter until creamy and whip it firmly into the egg and sugar mixture. Finally add the softened chocolate and, if liked, a little strong black coffee essence or rum.

Spread one round of cake with the butter cream filling, cover with the second round and then spread with the remaining cream over the top and sides. The gâteau can be decorated with chocolate 'vermicelli', finely grated chocolate, or little whirls of the cream.

CHOCOLATE GÂTEUX (2)

3 oz. (3 squares) bitter chocolate
5 oz. (scant ⅔ cup) sugar
4 eggs
3 oz. (¾ cup) plain flour

pinch of salt
butter cream filling (pages 139–
40) plus 8 oz. (8 squares) bitter
chocolate

Put the chocolate into a bowl, add about 1 tablespoon (1¼) of water, black coffee or rum and let it melt. Beat it until soft and creamy. Put aside to cool. Beat the sugar with the eggs until thick and creamy, then put over a low heat, stirring all the time to let the mixture become thick and creamy). Take from the heat and allow it to cool. Sift the flour with the salt, add it to the egg mixture, folding it in gradually. Finally add the chocolate and mix thoroughly but without beating. Pour into a well-greased 8-in. cake pan and bake at 370°F. (189°C.) Mark 5 for approximately 50 minutes. (Now I suggest that you should sit down and have a cigarette with a cup of coffee.) Prepare the filling. Make a butter cream. Melt the chocolate in a bowl over hot water, beat it until smooth and then beat in the butter cream. Test; if the chocolate cake is ready, take it from the oven, gently turn on to a wire rack and let it get cold. Cut into two or three layers. Spread each layer with the butter cream, put the layers together again and spread the remainder of the butter and chocolate cream round the sides of the cake. The sides can be sprinkled with chocolate 'vermicelli' or flaked almonds, if liked, and the top with whipped cream and finely grated chocolate.

CHESTNUT GÂTEAU

6 egg yolks
10 oz. (1¼ cups) sugar
½ lb. cooked, peeled and sieved
chestnuts
2 oz. (⅓ cup) ground hazelnuts or
almonds

a little vanilla flavouring
whipped cream and marrons glacés
for filling and garnish

Beat the egg yolks with the sugar until thick. Add the chestnuts, hazelnuts and the vanilla. Beat the egg whites until stiff and fold carefully into the mixture. Pour into a well-buttered deep 8-in. cake pan and bake at 375°F. (191°C.) Mark 5 for 30–35 minutes. Turn out to cool on a wire rack and then carefully split into two rounds. Cover one layer thickly with whipped cream, cover with the second layer and garnish the top with halved marrons glacés or a simple icing (frosting).

COFFEE CREAM GÂTEAU

An old fashioned coffee cream gâteau that everybody enjoyed at Gerbeaud's – the best pâtisserie in Budapest.

8 eggs, separated
9 oz. (full cup) caster sugar
5 oz. (1¼ cups) plain flour
5 oz. (1 cup) blanched, finely
chopped almonds

filling:
6 egg yolks
8 oz. (1 cup) caster sugar
½ cup (⅔) strong black coffee
6 oz. (¾ cup) butter
vanilla flavouring
chocolate-coated coffee beans, if
available

Whisk the egg yolks with the sugar until thick and creamy. Spoon in the flour gently, then add the almonds. Beat the egg whites until stiff. Fold into the cake mixture. Turn the mixture into three buttered and floured layer cake pans and bake for 12–15 minutes at 375°F. (191°C.) Mark 5, or put into a 9-in. deep cake pan, well greased and bake at about 350°–360°F. (175°–180°C.) Mark 4 for about 30 minutes. When the cake is baked, turn it out carefully on to a wire rack. To make the filling, beat the egg yolks with the sugar until thick, add the coffee and put it over a pan of very hot but not boiling water and go on stirring until the mixture is thick and creamy. Take it from the heat and beat until it is cold. Beat the butter until soft, then beat it into the coffee cream. Add the vanilla. If making 1 sponge cake, slice this into two rounds. Spread half the cream on one round and the remaining cream on the top and round the sides of the cake. If you have three rounds, spread the cream over the layers in the same manner. Garnish with chocolate-covered coffee beans.

HOT CHOCOLATE GÂTEAU

5 tablespoons (full ¼ cup) sugar
8 oz. (1 cup) butter
6 eggs, separated
4 oz. (4 squares) bitter chocolate
2 oz. (½ cup) plain flour

chocolate sauce:
½ cup (⅔) liquid chocolate
3 oz. (full ⅓ cup) sugar
2 – 3 tablespoons (2½ – 3¾) water
vanilla essence to taste
1 oz. (2 tablespoons) softened butter

Beat the sugar, butter and egg yolks together until quite thick and creamy. Melt the chocolate until soft over hot water, beat until cool, then beat into the creamed butter mixture. Beat the egg whites until stiff. Add gently and alternately the egg whites and flour, about 1 tablespoon (1¼) of each at a time. Blend thoroughly but do not beat. Prepare a round cake pan, butter it well and sprinkle lightly with flour. Pour the cake mixture into this and bake for approximately 10 minutes at 375°F. (191°C.) Mark 5. The centre should be soft and creamy. While the cake is cooking, make the sauce. Break the chocolate into small pieces, add the sugar and water and cook over a low heat or over boiling water until the chocolate is melted. Add the vanilla and butter and beat the sauce thoroughly. Pour over the gâteau, which should be cut in wedges, whilst still hot.

DATE GÂTEAU

4 egg yolks
4 oz. (½ cup) sugar
5 oz. (1 cup) chopped almonds
½ lb. dates, stoned and chopped

filling:
whipped cream flavoured with sugar and vanilla to taste

Beat the egg yolks and three-quarters of the sugar until thick. Add the almonds and the dates and mix well. Whip the egg whites until stiff, add the remaining sugar and continue beating until very stiff. Fold into the date mixture. Turn into a buttered and floured cake pan and bake in the oven at 375°F. (191°C.) Mark 5 for about 30 minutes or until the cake is a golden brown. Take from the oven, turn on to a cake rack and leave until quite cool. Cut into 2 and spread one layer thickly with cream, cover with the remaining layer and sandwich the two layers together.

DOBOS GÂTEAU (Hungary)

In Hungary every gâteau has a story behind it. This one was made for a duchess, that one for a lovely little countess; another was made for a princess and one perhaps for a gypsy band leader, but all of them have a happy or a sad romance behind them. The princess fell in love and the gypsy ran away with her; this was the Princess Stephanie and the gâteau was named after her. This *Dobos* gâteau, I am afraid, has no romance behind it, only an excellent and famous pastrycook called Dobos. It is a good gâteau and it is not very difficult to make. When I first came to England and before I had my own business, I could not buy one, and so I had to make it myself as it was my son's favourite birthday cake. I admit that the first one gave me one or two sleepless nights. To make a big *Dobos* gâteau presents some problems. But after my first effort I found that it was not really so very difficult. You can make anything if you want to very much and I wanted my cake to be as good as the ones my son was accustomed to in Budapest, when it had been made by professional pastry-cooks. I believe that everything can be successfully achieved. I believe that you can achieve anything if you want to please someone you love very much. I give you the recipe:

3 eggs, separated
2½ oz. (full ¼ cup) caster sugar
2 oz. (½ cup) plain flour

2 oz. (¼ cup) butter
2 oz. (½ cup) icing (confectioner's) sugar
1 egg yolk

filling:
2 oz. (2 squares) bitter chocolate

caramel topping:
3 oz. (full ⅓ cup) granulated sugar

Beat the egg yolks with half the sugar until thick. Sift the flour twice. Beat the egg whites until stiff, then fold in the rest of the sugar. Fold the egg whites into the beaten yolks, adding the flour alternately. Do not beat the mixture at this stage. Butter and flour 2 or 3 6-in. flan or sandwich pans and spread thinly with part of the mixture. Bake for 6–8 minutes at 365°F. (187°C) Mark 4–5 or until they are just done and a golden brown in colour. They may take a little longer. Take carefully from the pans and place on a flat surface. Repeat this process until you have 6 wafer-thin layers of sponge cake. When they are all cool, place the sponge rounds in wax paper, all piled high one on top of the other. Cover with a board and a weight.

Make the filling. Break the chocolate into small pieces and melt in a bowl over hot water. Do not let it get hot. Cream the butter and sugar, add the melted chocolate and egg yolk and beat until the filling is smooth and creamy. Spread a little of this over one layer of sponge, cover with a second layer, spread with the filling and repeat until all the layers but one are spread with cream. This last layer is the top layer and should be lightly dusted with sifted flour. Keep it aside for the moment.

Dissolve the remaining sugar in a small pan over a low heat, stirring and watching it all the time. The moment it has turned to caramel, pour the sugar over the last piece of sponge cake. With a palette knife dipped in oil, evenly spread the caramel over the cake and then mark it off firmly and evenly into slices with the knife frequently dipped into oil. You must work quickly to do this or the caramel will harden and cutting is then impossible. Put the top layer on the cake.

DELICIOUS GÂTEAU (Walnut Gâteau)

7 eggs
9 oz. (full cup) sugar
9 oz. (1½ cups) ground walnuts
25 roasted coffee beans, finely ground
a little vanilla flavouring

filling:
6 oz. (6 squares) sweet chocolate
5 oz. (full ½ cup) butter
3 egg yolks

Beat the eggs with the sugar until very creamy, thick and fluffy. Add the walnuts and the coffee beans and flavour with a little vanilla. Pour into a well-greased round 8-in. cake pan and bake in the oven at 350°F. (175°C.) Mark 4 for 40 minutes. Take from the oven. Gently turn out on to a wire rack and leave until cool. Prepare the filling. Break the chocolate into small pieces and put these into a bowl with the butter, equally cut into small pieces. Put the bowl over hot water and stir the mixture until soft but not too runny. Beat the egg yolks until smooth and slowly stir them into the chocolate-butter mixture and beat until it thickens. Leave it to cool. Slice the cake through to make 2 rounds. Spread 1 round with half the cream filling, cover with the remaining round and spread with the rest of the filling. The top can be decorated with fine cake crumbs or coarsely ground almonds.

FOURRIE GÂTEAU

This cake does give you a little trouble to make but in the end you will be pleased that you took the trouble. It will keep for 1 or 2 days in a refrigerator.

8 glacé cherries

2 oz. ($\frac{1}{3}$ cup) sultanas (white
   raisins)

$\frac{1}{4}$ cup ($\frac{1}{3}$) rum

$\frac{3}{4}$ lb. marzipan

6 oz. ($\frac{3}{4}$ cup) sugar

5 eggs

6 oz. ($1\frac{1}{2}$ cups) plain flour

2 cups ($2\frac{1}{2}$) whipping cream

2 tablespoons ($2\frac{1}{2}$) caster sugar

$\frac{1}{2}$ cup ($\frac{2}{3}$) thick custard

jam

white fondant (page 214)

flaked almonds, lightly roasted

Soak the cherries and sultanas in the rum. This is best done overnight. Soften the marzipan with a little water and beat it. Add the sugar and eggs and continue beating until the mixture is light and fluffy. Fold in the flour but do not beat at this point. Divide the mixture into 2 well-buttered 9-in. sandwich pans and bake at 375°F. (191°C.) Mark 5 for 30 minutes. Put aside 3 cherries and about 12 sultanas for decoration. Cut the remaining cherries into 4. Whip the cream, adding the second quantity of sugar, until thick, and gently mix it into the custard. Add the fruit (not that reserved for the decoration). Take the cakes from the oven, remove from the pans and let them cool. Slit one cake into 2 rounds (1 round for the base, the other for the top). Cut a 7-in. circle out of the remaining whole cake. Place the resultant ring on top of the base and fill the centre with filling, keeping a little for masking the sides. Cover with the remaining round of cake. Spread the top with jam and ice over with fondant. Spread the remaining whipped cream filling round the sides of the cake. Cut the remaining cherries into small pieces and sprinkle these with the sultanas on top of the cake. Sprinkle the sides generously with roasted and flaked almonds.

GÂTEAU ÉDOUARD

5 eggs, separated

5 oz. (scant $\frac{2}{3}$ cup) caster sugar

4 oz. (4 squares) bitter chocolate

1 teaspoon ($1\frac{1}{4}$) soft breadcrumbs

2 oz. ($\frac{1}{3}$ cup) ground almonds

1 teaspoon ($1\frac{1}{4}$) finely ground coffee

whipped cream

chopped roasted almonds

filling:

3 egg yolks, well beaten

3 teaspoons ($3\frac{3}{4}$) icing
   (confectioner's) sugar

$\frac{1}{2}$ cup ($\frac{2}{3}$) strong black coffee

4 oz. ($\frac{1}{2}$ cup) softened butter

whipping cream

roasted and chopped nuts

Combine the egg yolks with the caster sugar and beat until thick and fluffy. Soften the chocolate in a bowl over hot water. Beat it all the time. Add this to the beaten eggs and sugar, mix well, beating continuously. When the mixture is evenly mixed, fold in the breadcrumbs, the ground almonds and coffee. Beat the egg whites until stiff. Fold into the cake mixture. Pour into a buttered and lightly floured 8-in. cake pan and bake in the oven at 375°F. (191°C.) Mark 5 for 25–30 minutes. Test with a knitting needle, if it comes out clean the cake is done. Turn it out carefully on to a wire rack and leave until it is cool.

Prepare the filling. Combine the egg yolks with the sugar and coffee in a small bowl. Place it over slowly boiling water. Stir it well until the mixture begins to thicken and continue beating until the mixture is thick and smooth. Take the bowl from the heat but continue stirring until the cream is cool. Add the butter and beat it vigorously into the filling. Slice the sponge cake twice through to make three layers. Spread two layers with the filling and sandwich the three together again. Spread the top layer with thick whipped cream and sprinkle with roasted and chopped nuts.

GENOESE SPONGE

This is a light sponge cake which is used for petits fours or fancy cakes. It can also be served as a simple unadorned sponge cake, dusted with sifted icing (confectioner's) sugar.

6 oz. (1½ cups) plain flour   **8 eggs**
pinch of salt   **8 oz. (1 cup) caster sugar**
6 oz. (¾ cup) butter

Rub a shallow baking pan 12 × 8 in. with fat. Warm the flour and sieve it with salt. Soften the butter but do not let it become oily. Whisk the eggs slightly and then mix with the sugar and whisk over a pan of hot water for about 20 minutes until the mixture is thick and frothy but not sticky (this is caused by over-heating). Take from the heat and continue whisking until the mixture is cool. Mix in the butter and the flour gradually but quickly, adding them alternately to the eggs. Pour it into the prepared pan and bake in the oven at 375°F. (191°C.) Mark 5 with a steady heat all the time for about 30 minutes. The actual time depends on the depth of the cake, it might take another 15 minutes. Turn out on to a sugared sheet of paper and leave to get cold.

HAZELNUT GÂTEAU

1 white sponge cake (page 72)   **roasted hazelnuts, coarsely**
praline butter cream (page 141)   **chopped**
                                 sugar

Slice the sponge into 2 rounds and spread 1 round with praline butter cream. Cover with the remaining sponge and spread the top and sides with the butter cream. Pipe the butter cream over the top of the cake and sprinkle with hazelnuts over the top and round the sides. Heat a little sugar, enough to make a thin syrup, and sprinkle this with a spatula over the hazelnuts in thin filaments.

LINZER TORTE (Austria)

As we are discussing Austria, I would like to tell you about a very famous Austrian gâteau, mostly favoured by men, because it is neither sweet, rich nor creamy.

I wonder, how it is that certain articles, food or other materials, spread over the whole world. I am sure they are no better, or worse than the *Sacher*, the *Linzer* or the *Dobos* gâteaux. And yet they all have become internationally known.

Eventually I understood the *Sacher* gâteau. This came originally from Vienna, from the world famous Sacher Hotel which was then managed by the equally famous Madame Sacher. She was unique! Kings, archdukes, dukes, the whole world of geniuses, authors, poets, musicians went to her hotel and not only paid high prices, but also homage, to her. She commanded respect from everybody around her. She also created the famous *Sacher Torte*. Why is just the *Sacher Torte* still alive, very much alive? You have two *Sacher Torte* recipes, because there are several recipes for this. The same is the case with *Linzer* gâteau or *Torte*, therefore I am giving you two recipes for this as well.

Linzer Torte

LINZER TORTE (1)

8 oz. (1 cup) sugar
8 oz. (2 cups) plain flour
8 oz. (1⅓ cups) ground hazelnuts,
   unblanched
8 oz. (1 cup) butter

2 eggs
jam for filling
1 egg yolk
icing (confectioner's) sugar

Mix together the dry ingredients, cut the butter into small pieces and rub these into the dry ingredients. Add the eggs, one at a time and mix thoroughly. Work this all to a dough and chill for a short while. Pull off about a quarter of the pastry and put this aside. Roll out the rest on a lightly floured board to about ¼-in. thickness. Line the bottom and sides of a flan pan with this. Spread it generously with a good dark jam, raspberry is often preferred for a *Linzer Torte*. Roll out the remaining pastry and cut out into narrow strips. Arrange these in an even lattice-work pattern over the top of the jam. Beat the egg yolk, brush this over the pastry and bake at 390 °F. (200 °C.) Mark 5 − 6 for about 1 hour. Take the *Torte* from the oven and liberally sprinkle with sifted icing sugar.

LINZER TORTE (2)

6 oz. (1½ cups) plain flour
pinch of salt
pinch of ground cinnamon and
   cloves
5 oz. (full ½ cup) butter
4 oz. (½ cup) caster sugar
2 − 3 egg yolks

grated lemon peel
5 oz. (scant cup) ground
   unblanched almonds or walnuts
   or hazelnuts
raspberry jam
extra well beaten egg yolk

Sieve the flour on to a pastry board with the salt, cinnamon and cloves. Make a well in the centre and add the butter (chopped into small pieces), the sugar, egg yolks, lemon rind and ground almonds. Work this mixture to a smooth dough, kneading it thoroughly. Roll into a ball and leave for 1 hour. Put aside about a quarter of the paste. Roll out the rest of the paste to ¼ − ½ in. thickness. Line the bottom and sides of a flan pan with the paste. Spread with jam or, if available, with thick sweetened raspberry pulp. Roll out the remaining paste thinly and cut into thin strips. Arrange these in an even lattice-work pattern over the top of the jam. Brush with the extra egg yolk and bake in the oven at 375 °F. (191 °C.) Mark 5 for 1 hour. Take from the oven and when cool either sprinkle as in previous recipe with sifted icing (confectioner's) sugar or with warm redcurrant jelly.

MOCHA GÂTEAU (Austria)

Mocha is a variety of coffee bean grown in Arabia. The beans are roasted; the roasting is a very important part of the coffee process. Coffee can be ruined by over-roasting or by under-roasting. Coffee made from pure Mocha is generally served in special cups, smaller than those used for ordinary coffee. These little differences are important; people are pleased and impressed with them. This gâteau is made by covering round or square layers of cake made from the best genoese paste (page 121) with butter cream, flavoured with mocha. A layer of genoese paste is spread with the butter cream and another layer of cake placed on top, till the cake is two or three layers deep. Then the top is iced with mocha-flavoured fondant. Or it can be covered with the mocha-flavoured butter cream and decorated with butter cream piped through a fluted tube. Finish with roasted or chopped almonds or any other nuts.

6 eggs, separated	filling:
6 oz. (¾ cup) caster sugar	**4 egg yolks**
5 oz. (5 squares) bitter chocolate, melted	**4 tablespoons (5) caster sugar**
5 oz. (scant cup) ground almonds	**½ cup (⅔) strong black coffee**
1 tablespoon (1¼) finely ground coffee	**6 oz. (¾ cup) butter**
¾ pint (1) whipping cream	

Whisk the egg yolks with 5 oz. (scant ⅔ cup) sugar until the mixture is thick and fluffy. Whisk the egg whites until stiff, add the remaining sugar and continue whisking until the mixture is smooth. Add the chocolate, ground almonds and the coffee to the beaten egg yolks, then fold the egg whites in carefully. Generously butter an 8-in. round cake pan, sprinkle it lightly with flour. Pour in the cake mixture and bake in the oven at 360°F. (182°C.) Mark 4 for 30–35 minutes). Take from the oven, turn gently on to a wire rack and let the cake cool. Prepare the filling. Combine the egg yolks, sugar and the coffee. Mix well, then put the bowl over a pan of almost boiling water and cook, stirring all the time, until the mixture is thick. Take from the heat and continue stirring until the mixture is cool. Add the butter bit by bit beating it vigorously into the eggs. Slice the cake into 3. Spread the filling on 2 of the layers and sandwich all 3 together again. Beat the whipping cream until stiff and spread two-thirds of this over the top and round the sides of the cake. Put the rest of the cream into a piping bag and pipe round the top of the cake in a neat pattern.

NOUGATINE GÂTEAU

5 oz. (scant ⅔ cup) sugar
¼ lb. (1½ cups) flaked almonds
1 light sponge cake

coffee butter cream (page 139)
roasted flaked almonds
icing (confectioner's) sugar

First prepare the nougat. Put the sugar into a pan and cook over a low heat until it dissolves and then lightly browns and caramelizes. Gradually add the first quantity of almonds, mixing well with a metal spoon. Turn the mixture on to an oiled marble slab at once; while it is still warm, roll it out with a slim oiled rolling pin. Cut out 2 circles some 7 in. in diameter and cut each quickly into 12 pie-shaped pieces, i.e. triangles. It is important to work quickly. Roll 12 of the pieces quickly round the rolling pin, curving them to make crescents or tubes. Put the plain pieces and the curved pieces aside. Slice the sponge cake into 2 rounds. Spread 1 round with butter cream, cover with the remaining round. Spread the top and sides with the remaining butter cream, sprinkle round the sides with the roasted almond flakes. Arrange the flat piece of nougat evenly round the cake, the points meeting in the centre. Dust with icing sugar and then arrange the crescent pieces of nougat alternately between the flat pieces.

LOG CAKE

2 oz. (½ cup) plain flour
½ teaspoon (⅔) baking powder
pinch of salt
1 level tablespoon (1¼) cornflour
   (cornstarch)
4 oz. (½ cup) caster sugar
4 egg yolks

filling:
2 oz. (¼ cup) butter
milk
5 oz. (scant cup) walnuts
1 teaspoon (1¼) grated lemon peel
decoration:
2 oz. (¼ cup) sugar
2 egg yolks, well beaten
4 oz. (½ cup) butter
3 oz. (3 squares) bitter chocolate

Prepare a flat baking pan as for Swiss Roll (page 105). Sift the flour, baking powder, salt and cornflour three times into a bowl. Put aside 2 tablespoons (2½) of the sugar. Whisk the egg yolks until thick, beat in the sugar and continue beating until the mixture is very thick. Whip the egg whites until stiff, add the reserved sugar and continue beating until the mixture forms into peaks. Fold this into the egg yolks, lastly add the flour, folding it into the mixture. Pour this into the prepared sponge pan and bake in the oven at 350°F. (175°C.) Mark 4 for about 12 minutes. Turn the cake at once on to a sugared cloth, trim the edges and let it cool a little.

To make the filling, soften the butter with a little milk, beat well, then add the walnuts and lemon peel. Beat thoroughly before spreading it over the sponge cake. To make the covering, dissolve the sugar with a little water in a small pan over a gentle heat. Let it cook until the sugar forms a small thread. Pour the syrup on to the egg yolks, beating all the time until the mixture is thick. Beat the butter until creamy and gradually, still beating, add the egg and sugar mixture. Melt the chocolate over hot water, beat it until smooth and then beat it into the butter cream.

Spread the cake with the butter and walnut filling. Roll it up. Cover the roll with a light coating of butter cream. It is advisable to make the filling and decoration for the cake while it is baking.

PRINCESS ALEXANDRA CAKE

5 oz. (scant ⅔ cup) butter
5 oz. (scant ⅔ cup) caster sugar
3 eggs
8 oz. (2 cups) plain flour
1 teaspoon (1¼) baking powder

redcurrant jam
fresh cream (optional)
icing (confectioner's) sugar
  (optional)
lemon water icing (frosting)

Beat the butter until creamy and light. Add the sugar and again beat well. Add the eggs one by one, adding a little of the flour with each addition. Add the baking powder and the rest of the flour, mix well but do not beat the mixture. Pour it into a well-buttered and floured round cake pan and bake at 375°F. (191°C.) Mark 5 for 20–30 minutes or until the top feels firm to the touch. Turn out to cool on a wire rack. When cold, slice in half horizontally and layer with jam. Fresh cream may be added as well. The top can be covered with whipped cream or simply dusted over with icing sugar or spread with a lemon-flavoured water icing.

MORELLO CHERRY GÂTEAU

3 oz. (3 squares) bitter chocolate
3 oz. (6 tablespoons) butter
3 eggs, separated
3 oz. (full ⅓ cup) caster sugar
2 oz. (½ cup) plain flour

filling:
1 egg yolk

3½ oz. (scant ½ cup) caster sugar
1 oz. (1 square) bitter chocolate
4 oz. (½ cup) butter
1 tablespoon (1¼) rum
1 cup (1¼) stoned cooked morello
  cherries
1 cup (1¼) stoned uncooked
  morello cherries

Break the chocolate into small pieces and melt over hot water. Melt the butter but do not let it become oily. Whisk the egg yolks with half the sugar until thick. Whisk the egg whites stiffly, add the rest of the sugar and continue whisking until the mixture rises in peaks. Fold this into the beaten egg yolks. Sift the flour and fold it into the egg mixture. Gradually pour in the butter and chocolate. Pour into a 6-in. buttered and floured cake pan and bake in the oven for 40 – 45 minutes at 375°F. (191°C.) Mark 5. Take the cake from the oven, turn it out gently on to a wire rack and let it completely cool. In the meantime prepare the filling. Beat the egg yolk until smooth, add the sugar and continue beating, but over hot water until the mixture is thick. Melt the chocolate, beat it until smooth and add it to the beaten egg and sugar. Beat well. Add the butter bit by bit beating it all the time until the mixture is smooth and creamy. Add the rum, beat again. Divide the mixture into 2 portions. Into one half mix the cooked morello cherries. Slice the cooled cake into 2 rounds. Spread one round with the morello-flavoured butter cream. Cover with the remaining round and spread the cake over the top and round the sides with the rest of the butter cream. Decorate with the uncooked cherries.

NURNBERGI TORTA (Hungary)

6 oz. (¾ cup) sugar

5 oz. (scant cup) ground walnuts

8 oz. (8 squares) bitter chocolate, melted

2 oz. (⅔ cup) cake crumbs

8 egg whites

covering:

1 cup (1¼) whipping cream

sugar

4 oz. (4 squares) bitter chocolate

Combine the first 5 ingredients and mix thoroughly. The egg whites are not beaten in this recipe. Rub 2 shallow baking pans with butter, divide the mixture into these and bake at 250°F. (120°C.) Mark ½ until the cakes are set and a golden brown. Take from the oven, turn out on to a wire rack and let the cakes cool. Whip the cream with a little sugar until stiff. Spread this over one layer of the cake. Cover with the remaining layer. Melt the chocolate with a little water until it is of pouring consistency. Spread this over the top of the cake and leave until it dries.

ORANGE GÂTEAU (Tangier)

In Tangier where we were surrounded by orange trees – we naturally had oranges to eat – orange salads, orange sauce and orange cakes. One of the recipes I hand over to you.

6 eggs, separated
6 oz. (¾ cup) caster sugar
8 oz. (1⅓ cups) ground almonds
grated 3 oranges
juice 1½ oranges
4 teaspoons (5) cake crumbs
icing (confectioner's) sugar

filling:
8 oz. (1 cup) butter
6 oz. (¾ cup) sugar
3 egg yolks
grated peel 2 oranges

Grease and sprinkle with flour 3 flan or layer cake pans. Whisk the egg yolks until smooth, add 4 oz. (½ cup) sugar and continue whisking until the mixture is creamy. Add the almonds, rind and juice of the oranges and the crumbs. Whisk the egg whites until stiff, add 2 oz. (¼ cup) of sugar and continue whipping until the whites form peaks. Fold this into the cake mixture very carefully. Pour the mixture into the prepared pans. Bake in the oven at 375°F. (191°C.) Mark 5 for 15–20 minutes. Take from the oven, turn out and cool on a wire rack. In the meantime make the filling. Beat the butter with the sugar until soft and creamy. Add the egg yolks, beat vigorously – the cream must be stiff – then add the orange rind. Spread the cream on 2 of the layers of cake. Sandwich all 3 layers together and dust with sifted icing sugar. Or spread with orange-flavoured icing (frosting) or with orange sections dipped into sugar and boiled to the 'soft-boil' stage.

PISTACHIO GÂTEAU

Pistachio is one of the most delicate of flavours – as a matter of fact it has hardly any flavour. But it adds to the other ingredients something elegant and something very good. I love to use it, just because of that and the lovely pale, fine-green colour. I use it a lot for decoration, I use it in cooking. Here I give you a pistachio gâteau.

5 eggs, separated
6 oz. (¾ cup) granulated sugar
6 oz. (1 cup) ground almonds
1 oz. (¼ cup) chopped candied peel
grated rind 1 lemon
3½ oz. (scant cup) plain flour
4 oz. (⅔ cup) pistachio nuts

filling:
4 egg yolks
4 oz. (½ cup) caster sugar
juice and rind 2 oranges
grated rind 1 lemon
1 pint (2½ cups) whipping cream

Rub a 7-in. round cake pan with butter and dust lightly with flour. Beat the egg yolks with three-quarters of the sugar until thick and fluffy. Add the ground almonds, peel and grated rind and beat well. Fold in the flour, do not beat any more at this point. Whip the egg whites until stiff, add the remaining sugar and continue beating until the mixture forms peaks. Fold into the cake mixture. Pour into the prepared cake pan and bake at 350°F. (175°C.) Mark 4 for 30–40 minutes or until a knitting needle inserted into it comes out clean. Take the cake from the oven and leave in the pan until it is cool. Take carefully from the pan and slice into 2 rounds.

Blanch the pistachios in boiling salted water (the salt helps to keep their bright green colour). While the cake is cooling, prepare the filling and garnish. Beat the egg yolks until smooth, add the sugar, orange juice and peel and lemon peel. Put the mixture over hot but not boiling water and cook over a moderate heat, stirring all the time until it thickens. Take it from the heat and beat it until it cools. Beat the whipping cream until thick, then mix into the butter cream. Spread some of the filling on 1 layer cake, cover with the remaining layer, then spread the rest of the filling over the top and sides of the cake. Decorate the top with chopped and whole pistachio nuts.

PANAMA (ISCHLER) GÂTEAU (Austria)

One of the gâteaux I remember from my earliest childhood so very many years ago.

3 oz. (3 squares) bitter chocolate	filling:
5 oz. (scant cup) unblanched grated almonds	3 oz. (3 squares) bitter chocolate
7 eggs, separated	6 oz. ($\frac{3}{4}$ cup) butter
4$\frac{1}{2}$ oz. (full $\frac{1}{2}$ cup) caster sugar	6 oz. ($\frac{3}{4}$ cup) caster sugar
3 oz. ($\frac{1}{2}$ cup) blanched, toasted almonds, finely chopped	vanilla
	2 eggs

Grate the chocolate and mix with the ground almonds. Beat the egg yolks until smooth, add 3 oz ($\frac{1}{3}$ cup) of sugar and continue beating until the mixture is thick. Beat the whites until stiff, add the remaining sugar and beat until the mixture forms peaks. Fold the egg whites into the egg yolks alternately with the ground almond-chocolate mixture. Blend gently but evenly and pour into a deep buttered and floured cake pan. Bake in the oven at 375°F. (191°C.) Mark 5 for about 1 hour, but test after 45 minutes. Take from the oven, turn out on to a wire rack and leave until cool.

Make the filling. Break the chocolate into small pieces and melt over hot water until soft, beat it until smooth. Beat the butter, the sugar and vanilla together until the mixture is light and creamy. Beat the 2 eggs until thick, add to the butter cream, beat vigorously, then beat in the melted chocolate. Slice the cake to make 3 layers. Spread some of the cream on 2 of the layers, sandwich them back into shape, cover with the remaining layer and spread the cream over the top and sides of the cake. Sprinkle top and sides with toasted chopped almonds.

PRAVENIER GÂTEAU (Hungary)

10 egg whites
10 oz. (1¼ cups) caster or icing
   sugar
10 oz. (1⅔ cups) ground blanched
   almonds
roasted almonds, roughly pounded

filling:
8 oz. (1 cup) butter
8 oz. (1¾ cups) icing
   (confectioner's) sugar
2½ tablespoons (3) cold black coffee
6 oz. (1 cup) blanched almonds,
   roasted and ground

Beat the egg whites until stiff and gradually fold in the sugar, still beating hard until the mixture is very stiff. This is important as it is this beating which will ensure the success of the cake. Fold in the ground almonds. Fold the mixture into 3 well-buttered sandwich pans. Bake at 300°F. (146°C.) Mark 2 until the mixture is crisp, or about 35 minutes. Take from oven and leave the cakes in the pans until quite cool. Turn out carefully. Beat the butter until soft, add the icing sugar and continue beating until the mixture is creamy. Add the coffee and when this is blended into the butter cream beat in the ground almonds. Spread some of the cream on 2 of the layers of cake, sandwich all 3 together and spread the rest of the cream over the top and round the sides of the cake. Sprinkle the top and sides with the pounded and roasted almonds.

RIGO JANCSI (Hungary)

A type of rich sponge cake.

5 eggs, separated
2½ oz. (⅓ cup) caster sugar
2 oz. (½ cup) plain flour
1 dessertspoon (1 tablespoon) cocoa

4 – 6 oz. (4 – 6 squares) bitter
   chocolate
a little rum
½ pint (1¼ cups) whipping cream

Beat the egg yolks until smooth, add 1½ oz. (3 tablespoons) of sugar and continue beating until the mixture is thick. Beat the egg whites until stiff, add the remaining sugar and continue beating until the egg whites are stiff. Sift the flour and cocoa together. Fold the egg whites into the yolks gradually, then add the flour and cocoa mixture. Rub 2 square, shallow baking pans with butter and lightly flour. Divide the cake mixture into these and bake at 300 °F. (146 °C.) Mark 2 for about 30 minutes or until the mixture is set. Turn out with care. Melt the chocolate with a little rum until it is of thick pouring consistency. Whip the cream until thick and add as much of the melted chocolate as it will take. Spread this over 1 layer of the cake. Cover with the remaining layer and spread this with the remainder of the melted chocolate. If the cakes have been baked in small pans and are therefore deep, split each into 2 and continue as above.

RIVIERA GÂTEAU

This is one of the most useful gâteaux. It is usually made in a triangle. It is good because it is different from any other gâteau. I would call this a very useful cake for parties. You can add to the fresh cream chocolate, raspberry, or any other fruit. It is easy to decorate because it has only to be dusted over with vanilla-flavoured icing sugar. I always serve this gâteau with a punch sauce.

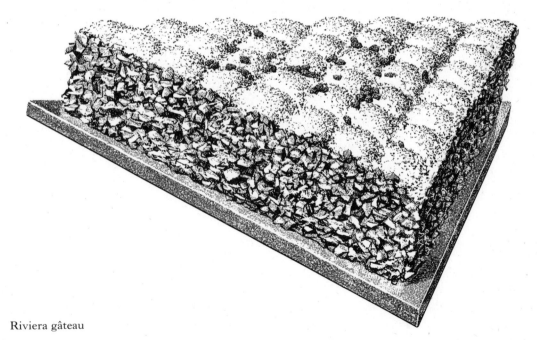

Riviera gâteau

1 lb. marzipan
¼ cup (⅓) warmish water
4 egg whites
4 oz. (scant ⅔ cup) icing
  (confectioner's) sugar
whipped cream
mixed fresh fruit

punch sauce:
a little custard
whipped cream
sugar to taste
curaçao or rum
raspberry juice

Beat the marzipan until soft, adding the water as you beat. Whisk the egg whites until stiff, gradually add the sugar and continue beating until the mixture is very stiff. Blend this into the marzipan. Pipe the mixture with a large plain piping nozzle on to a baking (cookie) sheet lined with greaseproof paper in triangles over an approximate 8-in. base. Dust over with sifted icing sugar and bake in the oven at 375°F. (191°C.) Mark 5 for about 30 minutes. Take from the oven and let the mixture cool. Build up into a triangular shaped cake by layering the triangles of baked marzipan with thickly whipped cream and fresh fruit, such as fresh raspberries. Dust over with sifted icing sugar.

To make the sauce, mix all the sauce ingredients together. Serve ice-cold. If a pink sauce is not liked, omit the raspberry juice.

GÂTEAU ST HONORÉ (France)

For over 40 years I have been grumbling – ever since I have owned a bakery and cake business – grumbling and rebelling, that God and man neglect my trade, my fellow-workers, pastrycooks and bakers. It is one of the most demanding kinds of work, day and night: but people don't appreciate it, they demand fresh and perfect pastries, rolls and bread. Sometimes they are quite indignant that we are not open on Sunday. As a matter of fact we do work on Sunday. We work every day of the week except on Saturday night.

I hope now you will sympathize with me and my colleagues. You can imagine how thrilled I was to read that the bakers and pastrycooks have their own patron saint. And what a lovely one – Saint Honoré.

I make hundreds of these very good, very decorative gâteaux, but I never knew that the name comes from Saint Honoré, who was Bishop of Amiens about 560 A.D. His cult began to spread in France in the middle of the eleventh century, and the Faubourg Saint-Honoré in Paris is named after him. His feast is celebrated on May 16. He is the patron saint of pastrycooks and bakers, though nothing in his life connects him with the food industry. I am, however, sure that he was a very nice bishop and now I know if I need help whom to ask; I am sure that my prayer will be answered. I will give you a very precise recipe for a gâteau St Honoré.

½ lb. choux paste (page 170)   vanilla cream:
¼ lb. short or flan   6 egg yolks
   pastry (page 157)   5 oz. (scant ⅔ cup) caster sugar
1 well-beaten egg   2 oz. (½ cup) plain flour
3 oz. (full ⅓ cup) granulated sugar   1 pint (1¼) milk
glacé cherries and angelica   1 vanilla pod
                                                8 egg whites

First make the vanilla cream. Beat the egg yolks with the sugar until the mixture is smooth and almost white. Add the flour, continue beating well, then add enough of the cold milk to make a smooth paste. Put the rest of the milk into a pan with the vanilla pod and bring it to the boil. Remove the pod and at once pour the milk into the egg mixture, stirring all the time. Return this to the pan and continue cooking over a low heat until the custard thickens, stirring all the time. Whip the egg whites until stiff. Pour a little of the hot custard into a bowl and fold in the egg whites. Pour this back into the pan, and over a gentle heat and stirring all the while continue cooking for about 3 minutes or until the egg whites have set. Pour the cream into a large bowl, cover and let the cream cool.

Make a choux paste as on page 170 and let it cool slightly. Roll out the short pastry to a round about ⅛-in. thick and roughly the size of a pudding plate. Place this on a greased baking (cookie) sheet, prick it well with a fork and brush ½-in. wide band round the edge with the egg. Put half the choux pastry into a forcing bag fitted with a plain nozzle and force a border round the edge of the pastry. Brush this with beaten egg and bake in the oven at 400°F. (205°C.) Mark 6 for about 25 minutes. Force the rest of the choux pastry on to another greased baking sheet into between 12–15 small nut-sized balls, much depends on their size and the size of the gâteau. Bake these in the same oven for about 12–15 minutes. As soon as you take the pastry from the oven, prick it with a fork to allow the steam to escape. Leave to cool.

Dissolve the sugar in 2 tablespoons (2½) of water and then boil it briskly to the crack stage or until it just begins to turn a pale strawberry pink. Dip the bottom of each of the choux balls into the syrup and at once place them round the ring of choux pastry, each close together, they may just touch. Pile the cream in the middle and decorate with halved glacé cherries and the angelica cut into neat shapes.

SACHER TORTE (1) (Austria)

5 oz. (5 squares) bitter chocolate

2½ oz. (scant ⅔ cup) plain flour

2½ oz. (⅓ cup) ground almonds

6 eggs, separated

5 oz. (1 cup) icing (confectioner's) sugar

5 oz. (full ½ cup) butter

apricot jam

coating:

7 oz. (scant cup) granulated sugar

7 oz. (7 squares) bitter chocolate

Grease and flour a 10-in. round cake pan. Put the chocolate into a bowl with 1 tablespoon (1¼) of water (rum or brandy) and melt over hot water. When it is soft, beat it until smooth and cool. Sieve the flour and almonds together. Beat the egg yolks and add 4 oz. (¾ cup) of icing sugar and beat until the mixture is thick. Add the chocolate. Beat the egg whites until stiff, add the remaining icing sugar and continue beating until very stiff. Fold this into the beaten egg mixture alternately with the sieved dry ingredients. Melt the butter and gently fold it into the mixture folding it with care in order not to spoil the aeration. Pour the mixture into the prepared cake pan and bake at 350°F. (175°C.) Mark 4 for 1–1½ hours. Take from the oven, turn on to a wire rack and leave until cool. Split into 2 rounds and spread with apricot jam. Spread round the sides and top with apricot jam.

To make the coating, dissolve the sugar in 2½ tablespoons (3) of water and then cook to the small thread stage. Break the chocolate into pieces and melt over hot water. Take the sugar from the heat, let it cool to luke-warm and then beat it into the melted chocolate. (Some cooks add a drop of olive oil to help the coating glisten.) Pour the chocolate coating over the top and sides of the cake, work as quickly and as neatly as possible. There are one or two points to note with a *Sacher Torte*. The thickness of the apricot jam should be the same as for the chocolate coating. Also it should not be very high. Whipped cream is often served with *Sacher Torte*, but this is neither traditional nor essential although very good.

SACHER TORTE (2)

6 oz. (6 squares) bitter chocolate
5 oz. (scant ⅔ cup) butter
5¾ oz. (full cup) icing
  (confectioner's) sugar
8 eggs, separated

4 oz. (1 cup) plain flour
apricot jam
coating:
7 oz. (7 squares) bitter chocolate

Melt the chocolate over a low heat and beat until smooth. Cream the butter with 4 oz. (¾ cup) icing sugar until the mixture is creamy; add the egg yolks, gradually, beating all the time. Beat the melted chocolate into the creamed butter mixture. Beat the egg whites until stiff, add the rest of the icing sugar and beat to a stiff meringue consistency. Add the egg whites and the flour alternately into the batter mixing gently but making sure the mixture is evenly blended. Grease 2 sandwich flan pans with butter and lightly dust with flour. Divide the mixture equally into these. Bake in the oven at 400°F. (205°C.) Mark 6 for about 1 hour – but test after 45 minutes. Take from the oven, turn on to a wire tray, dust with sifted sugar and leave for 24 hours. Brush 1 layer of cake with apricot jam (see previous recipe) and cover with the remaining layer of cake. Brush with apricot jam round the top and sides. Make a chocolate glaze coating with the sugar and the chocolate as in previous recipe and spread this over the top and sides of the cake. Slip the cake into a warm oven for a *few* seconds to dry the glaze.

SPITZBUB (Austria)

4 oz. (½ cup) butter
5 oz. (scant ⅔ cup) sugar
3¾ oz. (⅔ cup) ground
  walnuts
1 whole egg

a little cinnamon
a little grated lemon peel
5 oz. (1¼ cups) plain flour
raspberry jam

Cream the butter and sugar, add the walnuts. Beat well, add the egg, beat again; add the cinnamon, lemon peel and finally the flour. Work this to a stiff dough and divide into 2 portions, 1 larger than the other. Roll out the dough and line a baking (cookie) sheet. Cover with raspberry jam. Bake in the oven at 400°F. (205°C.) Mark 6 until the pastry is a light golden colour. While it is cooking, roll out the remainder of the dough until very thin and cut into long narrow strips. Place these criss-cross over the jam to make a trellis-work pattern. Return the tart to the oven and bake again until the top has browned, take from the oven and lightly dust with sifted caster sugar.

TUTTI FRUTTI TORTA (Hungary)

9 eggs, separated
10 oz. (1¼ cups) sugar
10 oz. (1⅔ cups) ground walnuts
4 oz. (1 cup) chopped stoned dates
4 oz. (⅔ cup) sultanas (white raisins)

4 oz. (1 cup) mixed chopped figs and candied peel
4 oz. (4 squares) bitter chocolate, melted

Beat the yolks until smooth, add two-thirds of the sugar and continue beating the mixture until it is thick and frothy. Add the walnuts, dates, sultanas, figs and peel, mix thoroughly, then add the melted chocolate (melted in a bowl over hot water and beaten smooth). Mix these ingredients together well. Beat the egg whites until stiff, gradually add the rest of the sugar and continue beating to a meringue consistency. Fold into the mixture. Rub a shallow square or oblong baking pan with butter and pour the mixture into it. Bake in the oven at 300°F. (146°C.) Mark 2 for about 1 hour or until the cake is brown. Take from the oven, turn on to a flat surface to cool. When cold the *torta* can be decorated with whipped cream and crystallized fruits.

WALNUT GÂTEAU (1)

I return now to my childhood – to a friend's birthday party. That friend is now living in London, and we see each other from time to time. A few weeks ago she came to see me and we talked, as usual, 'You remember . . .'. That, I think, makes a real friendship, things in common to remember.

She mentioned her birthday party and I remembered that I ate my first anchovy butter and caviar there. Her mother was very modern, much more advanced than any other mothers in those days and her own parties and those of her little daughter's were always different from everybody else's. For tea we had tea – not drinking chocolate or milk – but tea. We felt so grown-up. At each cup there was a plate with two half rolls. One had anchovy butter and the other caviar. After the rolls came the sweets. There was a walnut gâteau which I remember well. After this there came a chestnut purée with fresh cream. That was a sweet never missing from any party – and never failing at any party! Here is the gâteau:

4 eggs, separated
6 oz. (¾ cup) caster sugar
2 oz. (½ cup) plain flour

4 oz. (⅔ cup) ground walnuts
apricot jam
1 tablespoon (1¼) rum

Beat the yolks with 4 oz. (½ cup) sugar until the mixture is thick and fluffy. Add the flour and walnuts and mix well. Beat 2 egg whites until stiff and fold them into the cake pan and bake at 360°F. (182°C.) Mark 4 for 30–40 minutes. Test with a knitting needle before taking the cake from the oven; if it comes out clean the cake is done. Turn out on to a wire rack, cool and slice into 2 rounds. Mix enough jam with the rum to spread over 1 round, cover with the remaining round and spread round the top and sides with jam. Beat the remaining egg whites until stiff, add the remaining sugar gradually and continue beating until the mixture is of a stiff meringue consistency. Put the bowl over hot water and, stirring all the time, cook until the mixture thickens. Cool, pour on the top of the cake and finally roughen with a fork. That's all.

WALNUT GÂTEAU (2)

12 oz. (3 cups) plain flour
pinch of salt
10 oz. (1¼ cups) butter
6 oz. (¾ cup) sugar
5 egg yolks
¼ cup (⅓) sour cream

filling:
7 egg whites
8 oz. (1 cup) caster sugar
5 egg yolks
9 oz. (1½ cups) ground walnuts

Sieve the flour and salt into a bowl. Break the butter into small pieces. Add this to the flour and rub it in until the mixture looks crumbly. Add the sugar, mix well, add the egg yolks, one by one, the sour cream and work the mixture to a stiff dough. Knead it well until it is almost silky. Divide the dough into 2. Put 1 piece aside and roll the other into a rectangle about ¼ in. thick. Place it on a greased baking (cookie) sheet and bake in the oven at 375°F. (191°C.) Mark 5 for 12–15 minutes. Take from the oven and place on a flat surface. Cool. To make the filling, beat the egg whites until very stiff, gradually add half the sugar and continue beating until the mixture is again stiff. Add the yolks one by one and mix well. Add the remaining sugar and when all this is thoroughly blended, slowly and carefully add the walnuts. Spread this mixture over the cooled pastry.

Quickly roll out the remaining paste the same size and thickness as the first piece and lay it over the filling. Prick it lightly with a fork and bake in the oven at the same heat for 15–20 minutes. Take from the oven, cool on a wire rack and slice to serve.

WALNUT GÂTEAU (3)

7 eggs, separated
5 oz. (scant ⅔ cup) caster sugar
5 oz. (scant ⅔ cup) butter
5 oz. (5 squares) melted chocolate
6 oz. (1 cup) ground walnuts
cake crumbs

filling:
1 cup (1¼) whipping cream
5 oz. (scant ⅔ cup) sugar
rum to taste
6 oz. (1 cup) shelled walnuts

Whisk the egg yolks with 3 oz. (full ⅓ cup) of sugar and beat until the mixture is thick. Gradually add the butter and chocolate. Beat vigorously until the mixture is thick and creamy. Add the walnuts and as many crumbs as needed to make a firm paste. Beat the egg whites until stiff, add the remaining sugar gradually and continue beating to a stiff meringue consistency. Fold this into the walnut mixture with great care. Rub an 8–9 in. round cake pan generously with butter, pour in the cake mixture and bake in the oven at 375°–400°F. (191°C.–205°C.) Mark 5–6 for 40–45 minutes. Test with a knitting needle, if it comes out clean the cake is ready. Take from the oven, turn on to a wire rack and cool. Slice into 2 rounds.

To make the filling, beat the cream with the sugar until stiff. Add the rum and walnuts. Spread this on 1 round of the cake, cover with the second round. The cake can be spread with a chocolate icing, if liked, or spread with apricot jam and sprinkled with roasted coarsely ground walnuts, or shelled halved walnuts, or simply sprinkled with sifted caster sugar or icing (confectioner's) sugar.

STRAWBERRY GÂTEAU

3 eggs
3 oz. (full ⅓ cup) butter
3 oz. (full ⅓ cup) caster sugar
2 oz. (⅓ cup) ground almonds
1½ oz. (full ⅓ cup) plain flour
biscuit or cake crumbs

filling:
¼ lb. (¾ cup) icing (confectioner's) sugar
1 lb. strawberries, preferably wild
few drops maraschino and lemon juice
redcurrant jelly
glacé fruits, chopped
thin water icing (frosting) (page 143)

Separate the eggs. Cream the butter with 2 oz. (¼ cup) of sugar and add the egg yolks one by one. Beat until the mixture is thick. Beat the egg whites stiffly, add the remaining sugar and continue beating until the mixture is meringue stiff. Fold this into the creamed butter and eggs alternately with the ground almonds, the flour and enough crumbs to make a batter of dropping consistency. Pour into a well-buttered and floured 6-in. cake pan and bake in the oven at 375°F. (191°C.) Mark 5 for about 40 minutes; test with a knitting needle, if it comes out clean the cake is ready. Take from the oven and turn on to a wire rack. Let it cool. Slice through to make 2 rounds.

To make the filling, sift the icing sugar over the strawberries and rub them through a sieve. Add maraschino and lemon juice – to taste but not too much or the mixture will be sodden. Bind with redcurrant jelly. Spread 1 round of the cake with two-thirds of the strawberry purée. Spread the rest over the top of the cake, sprinkle with the chopped glacé fruits and then cover with a thin layer of water icing. Another suggestion is to arrange a layer of halved garden strawberries over the top of the purée (instead of the glacé fruits) and to make the icing with lemon juice instead of water, which gives a lovely sharp taste to it.

FILLINGS AND ICINGS

The best filling of all for cakes and gâteaux is fresh cream; the next best is butter cream, which is good for layering and decorating. I give you giveral recipes for butter cream which I hope will be useful. For all butter cream recipes, use unsalted (sweet) butter.

BUTTER CREAM (1)

3 oz. (⅓ cup) granulated sugar   **2 egg yolks**
¼ cup (⅓) water   **4 – 6 oz. (½ – ¾ cup) butter**

Dissolve the sugar in the water over a low heat, bring to the boil and to a temperature of between 216°–218°F. (99°–100°C.) until it forms a thin thread. To test this put your finger and thumb into ice-cold water and then very quickly dip into the boiling sugar; take a pinch between the finger and thumb and if the mixture cracks or breaks, it is ready. It should look like a piece of glass. Take the mixture from the heat. Beat the egg yolks thoroughly and pour the sugar syrup into them in a steady stream, stirring vigorously all the time until the mixture is smooth and mousse-like. Now work the butter, using a wooden spoon, until it is soft and creamy, and gradually add the egg mixture. Flavour to taste, with melted chocolate (bitter or sweet), strong black coffee, the zest of orange or sieved raspberries or strawberries etc.

BUTTER CREAM (2)

4 oz. (½ cup) granulated sugar   **3 egg yolks**
¼ cup (⅓) water   **½ lb. (1 cup) butter**

Dissolve the sugar in the water over a low heat, then raise the heat and let the mixture boil steadily until it forms a thin thread (see previous recipe). Take from the heat and leave until the syrup ceases to bubble. In the meantime beat the egg yolks until thick and creamy and pour the cooled syrup over them in a steady stream, beating all the time until the mixture is thick and mousse-like. Cream the butter with a wooden spoon and beat in the egg and syrup mixture. Continue beating until the mixture is thick and creamy. Flavour to taste (see previous recipe).

BUTTER CREAM (3)

¾ cup (1) milk   **2 egg yolks**
4 oz. (½ cup) caster sugar   **½ lb. (1 cup) butter**

Put the milk in a pan with half the sugar and, over a low heat, cook until the sugar is dissolved. Beat the eggs in a largish bowl with the remaining sugar and then add the butter. Beat this mixture until it is light and creamy. Slowly add the milk, beating all the time. The mixture must be light and creamy and can be flavoured to taste.

CHOCOLATE BUTTER CREAM

2 oz. (2 squares) bitter chocolate   **½ lb. (1¾ cups) icing (confectioner's)**
½ lb. (1 cup) butter   **sugar**

Melt the chocolate until it is soft and beat until creamy. Beat the butter until soft, add the icing sugar and continue beating until the mixture is light and fluffy. Finally beat in the melted chocolate and continue beating until blended and the cream is smooth. Instead of chocolate, the same quantity of cocoa may be used.

MERINGUE BUTTER CREAM

8 oz. (1 cup) butter   **4 oz. (¾ cup) icing (confectioner's)**
2 egg whites   **sugar**

Cream the butter until very soft. Put the egg whites and sugar into a bowl and place over a pan of simmering water. Whisk together until the mixture starts to thicken and holds it shape. Add a little of the softened butter to the meringue and continue stirring (over the simmering water) until the mixture is very thick, yet creamy. Flavour as for any other butter cream.

MOCHA BUTTER CREAM

4 oz. (½ cup) butter   **coffee essence**
**6 oz. (1 cup) icing (confectioner's)
   sugar**

Cream the butter, add the sugar little by little, beating the mixture until it is smooth and creamy. Add the coffee essence, about 1–2 teaspoons (1¼–2½) is usually sufficient.

PRALINE BUTTER CREAM

½ lb. (1 cup) butter   **praline paste (see below)**
**½ lb. (1½ cups) icing
   (confectioner's) sugar**

Beat the butter until creamy, gradually add the sugar and continue beating until the mixture is soft and creamy. Beat in the praline paste and continue beating until it has been evenly blended.

PRALINE PASTE

2 oz. (scant ½ cup) brown sugar   **vanilla or almond flavouring**
2 oz. (⅓ cup) ground almonds

Put the sugar and almonds into a small pan and cook slowly to a nut brown, stirring well all the time with a metal spoon, especially when the sugar starts to melt. Add the flavouring and turn the mixture on to an oiled board or slab to cool. Bunch it to a paste. This will harden. To use, crush the praline, then pound it to a smooth paste. Praline is also made more usually with equal quantities of caster sugar and chopped blanched almonds and treated as above.

LEMON ICING

2 egg whites   **1 lb. (3 cups) icing (confectioner's)**
1 lemon   **sugar**

Slightly whisk the egg whites. Squeeze the oil from the lemon skin on to the icing sugar. Mix half the sugar with the egg whites. Stir until the mixture is well blended, then stir for 5–10 minutes or until the mixture is smooth and glossy. Cover with a slightly damp cloth and leave until bubbles rise to the top. Gradually add the remaining sugar until the required consistency is achieved, this icing should rise in peaks. Add enough of the lemon juice to flavour – but take care you do not add too much or the icing will become too thin. If liked, add grated lemon rind. This icing is useful for petits fours or for covering gâteaux.

FRANGIPANE

A useful filling for flans, tarts and sponge cakes.

4 oz. (½ cup) butter   flavouring:
4 oz. (½ cup) caster sugar   **orange-flower water, lemon juice,**
2 eggs   **vanilla, kirsch etc.**
1 oz. (¼ cup) plain flour
4 oz. (⅔ cup) ground almonds

Cream the butter using a wooden spoon, gradually add the sugar beating the mixture well. Beat in the eggs one at a time and then stir in the flour, mix well, add the almonds and any of the chosen flavourings. Use as required. Frangipane can be used in small pastry cases and baked in the oven at 375 °F. (191 °C.) Mark 5 until the filling is firm to the touch.

ROYAL ICING (Frosting)

2 lb. (7 cups) icing (confectioner's)   **4 egg whites**
sugar   **2 teaspoons (2½) glycerine**

Sift the sugar. Put the egg whites into a bowl and stir just a little, enough to break up the albumen but without making too many air bubbles. Add half the sugar and beat with a wooden spoon until the mixture is well blended. Stir briskly for 5–10 minutes. Cover with a slightly damp cloth and leave until bubbles form at the top. Gradually add the remaining sugar until the required consistency is required, the icing should be stiff and firm. For a wedding cake, for example, or so-called flat work, an easy test is thus; place a wooden spoon in it. If it slowly slips to one side, the consistency is correct. For rough icing the mixture should fall in peaks. Add the glycerine (this is to make the icing glossy and can be omitted). Add flavouring or colouring if required. If possible, icing should be left overnight in an airtight container. A good tip to ensure really smooth icing, is to take 1 tablespoon (1¼) of the icing (before using it) and mix it with enough water to make a coating consistency. Mix it well and then mix it back into the bulk of the icing and mix it thoroughly.

CUBE SUGAR ICING (Frosting)

1 lb. (4 cups) cube sugar
4 egg whites

1 oz. (2 tablespoons) cornflour
(cornstarch)

Pound the sugar until fine. Beat the egg whites until frothy, gradually add the sugar, beat well, then add the cornflour, beating all the time. Spread this over the cakes and put them into a cool oven to let the coating dry and harden but do not let it change colour. If a coloured icing is required, add cochineal, strawberry or redcurrant juice or other colourings to choice. If cakes are iced with this icing straight from the oven, when still hot, the icing will become firm as the cakes cool.

WATER or GLACÉ ICING (Frosting)

Basic recipe:
**1 lb. (3 cups) icing (confectioner's)
sugar**

5–6 tablespoons water
flavouring and colouring to taste

Sieve the sugar into a bowl and slowly add enough water to make a coating consistency. The above quantity will coat 1 large cake and two 6-in. cakes.

VARIATIONS ON WATER OR GLACÉ ICING

For orange or lemon icing, replace the water with strained orange or lemon juice. For chocolate icing, melt 4 oz. (4 squares) bitter chocolate in the water and boil for 2 – 3 minutes. Take from the heat, cool, add the icing sugar and beat thoroughly; or mix 2 tablespoons (2½) sieved cocoa with the water, boil for 2 minutes, cool and mix into the icing sugar. For coffee icing, use half and half water and coffee essence.

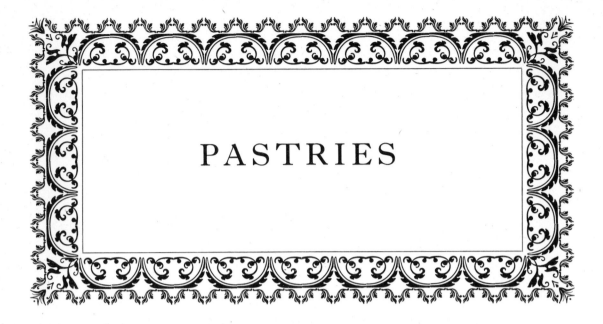

PASTRIES

GENERAL INSTRUCTIONS

There are fewer rules to be observed for pastry making, and such as they are are no more than commonsense. It is very easy to make pastry successfully and this requires the minimum of utensils. All that is needed is a bowl, baking board, rolling pin, spoon, fork and jug. The essence of successful pastry making is speed of work, lightness of touch and a cool, even temperature in both cook and kitchen.

Materials
The materials used are flour, fat, and liquid. The fat may be butter, lard, vegetable fat or a combination of these. The minimum of liquid necessary to form a workable paste is the ideal for shortcrust pastry. The methods for puff pastry and choux pastry have been described in the chapter on pastries.

Lightness and sureness of the fingertips when rubbing the fat into the flour and the speed at which this is done are essential to success. It is however possible to achieve this with a fork when using vegetable fat or lard. The liquid – ice-cold water, egg yolk or lemon juice – must be added after the fat, again with the exception of puff pastry. Rolling is an art that only experience can perfect. It needs quick, firm, but not heavy, movements away from the body to ensure even pressure on the pastry which should be turned between rollings. Reflour both the rolling pin and your hands as necessary to prevent sticking. Many experts state that resting the pastry in a cool place before final shaping and baking will improve the result and prevent shrinking during cooking.

Pastry is more often spoiled by baking at a too low temperature than the reverse. Eggs will add richness but will make it more liable to crumble and break while it is being handled. Be careful with sugar. Granulated sugar is apt to spot the pastry in cooking. It is safer to use icing sugar. Nut pastry is delicious, but requires care in handling.

PUFF PASTRY

For the last two hundred years, the most popular of all pastries has been puff pastry. In my childhood in Hungary we had cream slices with yellow vanilla cream mixed with egg yolks, sugar and fresh cream. The flavour was unforgettable and very difficult to repeat. I wonder whether they were really so good or that my childhood appetite added to the flavour. Very likely the famous Hungarian flour had something to do with it. Of course, the eggs were different; the chickens were different – they were all very happy chickens: no batteries, not enclosed in little prisons; they wandered about in the yard or the fields and three times a day their mistress threw maize to them with love and care.

Another important ingredient in the making of continental cream slices is vanilla pod. There are many kinds of vanilla; very good thin pods, with an especially good flavour; much thicker ones, much cheaper and with less flavour. Hungarian importers bought the very best kind of vanilla, tea or coffee because the duty was the same. The differences in the prices didn't matter very much, therefore the Hungarian coffee was always good. As long as I can remember, I drank only Darjeeling tea in Hungary, because the price was hardly different from that of the poorer quality.

For forty years I have fought actively for better food, better pastry, better everything. But to go back to puff pastry, I want to tell you how many kinds of pastries you can make out of it. First the cream slice of which there are at least three kinds: one is the famous *millefeuille*; another is a coffee slice filled with whipped cream and coffee cream, again in three layers; and lastly whipped cream and chocolate cream. Of course, only fresh cream is used – that wonderful Jersey cream is best. You can make hundreds of kinds of pastries from puff pastry: sweet ones and savouries, vol-au-vents, pie cases and tarts, sausage rolls, pie crusts and fruit tarts, large ones and tiny ones. To make really good puff pastry is not one of the easiest things to do. I remember at home, when we engaged a cook, one of the most important questions was 'Can you make puff pastry?' It is a difficult procedure because the temperature of your hand plays a part as well. A cook with a naturally warm hand can seldom make good puff pastry, as everything should be kept cool, including utensils and ingredients. I will try to give you a recipe for the making of puff pastry which is interesting because it is not so much different from that which pastrycooks made in 1760, over two hundred years ago.

I like everything in the puff pastry line made with butter. I do not know whether I am right in sticking so much to butter but what can you do with your upbringing? It is difficult to shake it off. I was born into a farmer's family, and in Hungary butter was taken for granted, being an agricultural country. In my youth, which was a long, long time ago, the margarine was not good – I only suppose so, because I never tasted it, to be truthful. There were margarine factories in my time but we never used it either at home or in the business. I have even had arguments in Hungary with margarine-factory owners who wanted to convert me, but without success. I am still a butter believer. Making puff pastry needs precision. As with most things you cannot take short cuts in the pastry kitchen; of course, there are daily routines and so it is very simple. In making puff pastry it is very important to have the best pastry flour, I was told by my miller. This flour is called pastry flour everywhere.

As a general rule in the making of puff pastry it is very important that your water should be ice cold and you should use the lemon juice with the water. You make the pastry by first mixing the flour with the water and lemon juice. The pastry should not be soft and not hard. But it must be hard enough to hold your butter. It often happens that the pastry is too soft when you roll it out and so the butter is squeezed out. It is important that when you add the butter to the pastry the butter should be firm, but again not too hard and not too soft. I am afraid these things have to be learnt by practice and experience. The pastry and the butter should be the same consistency. If you can achieve this then the mixing will not be difficult. If it is reasonably firm it is easy to roll out. Where most experience is needed is in the technique of rolling out the pastry. This must be done firmly using a big, heavy rolling pin. Then roll backwards and forwards, repeating the movement several times. Again experience is far more helpful than any recipe. If you press too much you will push out the butter and then the pastry will not rise properly. You have to be pretty careful for the first two or three turns because the butter must not come through the pastry, which would make it sticky; if this happens you have to use more flour and you have to be very sparing with extra flour. Too much flour ruins the pastry. I must warn you, if I have not done so before, that it is difficult to make puff pastry if you happen to have very warm hands. Let us assume however that you have mastered the art because I would like to give you a few recipes made with puff pastry.

Flaky pastry and puff pastry are made in much the same way, but all my pastry-cooks – in Hungary, in Vienna, Prague, Berlin and London – made them a little bit differently. Old-fashioned puff pastry contained eggs. But in modern puff pastry we no longer use them. We used to start with the flour, a very small piece of butter, a pinch of salt, 2 yolks of eggs and about $\frac{1}{4}$ cup ($\frac{1}{3}$) of water. This was made into a very silky dough, neither too hard, nor too soft.

In contrast, a modern puff pastry contains no eggs, but plenty of butter. You can, indeed, have in a puff pastry the same amount of butter as flour; in such a case, ice-cold water is needed. Proportions should be 6 oz. flour ($1\frac{1}{2}$ cups) the same of butter to $\frac{1}{4}$ pint ($\frac{1}{3}$ pint) water. Sieve the flour in a bowl. Take about $\frac{1}{2}$ oz. of butter and mix a $\frac{1}{4}$ pint ($\frac{1}{3}$ pint) cold water and make a soft dough from this. Then roll it out on a pastry board to about $\frac{1}{2}$ in. thickness. Then flatten the butter with your rolling pin, put it in the middle of the pastry and pack the butter into the dough as if making a parcel. Put the pastry in a cold place or in a refrigerator, then roll it out again and fold it six times. Then put it back in the cold place or the refrigerator for another hour. Repeat the operation once more. Then yet once again – three times altogether.

You can make really hundreds and hundreds of different kinds of savouries and sweets from puff pastry. You can also make the famous *rissoles* used to garnish soups. These *rissoles* are three cornered and filled with mushrooms which are first fried with a little onions and chopped mushrooms. These are then fried in deep fat. You can make the filling with cream cheese; for a sweet add sugar and a yolk of egg, and fill your little three-cornered pastry. If it is savoury you add to cream cheese, salt and quite a bit of chopped dill. You can put with the cream cheese chopped chives and salt; you can also fill the savoury puff pastry with ham, anchovy or with any other meat or fish.

I have already given you several puff pastry recipes, but one night – not able to sleep because of troubles and bad conscience – I started to read a very, very heavy book, which is difficult in bed. I thought my arm would break, but I went on reading till I found a passage about puff pastry. There it was said that puff pastry was one of the most fashionable and most popular culinary products very many years ago. There was a lot of discussion as to who had been the first maker of this delicacy. Somebody said in France that a very famous painter in the seventeenth century was the original founder. The other party said that it was a very famous pastrycook. But the historian said that the Greeks and the Romans had already made this pastry.

I read and read in the night. I was so tired in the end that I could not make any notes and decided to look up the passage again next morning. Of course, the 'next morning' for me means to get up and rush to my office. But puff pastry was in my mind during the whole day. I came home earlier than usual in the afternoon, sat at my desk surrounded by books and started to look for the interesting story about puff pastry. You would not believe it, but for four solid hours I looked through all the heavy books and could not find the piece about puff pastry.

In the end from irritation I got a headache and left the books and came out to watch television. I hardly believe that this is the best medicine for headache. Anyway,

I watched for a while and then went back and looked for another half-hour, but without result. Angry I went to bed and read a little, then went to sleep.

The next morning I woke up, still annoyed. I looked at all the books, especially at one which I had suspected the most, and I said aloud: 'I look for you once more and . . .'. In that moment I opened the book – a huge book – exactly on the page where my puff pastry was. Yet it was not called 'puff pastry', but *flaky* pastry. That was the silly reason why I could not find it before.

PUFF PASTRY (1)

1 lb. (4 cups) plain flour   **½ lb. (1 cup) butter**
1 whole egg

Sieve the flour into a bowl. Take out about a quarter. Put aside. Beat the egg until it is smooth. Add the egg to the flour, work it in and add as much water as the flour will absorb. The result should be a pretty stiff paste. Roll it out with a rolling pin to a thin oblong sheet. Lay about a quarter of the butter over it, cut into small pieces. Dredge it with some of the reserved flour. Roll it up, tightly and then roll out again with the rolling pin. Repeat this procedure four times until all the butter is mixed into the flour and the paste is rolled out flat. Fold the paste in three, folding the first lap away from you and the second one towards you. Turn the paste half-way round bringing the edges to one side. Repeat this rolling and folding and closing the edges, four times in all but allowing a rest between the second and third rolling. Put into a refrigerator for between 1–2 hours. The paste is now ready to use: suitable for *vol-au-vent* cases, cream horns, *palmiers*, cream slices etc.

PUFF PASTRY (2)

8 oz. (2 cups) plain flour   **1 teaspoon (1¼) lemon juice**
pinch of salt   **8 oz. (1 cup) butter**
about ¼ cup (⅓) ice-cold water to
  mix

Sieve the flour and salt into a bowl and mix with the water and lemon juice to a stiff paste. Turn on to a floured board (or marble slab) and knead it for 10 minutes or until the paste is elastic and no longer sticks to the fingers. Roll the dough into a strip long and wide enough to enclose the butter. Place the butter on it (if the butter is hard, beat until it is pliable), roll the pastry over the butter, flatten it in 2 or 3 places with a rolling pin and then roll it out into a long strip again, taking care the butter does not break through. Fold the strip of pastry in 3, press down the folds and put the pastry aside to rest for 15 minutes. Do not seal the edges of the pastry. Roll out the paste again with the folded edge to the right and fold twice, then put aside again to rest. Roll out another five times and finally roll out to the size and thickness required. Before baking, let the paste rest in a cool place.

Bake in a very hot oven 450°F. (233°C.) Mark 8, and it is important the door is not opened until the pastry has set and that no draught enters.

PALMIERS (France)

puff pastry   **caster sugar**

Palmiers can be made with the trimmings of left-over puff pastry. Roll out the pastry to a thin strip, sprinkle generously with caster sugar, roll up tightly from one end lengthwise to the centre of the strip and then from the other end to the centre as well. Cut across in slices, which can be either thick or thin. Place on a dampened baking (cookie) sheet, sprinkle again with sugar and bake for 10 – 12 minutes at 425°F. (216°C.) Mark 7. When the tops begin to go brown, turn them over, sprinkle again with sugar so that both sides will caramelize. When they are brown and somewhat sticky, the *palmiers* are done. Take from the oven, carefully lift on to a wire rack and leave to cool. Serve plain or put two together, sandwiched with thick whipped cream.

CREAM SLICES

Cream slices are one of the most tempting of puff pastries. I remember that as a child I stopped at every shop window where I saw these lovely cream slices. I just never could understand how any man or woman who had enough money in their pocket or purse could pass a shop and not go in and buy and take one home or eat it there and then. Where are these lovely young years when these little things were such a temptation? I give you one kind of cream slice recipe:

½ lb. puff pastry   1 tablespoon (1¼) cornflour
3 eggs, separated   (cornstarch)
5 oz. (scant ⅔ cup) caster sugar   ¾ pint (1½ cups) milk
                                           small piece vanilla pod

Roll out the pastry as thinly as possible to a large rectangle and cut it into 2 equal strips. Lay these on slightly dampened baking (cookie) sheet, prick well all over with a fork and chill for 10 minutes. Bake in the oven at 425°F. (216°C.) Mark 7 for 10–15 minutes or until it is a pale brown. Turn the pastry over carefully with a palette knife and cook for another 5 minutes. Take from the oven, carefully place on a wire rack to cool.

Make the filling. Beat the egg whites until stiff, gradually add two-thirds of the sugar. Beat the egg yolks lightly with the remaining sugar and the cornflour. Bring the milk with the vanilla pod to the boil, pour it into the beaten egg yolks, stirring all the time to avoid lumps. Beat the mixture well, return it to the pan and continue cooking and stirring until the custard thickens. Add the egg whites while the custard is cooking and continue cooking for another 3 minutes. Let the mixture cool. Spread the custard thickly over one layer of pastry – it should be at least $1\frac{1}{2}$ in. thick – and cover with the second piece. Cut into slices with a very sharp knife, dipping it into boiling water. Dust with sifted icing (confectioner's) sugar. The cream slices are ready to serve. And they are very good too.

CARLTON MILLEFEUILLE PASTRY

Many years ago I went to Cannes and stayed in the Carlton Hotel. The Managing Director and his wife were most kind and good to me and I never felt lonely there. I learned much and tasted wonderful food, very especially pastries and gâteaux. The *millefeuille* pastry, the recipe for which I want to give you, was the best I have ever tasted. The puff pastry from which the gâteau was made was a different puff pastry from the English one or, indeed, from any other puff pastry I have tasted before. I suppose it was so good because it was made differently. It was very light, and tasted heavenly. The chef told me that the most important factor was the very careful mixing of materials and a light touch. In the Carlton Hotel the pastrycooks, all very young men, were quite outstanding. This was their method.

The chef sifted the flour on a marble slab, and made a well in the flour; he then put the butter, which was very fresh and unsalted, in the well, Next he added the sugar and eggs, and at this point no more liquid. In this way the pastry will not shrink and will not lose shape during the cooking. He told me he preferred icing sugar as this made the pastry lighter. He mixed the butter, sugar and eggs together, blended the mixture well, very slightly drawing the flour to it. He used only his finger-tips and very gently, little by little, he mixed the whole dough. It was a joy to see him working, his hand was not sticky, not even floury. He worked only with one hand and only the finger-tips. When the dough was ready and the flour was used slowly, his finger-tips were quite clean, then he used the heel of his palm and kneaded the whole dough together. He said you should not work the pastry too long or too much because the pastry then will be sticky and it will be difficult to turn. If you work it too hard and long you have to use more flour and that would spoil your whole pastry. When the pastry is formed, shape it into a nice square piece, pack it in a greaseproof paper and set aside in a cool place or keep it in the refrigerator overnight and use it the next day. Here are the ingredients.

8 oz. (2 cups) plain flour   **4 eggs**
4 oz. (½ cup) butter   **a little icing (confectioner's) sugar**

Mix the ingredients as on page 150. Cut 4 rounds. Roll out as thinly as possible Place on a slightly dampened baking (cookie) sheet and bake as in previous recipe. Cool. Put a layer of *crème patissière* between each round or use whipped cream. Vanilla flavouring may be added if liked, or flavour the cream with very strong coffee. You can cover it with water icing and ring your gâteau with fresh cream and very finely roasted almonds or hazelnuts. Alternatively, you can leave it plain and eat it dry.

Millefeuille gâteau

You can also make puff pastry horns. I think these are very popular in England. Roll the puff pastry on little wooden or steel cones. Bake the pastry on these, let them cool and fill with whipped cream; you can also use chocolate or coffee cream.

MILLEFEUILLE GÂTEAU (France)

A few years ago *millefeuille* was very fashionable and very popular. I do not think people could buy *millefeuille* in many places, so we found we had to make much more than I ever reckoned with, but slowly it has become less and less popular. I think this is inevitable as people will always want something new. People in our shop sometimes look round and ask if that is all we have. We never have less than two or three hundred different cakes, buns, pastries and gâteaux. So sometimes I ask the customer 'Oh, what do you want, if there is not enough here?' 'Oh, I only want one or two'. What can we do but smile! I find in any difficulty a smile helps you, and the customer, perhaps, goes out a satisfied one. But let me deal now with the *millefeuille* gâteau.

To make this, roll out about 1 lb. of puff pastry very thinly and cut out 6 rounds 7-in in diameter. Prick them well with a fork. Place the rounds of pastry on a slightly dampened baking (cookie) sheet and bake them in the oven at 425 °F. (216 °C.) Mark 7 for 10 – 15 minutes or until they are a pale golden colour. Turn them over to bake for another 5 minutes, take from the oven and cool on a wire rack. When they are quite cold spread one round with sweetened whipped cream. Cover with a second round and spread this with raspberry jam. Repeat this until all the rounds are finished and cover the top round with thin lemon icing (see page 142).

VANILLA CUSTARD SLICES

1 lb. puff pastry (page 148)	**whipped cream**
crème patissière (page 173)	**lemon icing (page 142)**
raspberry jam	**pistachio nuts, finely chopped**

Roll out the pastry very thinly into a rectangle. Cut into 2 long strips and each strip into smaller strips about 2½ × 1 in. Place on a slightly dampened baking (cookie) sheet and bake in the oven at 425 °F. (216 °C.) Mark 7 for 10 – 15 minutes or until a golden brown. Turn the slices to brown on the other side for 5 minutes. Take from the oven and cool on a wire rack. Divide the slices into stacks of 4 layers. Spread one layer of pastry with *crème patissière*, cover with a layer of pastry, spread this with jam, cover with a third layer of pastry and spread this with whipped cream. Add the final layer and spread this with lemon icing. Sprinkle with finely chopped pistachio nuts.

RICHMOND MAIDS OF HONOUR

½ lb. puff pastry (page 148)   1 oz. (2 tablespoons) butter,
4 oz. (½ cup) curd cheese   melted but lukewarm
1 egg, well beaten   2 oz. (2 tablespoons) caster sugar

Make the pastry, preferably the night before, and roll to about ¼-in. thickness.
Cut into rounds with a pastry cutter. Line 12–18 patty pans with the pastry rounds,
press the pastry well into the pans and then, with the finger and thumb, work the
paste from the bottom upwards so that the bottom of the pastry case is much thinner
than the top which should bulge slightly all round.

   Make the filling. Sieve the curd cheese, add the egg and butter, finally flavour with
sugar. Mix thoroughly. Half-fill each pastry case with filling and bake at 400°F.
(205°C.) Mark 6 for 30 minutes.

   Home-made curd cheese is the most suitable for this recipe and of a somewhat
rubbery texture before it has been sieved.

MINCE PIES

You can make these with either puff pastry or short pastry, they both taste very good.

puff, flaky or shortcrust pastry   mincemeat

Roll out the chosen pastry – puff is the most traditional – to ¼-in. thickness and cut
with a cutter into rounds 3-in. in diameter. Roll out the trimmings and cut into an
equal number of rounds but much thinner. Line patty pans with the thinner rounds,
fill up with the mincemeat (as much as the tart will take) and moisten the edges of the
pastry with cold water or slightly beaten egg white. Lay the thicker rounds of pastry
on the top and press the edges together with a fork. Make a hole in the top of each one
with a skewer to let the steam escape, brush over with egg white, milk or egg yolk and
dredge with caster sugar. For puff pastry bake at 475°F. (246°C.) Mark 9, and for
short pastry bake at 400°F. (205°C.) Mark 6 for 20 minutes or until the pies are well
browned and nicely risen.

BANBURY CAKES

1 lb. puff or flaky pastry (pages 148, 154)
4 oz. (½ cup) butter
2 oz. (¼ cup) sugar
4 oz. (1 cup) finely chopped peel
½ lb. (1⅓ cup) currants

1 tablespoon (1¼) brandy
½ teaspoon (⅔) ground allspice or nutmeg
1 egg white, beaten
caster sugar

Cream the butter and sugar together. Add the peel, currants, brandy and allspice. Mix well. Roll out the pastry thinly. Cut it into circles 3-in. in diameter. Put a little of the filling on each. Dampen the edges and draw them into the centre and seal them. Turn the cakes over and roll lightly into an oblong. Pinch each end to a point to give them the traditional Banbury cake shape. Mark 3 slashes on the top with the back of a knife and bake at 425°F. (216°C.) Mark 7 for 15 minutes. Brush with the beaten egg white and sprinkle with sugar and continue baking at the same temperature for another 5 minutes. Sprinkle again with sugar just before serving.

SACRISTANS

½ lb. puff pastry (page 148)
1 egg, beaten

coarsely chopped almonds
icing (confectioner's) sugar

Roll out the pastry to a thin strip 4-in. wide. Paint with beaten egg leaving a ½-in. border at each side. Sprinkle with almonds and dredge with sifted icing sugar. Cut into strips about ¾-in. long. Twist these three or four times and place on a slightly dampened baking (cookie) sheet. Press the ends down firmly and bake at 425°F. (216°C.) Mark 7 for 8–10 minutes. Carefully lift off the sacristans from the baking sheet and leave to cool on a wire rack.

FLAKY PASTRY

8 oz. (2 cups) plain flour
¼ teaspoon (⅓) salt
6 oz. (¾ cup) butter or other fat

½ teaspoon (⅔) lemon juice
cold water to mix

Sieve the flour with the salt into a bowl. Divide the butter into 4 portions. Rub one portion into the flour until the mixture looks crumbly. Add the lemon juice and enough water to make a firm dough. Knead lightly on a floured board. Roll out into a strip about 18-in. long and 6-in. wide, and a little less than ¼-in. thick. Spread one of the three remaining portions of fat over two-thirds of the paste in even rows to about 1 in. of the edge of the paste. Dredge the butter lightly with flour. Fold the pastry into three with the unbuttered portion in the centre. This means there is an alternate layer of fat and of paste. Turn the paste right round with the folded edge towards yourself. Press the edges sharply together to enclose the air and press the pastry in 2 or 3 places to form ridges. Roll out again in a narrow strip, being careful not to roll over the edges. Proceed as before with the remaining 2 portions of fat. Lastly roll out to the thickness required.

To bake flaky pastry, have a very hot oven, 450°F. (233°C.) Mark 8 for 8–10 minutes for patties or tartlets and 425°F. (126°C.) Mark 7 for 20–30 minutes for pies.

Variations

1. *Bun :* you can make several different shapes; cut out a piece and roll it very thin and narrow. Brush it over with melted butter; mix cinnamon, chocolate and sugar together and sprinkle it over the paste. Fold over once and roll up like a Chelsea bun.

2. *Square :* cut out squares 2 in. in diameter, put softened marzipan in the middle and roll up like a *croissant*.

3. *Envelopes :* have ready a pretty stiff custard and place into a pastry which should be cut in a square and then folded like an envelope.

4. *Rectangle :* cut a rectangle 2 in. wide and 3 in. long and pipe apricot jam into the middle and fold over.

You can vary these fillings according to your taste; the important thing is to butter a baking dish and put the pastries on it; mix a little yolk of egg with a little milk and sugar and wash over each pastry. Let them rest for an hour and repeat the washing once more before baking in a medium oven till cooked and nice and golden-brown.

SHORT PASTRY OR SHORTCRUST PASTRY

Short pastry is one of the most useful pastries you can make. It keeps uncooked in the refrigerator for a few days, or, cooked, it may be kept for a fortnight. You can make pastries, petits fours, pies, tartlets and a variety of savouries from this pastry. Short pastry if it is carefully made, can be very good and very pleasant. I prefer to make it with butter, but you can make very successful pastry with margarine or with one of the new vegetable shortening. If the weather is cold, rub the butter or margarine well into the flour with your finger-tips. You have to be careful not to work it into a greasy cake or into lumps. If in warm weather the fat used is too soft, it is better to place it in the basin with other ingredients such as eggs and sugar, and mix well before adding the flour. The moistening to use depends on the kind of pastry you want to make. For some purposes, water alone is used; for a richer pastry use eggs instead. In making the dough it is not necessary to rub it too hard and too much, as you will then produce a very greasy pastry. This is a common fault. The ingredients are made smooth and clear by pinching. There is no need to rub the fat into the flour, no need to rub it hard. It is very easy to make short pastry too wet and this is also a common fault. Here are three shortcrust or short pastry recipes for you to try:

SHORT PASTRY (1) (Sweet)

1 lb. (4 cups) plain flour	2 oz. ($\frac{1}{4}$ cup) caster sugar
4 oz. ($\frac{1}{2}$ cup) butter	1 egg yolk
4 oz. ($\frac{1}{2}$ cup) lard	$\frac{1}{4}$ cup ($\frac{1}{3}$) cold water

Sieve the flour into a mixing bowl. Cut the fat into the flour with a round-bladed knife and as soon as the pieces of fat are coated with flour rub in with the finger-tips until the mixture looks like fine breadcrumbs. Mix in the sugar (omit this if making pastry for a savoury filling). Make a well in the middle, add the egg yolk and the water. Mix quickly with a knife or, if preferred, still working with the fingers. Work to a firm dough. Turn this out on to a floured pastry board and knead the pastry until smooth. Wrap in greaseproof paper and chill in the refrigerator for about 30 minutes before using.

A richer pastry can be made by increasing the quantity of fat by another 2 oz. (4 tablespoons).

SHORT PASTRY (2) (Rich)

1 lb. (4 cups) plain flour	**3 egg yolks**
8 oz. (1 cup) butter	**¼ cup (⅓) cold water**

Sieve the flour into a bowl, add the butter cut in small pieces; when these are well coated with flour, rub in until the mixture looks like fine breadcrumbs. Make a hole in the middle, add the egg yolks and half the water. Mix to a firm dough, adding if required the rest of the water. Continue as in previous recipe. Use for rich pies.

FRENCH SHORT PASTRY (3) (Pâte Brisée)

8 oz. (2 cups) plain flour	**1 whole egg**
pinch of salt	**5 oz. (½ cup + 2 tablespoons) butter**
1 teaspoon (1¼) caster sugar	**2–3 tablespoons (2½–3¾) iced water**

Sieve the flour into a mixing bowl with the salt and sugar. Make a well in the middle, add the egg. Add the butter, cut into pieces, and work the mixture until it resembles breadcrumbs or oatmeal. Add the water and blend quickly (with the hand). Work to a firm dough until it just holds together and then place on a floured board. Knead it gently but firmly until a smooth dough has been achieved, also the complete blending of all ingredients. Wrap in a slightly damp cloth or greaseproof paper and keep for 1 hour in the freezing compartment of the refrigerator or in the main part overnight which is preferable. For savoury fillings omit the sugar.

FRENCH FLAN PASTRY

4 oz. (1 cup) plain flour	**2 oz. (¼ cup) caster sugar**
pinch of salt	**2–3 drops vanilla**
2 oz. (¼ cup) butter	**2 egg yolks**

Sieve the flour with a pinch of salt on to a floured board. Make a well in the centre, add the butter, sugar, vanilla and egg yolks. Work the ingredients together with the finger-tips until completely blended. Knead the mixture to a firm dough and chill for 2 hours before using.

WOMAN'S MOOD CAKE (Redcurrant Tart)

2½ oz. (5 tablespoons) butter	1 lb. redcurrants
4 oz. (1 cup) plain flour	granulated sugar
1½ oz. (3 tablespoons) caster sugar	2 egg whites
1 teaspoon (1¼) grated lemon peel	4 tablespoons (5) icing
1 large egg	(confectioner's) sugar

Rub the butter into the flour, add the caster sugar and grated lemon peel, mix well, add the egg and mix to a firm dough. Leave in a cool place for 30 minutes. Clean the redcurrants, freeing them from their stalks. Cook 2 tablespoons (2½) of water with sugar to taste until the sugar is dissolved. Add the redcurrants and cook for a few minutes only. Take the fruit out with a slotted spoon and put aside. Let the syrup continue cooking until it is a thick syrup. Roll out the pastry very thinly and bake it blind in a round flan pan until it is a pale golden colour. Leave it to cool, then brush with the sugar syrup. Arrange the redcurrants on top. Whip the egg whites until stiff and gradually beat in the icing sugar. Spread this over the top of the redcurrants and bake at 350°F. (175°C.) Mark 4 until the meringue top is dry rather than either browned or baked. The tart can be eaten hot or cold.

APPLE TART

I have never in my life made so many apple tarts, flans, turnovers and pies as here in England. Except for the famous *Apfel Strudel* and apple slices, we never baked anything else with apples in Hungary. Just lately one of our new Scottish pastrycooks made a very successful apple tart. Here is the recipe.

½ lb. shortcrust pastry	3½ oz. (scant ½ cup) sugar
1 lb. cooking apples	1 cup (1¼) cream
2 oz. (½ cup) plain flour	

First roll out the pastry and line an 8-in. tart pan. Peel the apples and cut them into thin rings – drop these into water as you work for apples brown quickly. As soon as all the apples are ready, pat them dry and arrange neatly round the inside of the pan, on top of the pastry with the slices slightly overlapping. All the pastry must be covered. Put into the oven at 400°F. (205°C.) Mark 6 and bake for 10 minutes.

In the meantime make the covering. Mix the flour with the sugar in a bowl, stir in the cream. After the apples have been baking for 10 minutes, take from the pan and pour the covering over the top. Lower the heat to 325°F. (162°C.) Mark 3, and return the tart to the oven to bake for a further 10–15 minutes.

BANANA MERINGUE TART (Brazil)

6 bananas
2 oz. (¼ cup) butter
½ lb. shortcrust pastry

1 teaspoon (1¼) ground cinnamon
6 oz. (¾ cup) caster sugar
3 eggs, separated

Peel the bananas and cut into long strips. Warm the butter in a pan and gently fry the banana strips till they are golden brown. Line a flan tin with shortcrust pastry and cover the pastry with the bananas arranged carefully in rows. Sprinkle with the cinnamon mixed with a spoonful of the sugar. Melt one-third of the sugar in a double boiler or over a pan half filled with water, add the yolks, slightly beaten, and cook, stirring all the time till the mixture thickens. Pour this over the bananas. Whisk the whites till stiff, fold in the remaining sugar and continue beating until the mixture is very stiff forming peaks. Spread this over the top of the flan completely covering the filling. Cook at 375°F. (191°C.) Mark 5 for 35–45 minutes. Leave till cool and sprinkle with sugar.

Meringues and pastries: 1. meringues; 2. vol-au-vent cases; 3. and 4. chocolate éclairs.

BAKEWELL TART

A traditional British recipe which varies slightly in different counties.

½ lb. shortcrust pastry
raspberry or strawberry jam
2 oz. (¼ cup) butter
2 oz. (¼ cup) caster sugar
1 egg, well beaten

2 oz. (⅓ cup) ground almonds
2 heaped tablespoons (2½) soft
    bread or cake crumbs
almond essence to taste

Line an 8-in. sandwich pan with rolled-out pastry. Spread the pastry with jam (although a red jam is usual, other jams may be used and some recipes also add lemon curd). Cream the butter in a bowl, add the sugar and continue beating until the mixture is light. Gradually beat in the egg, then add the almonds and cake crumbs. Add almond essence and spread this mixture over the jam. Bake in the oven for 35–45 minutes at 375°F. (191°C.) Mark 5. Serve hot or cold.

BRAMBLE TARTLETS

6 oz. shortcrust pastry
½ lb. brambles or blackberries

sugar to taste
whipping cream to taste

Roll out the pastry thinly and line 12–14 tartlet pans, depending on their size. Prick well all over and bake in the oven at 375°F. (191°C.) Mark 5 for 12–15 minutes or until golden brown. In the meantime clean and hull the brambles and cook them in a little water, sweetened to taste, until just cooked – keep them as whole as possible. Take the tartlets from the oven, cool on a wire rack and then fill each with a little of the sweetened fruit. Whip the cream until it makes peaks, sugar may be added if liked, and drop a small blob of this on top of the tartlets. Blueberries can be used in the same manner.

CONGRESS TARTS

2 oz. shortcrust pastry
raspberry jam
2 oz. (4 tablespoons) butter
2 oz. (¼ cup) caster sugar

3 oz. (½ cup) ground almonds
grated rind and juice ½ lemon
1 large egg white

Roll out the pastry and line about 10 tartlet pans. Spread the bottom of each with jam. Cream the butter with the caster sugar, add the almonds, beat well, add the lemon rind and juice. Beat the egg white until stiff – a little caster sugar may be added, if liked, to make it of meringue stiffness. Mix this into the butter-almond mixture. Put a little of the filling into each tartlet case and bake near the top of the oven at 425°F. (216°C.) Mark 7 for about 15 minutes. Cool on a wire rack. Congress tarts can be decorated if liked with a few slivered almonds or glacé cherries or with a cross made over the top with a strip of pastry – all added before baking.

JAM TARTS

Jam tarts and fruit pies and tarts are very popular. The jam should be a bright colour and should be of good quality. It should be thick, otherwise it boils out in the cooking. If the jam is too thick, you can thin it with a little water. For jam tarts roll out the pastry to $\frac{1}{6}$ in. thick. Cut out with an oval cutter or a round one – whichever you prefer. Place each piece in a patty tray and seal down with your fingers, making a pattern round the edge. It should be a quarter of an inch higher than the mould. Prick the bottom of it lightly with a pointed knife and fill with jam and bake in a hot oven.

Another method of making tarts is to cut the pastry with a crinkled cutter and thumb up the edge before adding the jam. For variety, small diamonds or strips can be baked separately on a baking sheet. When cooked these should be placed in the centre of the tarts.

It is, perhaps, ridiculous that somebody can be very sentimental about a pastry and about a jam tart. But I am very, very sentimental about this special pastry because

A selection of tarts: 1. Congress tarts; 2. jam tarts; 3. fruit tarts; (*centre*) lemon curd tart

many years ago one of Sir Winston Churchill's secretaries told me how much Sir Winston liked jam tarts. She told me that it was his favourite pastry. It is a very plain pastry but it had to be perfect if it was to be made for him. He was a perfectionist in every way and in everything. The next best would never do for him. Once, another secretary told me that Churchill was dictating to him and suddenly he stopped because he had not got the word he wanted to use and he asked the secretary to go away. At 4 o'clock in the morning the secretary was called in and jubilantly he told him that he had found the right word! He was just as precise about his food as well. His favourite pastry was jam tart and I started to experiment with this simple, very English pastry. I made several shortcrust pastries and looked for the best existing jam which I must admit was not always a home-made one.

JAM TARTS (1)

4 oz. (1 cup) plain flour   **2 oz. (¼ cup) butter**
pinch of salt   **a little milk**
½ oz. (1 tablespoon) caster sugar   **jam**

Sieve the flour, salt and sugar into a bowl. Rub in the butter until the mixture resembles crumbs. Add just enough milk to mix to a dough. Knead until smooth and leave for 2½ hours in a cool place to rest. Roll the pastry about ⅛-in. thick and cut into rounds with a floured cutter (the rounds should be one size larger than the patty pans to be used). Line the small pans with dough, evenly pressing it gently into the sides. Add the chosen jam, remembering not to overfill, and bake in the oven at 400°F. (205°C.) Mark 6 for about 10–15 minutes.

JAM TARTS (2)

I tried a new short pastry recipe recently. I remembered suddenly that my mother made a short pastry with hard-boiled egg yolks. Jam tarts with a difference.

8 oz. (2 cups) plain flour   **2 hard-cooked egg yolks**
4 oz. (½ cup) butter   **jam**

Mix all the ingredients (except the jam) together. It makes mixing easier if the butter is softened a little before use. Mix thoroughly and pack in greaseproof paper and put in the refrigerator to rest for a few hours – or overnight. Roll out thin and cut into rounds. Press into tartlet moulds and fill well with jam. Bake for 20 minutes in a moderate oven, 370°F. (189°C.) Mark 5 for 20 minutes.

LEMON CURD TARTS

6 oz. shortcrust pastry   **lemon curd**

These are made in the same manner as jam tarts except the filling is of lemon curd.

PECAN PIE (U.S.A.)

I first ate pecan pie in an American hotel, which was really a road house; the food was excellent and the restaurant good though very homely. After a very good dinner they served an excellent pecan pie. I give you the recipe for this pie, but remember, it is extremely rich.

½ lb. shortcrust pastry   **¼ teaspoon (⅛) salt**
8 oz. (1¼ cups) broken pecan nuts   **½ cup (⅔) dark corn syrup**
2 oz. (¼ cup) butter   **3 eggs, beaten**
½ cup (⅔) soft brown sugar   **¾ teaspoon (1) vanilla essence**

Roll out the pastry and line a shallow 8-in. pie pan with pastry. Sprinkle it with pecans. Cream the butter and sugar together until fluffy. Add salt, corn syrup, eggs and vanilla. Beat the mixture thoroughly and then pour it over the pecans. (The pecans will rise to the top during cooking.) Bake at 450°F. (233°C.) Mark 8 for 10 minutes, reduce the temperature to 350°F. (175°C.) Mark 4 and continue baking for another 35 minutes or until a knife inserted in the middle comes out clean.

The pie can be garnished with pecan halves, also spread with whipped cream to serve.

REDCURRANT FLAN

½ lb. rich shortcrust pastry   **2 egg whites**
redcurrants   **4 oz. (½ cup) caster sugar**

Make the pastry according to the recipe on page 156. Line a buttered and floured rectangular flan pan. Prick it well all over and bake in the oven at 375°F. (191°C.) Mark 5 until a light brown. Clean the redcurrants – there should be enough to thickly cover the pastry. Whisk the egg whites until stiff, gradually fold in the sugar and continue beating to a meringue consistency. As soon as the pastry is baked, pile redcurrants on top of it, spread with the meringue mixture, completely covering the redcurrants, and bake in the oven at 325°F. (162°C.) Mark 3 until the meringue has set and begins to be tinged with faint golden-brown specks. Leave until cold and cut into slices to serve.

STRAWBERRY TARTLETS

6 oz. shortcrust pastry (rich)	**cream**
sugar to taste	**½ lb. small strawberries**
½ lb. (1 cup) cream cheese	**¼ pint (full ½ cup) redcurrant jelly**

Roll out the prepared pastry thinly and with a cutter cut into rounds. Line the pastry on to 2-in. tartlet pans and bake blind for about 8 minutes at 375°F. (191°C.) Mark 5. When they are golden brown take from the oven, turn out to cool on a wire rack. Add sugar to taste to the cream cheese and if this is a little dry, add enough cream to moisten it. When the tartlets are cold fill with cream cheese and then arrange the strawberries on top. Beat the jelly until smooth and heat it just a little but do not let it boil. Brush this over the strawberries. The amount of redcurrant jelly should be sufficient to fill the tartlets and hold the strawberries firmly in place.

LEMON MERINGUE PIE

½ lb. rich shortcrust pastry (page 157)	**1 tablespoon (1¼) sugar**
1 tablespoon (1¼) cornflour (cornstarch)	**2 egg yolks**
	grated rind and juice 1 lemon
	2 egg whites
1 cup (1¼) milk	**4 oz. (½ cup) caster sugar**

Make the pastry and let it rest in a cool place for 30 minutes. Line an 8-in. flan tin with the pastry, prick well and bake 'blind' at 425°F. (216°C.) Mark 7. Take from the oven and lower the heat to 325°F. (162°C.) Mark 3. While the pastry is baking, make the filling. Mix the cornflour with enough of the milk to make a thin paste. Bring the rest of the milk to the boil, pour this over the cornflour paste, stirring all the time, then return the mixture to the pan and cook over a moderate heat, stirring all the time until it is smooth and thick. Add the sugar, stir well and take from the heat. Leave to cool. Beat the egg yolks until smooth and beat into the cornflour cream. When well blended, add the rind and juice of the lemon. Pour this mixture into the pastry case and bake for about 10 minutes. Meanwhile prepare the meringue. Beat the egg whites (a third egg white may be used), whisk in 1 tablespoon (1¼) of the sugar and then fold in the remainder. Take the pie from the oven and pile the meringue on the top, spreading it over completely and extend to the pastry edge. Lower the oven heat to 275 °F. (133 °C.) Mark 1 and bake for 10–15 minutes or until the meringue topping is firm yet soft, rather like marshmallow with a crisp pale golden coating.

MIRLITONS (France)

Very many years ago I had a French pastrycook who stayed with me a long time. He made the most wonderfully light French pastries. One of these pastries is *mirliton*. Here is the recipe:

6 oz. shortcrust pastry (page 156)
apricot jam
4 macaroons
slivered blanched almonds

2 eggs
3½ oz. (scant ½ cup) caster sugar
icing (confectioner's) sugar

Roll out the pastry about ¼-in. thick and cut into rounds to fit patty pans. Line the pans, prick the bottoms with a fork and brush each with apricot jam. Coarsely break up the macaroons and dry them in a hot oven. Crush them with a rolling pin. Mix the eggs and sugar and beat until the mixture is very thick and mousse-like. Add the macaroons. Fill this mixture into the pastry cases and top with slivered almonds arranged like a clover leaf and generously dust with icing sugar. Bake at 300°F. (146°C.) Mark 2 for 15 minutes.

POPPYSEED or WALNUT ROLL (Hungary)

paste:
1 lb. (4 cups) plain flour
1 oz. (1½ cakes) yeast
4 oz. (½ cup) sugar
milk or sour cream
½ lb. (1 cup) butter
2 egg yolks
1 whole egg

filling:
4 oz. (½ cup) sugar
about 1 lb. ground walnuts or poppyseeds
1 tablespoon (1¼) rum
2 tablespoons (2½) milk

glazing:
1 – 2 egg yolks
icing (confectioner's) sugar

Put into a small bowl the yeast, 1 tablespoon (1¼) sugar and ¼ cup (⅓) of milk. Stir well then let it rise. Sift the flour into a bowl, lightly rub in the butter. Beat the egg yolks with the whole egg, add to the flour, mix well and add the remaining sugar, the yeast mixture and enough milk (warmed) to make a smooth dough. Knead thoroughly, cover and put into a refrigerator overnight. Next day weigh the paste. Mix the filling sugar with enough walnuts or poppyseeds to equal the weight of the paste. Put this into a pan, add the rum and milk, mix well, bring to the boil and let it cool. Knead the pastry until it is smooth and pliable, then roll it out to a neat rectangle about $\frac{1}{3}$ in. thick. Spread the cooled filling over it and then roll it up as you do roly-poly pudding. Place it folded upside down on a well-greased baking (cookie) sheet. Beat the egg yolk(s) with 1 teaspoon ($1\frac{1}{4}$) icing sugar and brush this lightly over the pastry. Allow it to rest for 2 hours and then brush it again with the glaze. Repeat this after another 15 minutes. Leave the roll again to rest for 15 minutes and then bake at 375°–400°F. (191°–205°C.) Mark 5–6 for 1 hour or until the pastry is a golden brown.

DANISH PASTRY

Danish pastries were introduced into England about fifteen years ago. I went to Copenhagen where I think I visited all the existing bakeries. These are mostly small businesses. The biggest, which holds the Royal Warrant, employed sixteen pastrycooks; the others were all family businesses where parents and children worked together. They were all delightful people, the bakeries were small, spotlessly clean and tidy, but oh my poor legs, they still hurt me because I had to toil up the stairs in the three- or four-storied houses in which the bakeries were housed; all of them showed me round everything very thoroughly and I did this for eight solid days. In each establishment I tasted their products which were extremely good, but must be eaten fresh from the oven: the pastries were sold in small shops throughout the day and one small boy does nothing else but carry the freshly baked pastries to the shops, still on the baking trays, puts them in the window and they are sold then and there.

Every day we make thousands of Danish pastries. I really do not know why we call them Danish as I have never seen pastries like these in Denmark. What we call Danish pastry does not resemble the true rich Danish pastry at all but is more a kind of flaky pastry. However, I give you our recipe and here it is:

$1\frac{1}{2}$ oz. ($2\frac{1}{4}$ cakes) yeast	1 lb. (4 cups) plain flour
$2\frac{1}{2}$ oz. (scant $\frac{1}{3}$ cup) sugar	8 oz. (1 cup) butter
2 eggs, lightly beaten	pinch of salt
2 tablespoons ($2\frac{1}{2}$) warm milk	

Put the yeast with the sugar into a wooden bowl and mix with a spoon until it is smooth and creamy. Add the eggs, milk and flour and mix thoroughly. Add half the butter and the salt and work with your hands until the dough is smooth and silky. Cover with a cloth and put into a fairly warm place to double its size. Put the rest of the butter into the refrigerator. When the dough has risen, put it on a floured pastry board and roll it out. Take the chilled butter and cut into half. Cut one half into small pieces and spread these over the rolled-out dough and fold the dough in three over the butter. Roll it out again, add the rest of the butter, cut into small pieces and again fold in three over the butter. Roll it out again and let it rest for 20 minutes. Fold over again and put into the refrigerator for 20 minutes. The dough must be firm before it is finally cut and rolled in a variety of ways – into stars, oblongs, rounds, triangles, buns etc.

For Danish pastries, different fillings may be used: custard, almond paste, any dried fruits, cherries, sultanas, raisins, or any combination of fruits. Almond paste filling is one of the most popular and here is the recipe.

3 oz. (½ cup) ground almonds
1 egg, well-beaten

3 tablespoons (3¾) sugar
grated peel of lemon

Mix the almonds with the sugar, work in the egg then work till it is firm and paste-like. Fill your dough with this. Add a little vanilla flavouring if liked.

CHEESE PASTRY

8 oz. (2 cups) plain flour
pinch of salt
pinch of black pepper
pinch of red pepper

4 oz. (½ cup) butter
4 oz. (1 cup) grated cheese
1 egg yolk
milk

Sieve the flour into a mixing bowl with the salt and peppers. Add the butter, cut into small pieces and rub it well into the flour with the finger-tips. When the mixture looks like breadcrumbs, add the cheese and stir gently with a fork. Mix the egg yolk with about 2 tablespoons (2½) of milk and put into the other ingredients. A little more milk may be required. Mix carefully to a firm dough and place on a floured board. Knead lightly until it is smooth. Place in the refrigerator for about 1 hour before using. Use for savoury biscuits (cookies), straws, canapés and savoury tarts.

CHEESE SACRISTANS or TWISTS

4 oz. (1 cup) plain flour
pinch of salt
pinch of Hungarian paprika
    (optional)
2 oz. (¼ cup) butter

2 oz. (⅔ cup) grated
    Parmesan cheese
1 egg yolk
a little milk or water to bind

Sieve the flour, salt and paprika together into a bowl. Rub in the butter until the mixture resembles breadcrumbs. Add the cheese, stir well, add the yolk and as much liquid as required to make a firm but pliable dough. Put on to a floured board, roll out to about ⅛-in. thickness and cut into strips 4 in. long by 1 in. wide. Twist the strips, holding one end with one hand and rolling with the other hand. Put the sacristans on to a well-buttered baking (cookie) sheet and bake in the oven at 425°F. (216°C.) Mark 7 for 7–10 minutes or until a golden brown and firm to the touch. Take from the oven and cool on the baking sheet.

CHEESE STRAWS

Prepare a pastry exactly as for sacristans. Roll it out thinly and evenly into a 4-in. wide strip. Trim the edges. Cut the pastry strip into fingers about ¼-in. wide. Place on a well-buttered sheet. Roll out the left over strips and shape into large rings. Put these on to the baking (cookie) sheet and bake as for sacristans. Cool on the baking sheet and serve bundles of cheese straws in the rings.

NUT PASTRY (Austria)

8 oz. (2 cups) plain flour
6 oz. (1 cup) ground almonds or
    hazelnuts
3 egg yolks, lightly beaten
3 oz. (full ⅓ cup) sugar

½ teaspoon (⅔) grated lemon rind
pinch of ground cloves and
    cinnamon
7 oz. (scant cup) butter

Make sure all the ingredients are cool and, where possible, use a cold marble slab for working. Sieve the flour on to the marble slab or pastry board and add the nuts. Make a well in the middle. Drop in the egg yolks, sugar, lemon peel and spices. Stir it with the blade of a knife. Cut the butter into slivers directly into the flour mixture and work, with the hands, to a dough, working as quickly and as lightly as possible.

As soon as the paste is properly blended and smooth, wrap it in greaseproof paper or a cloth and leave for at least 1 hour in a cool place. The paste is useful for making biscuits (cookies) or as the base for a *Linzer Torte* (see page 123) etc.

CHOUX PASTRY

Choux pastry is perhaps the best known of all paste or pastries. I cannot tell you for how long choux paste or pastry has been made; it is very easy to make, very light. It is suitable for the most delicate stomach. You can make many kinds of pastries from it including eclairs and chocolate buns. These are usually filled with fresh cream, vanilla cream or chocolate cream, but are also very good filled with an enormous variety of savoury fillings such as sardines, mashed and flavoured with anchovies, or chopped ham or mushroom in a thick cream mixture.

I personally like choux pastry just as it is without any filling, and I like it when it is hard and crispy. Choux pastry may be easy to make but you have to be precise when making it, as in nearly everything else. My experience is that short-cuts do not help, but rather hinder because they often lead to double work in the end. It requires also some experience so please be patient. If you beat the pastry too much it will be spoiled, so be careful and beat it just right. If the pastry is overworked, it will not rise. When you have made choux pastry once or twice you will discover exactly how much to beat. You might be lucky and beat the pastry exactly right the first time. When the pastry is baked it should be firm, crisp and a good golden brown. Eaten fresh it is lovely. The time to prepare the dough from start to putting it into the oven is less than 30 minutes.

The shapes you can make vary. There are tiny balls of choux pastry filled with whipped cream or a chocolate or vanilla cream. These are called *profiteroles*. They can be very pretty when built into a pyramid with a little burnt sugar between each one to hold them together. This makes a decorative centre-piece for the sideboard for a buffet meal. It can be served with a chocolate sauce or with raspberry ice-cream. This pyramid of profiteroles is the traditional wedding cake in France (see page 181). And choux pastry is the basis for Gâteau St Honoré (see page 132) which also makes a very decorative sweet.

CHOUX PASTE

1 cup (1¼) water   4 oz. (1 cup) plain flour
pinch of salt   3 eggs
3 oz. (6 tablespoons) butter

Bring the water, salt and butter slowly to the boil. When the butter is dissolved place the pan at the side of the stove and immediately add the flour, all of it at once. Beat with a wooden spoon only until the mixture is smooth but at this moment do not overbeat. Then return the pan to the heat and beat vigorously over a high heat until the mixture leaves the sides of the pan, forms a mass and begins to leave a fine film at the bottom of the pan. Take the pan again from the heat, cool the pastry a little, make a well in the middle of the dough and break an egg into it. Beat this into the pastry until it has been absorbed – the first egg takes a matter of seconds. Continue with the remaining eggs until they are all absorbed into the paste and beat the pastry until it looks glossy. If using the choux with a sweet filling, 1 teaspoon (1¼) of caster sugar is added to the butter and water – not a suggestion more.

A forcing bag produces the neatest of puffs but if you do not have one, use a spoon. Place the mixture into a forcing bag with a plain tube and pipe in any of the following shapes. (1) Finger shape for éclairs about 3 in. long; (2) large rounds for buns or puffs about 2 in. in diameter, and (3) very small rounds for *profiteroles*. Pipe the choux pastry on to a greased and floured baking (cookie) sheet in mounds about 2 in. apart and bake in the oven at 450 °F. (233 °C.) Mark 8 for about 20 minutes. Do not open the oven door for at least the first 8 minutes of cooking. The puffs are done when they have doubled their size, are a golden brown and firm and crisp to the touch. Take from the oven, pierce the side of each puff with a sharp knife. Return to the oven and leave with the door ajar for 10 minutes. Cool the puffs on a rack. If making larger puffs you can put a deep baking pan on top of them before putting them into the oven or after they have been cooking for 20 minutes, lower the heat to 375 °F. (191 °C.) Mark 5 and continue baking until the puffs are a golden brown and firm to the touch.

The method given for making and baking choux pastry which I have given is the usual one. There are cooks who prefer to bake the pastry on a dampened baking (cookie) sheet. Some also cook it in a hot oven but with a rising temperature, i.e. they start at 400 °F. (205 °C.) Mark 6 and after 10 minutes increase the heat to 425 °F. (216 °C.) Mark 7. What is important is that if the pastry, in whatever shape it is baked, is taken out of the oven before it is brown and crisp it will collapse. It is best not to make more choux pastry than is required for once baked it does not keep well and should be used within 2–3 hours at the most. The fresher it is eaten, the better. The quantity will make enough dough for about 4–6 people. However, deep-freeze enthusiasts will know that choux shells freeze perfectly. Plain flour can be used for choux pastry but if a 'strong' flour is available this is better and the pastry will be particularly crisp when baked.

CHOUX PASTRY BUNS OR PUFFS

4½ oz. (scant 1¼ cups) plain flour
1 oz. (2 tablespoons) caster sugar
pinch of salt

1 cup (1¼) water
4 oz. (½ cup) butter
4 small eggs

Sift the flour, sugar and salt together. Heat the water and butter together in a pan to boiling point. Take the pan from the heat at once (in order not to lose any of the liquid) and immediately add all the flour at once – this is important. Return the pan to the heat beating the mixture vigorously with a wooden spoon and continue beating until it is smooth and comes away from the sides of the pan. Let the paste cool slightly. Beat the eggs and gradually beat these into the cooled mixture, beating thoroughly if the pastry is going to rise. The consistency should be soft but capable of holding its shape, so watch carefully as the last of the egg is being added, all of it may not be required. Drop tablespoonfuls of the mixture in small rounds on to a lightly greased baking (cookie) sheet and bake at 400°F. (205°C.) Mark 6 for 15 minutes, then lower the heat and let them remain a few minutes longer until crisp and lightly coloured. Serve generously sprinkled with sifted icing (confectioner's) sugar. The mixture can also be piped on to the baking sheet.

CREAM-FILLED PUFFS

choux pastry (page 170)
½ pint (1¼ cups) whipping cream

caster sugar to taste
icing (confectioner's) sugar

Prepare the choux pastry and pipe into large balls or rounds on to a prepared baking (cookie) sheet. Bake at 400°F. (205°C.) Mark 6 for 20 minutes or until the pastry is brown and crisp. When quite firm to the touch, take from the oven and cool on a wire rack. Make a slit with a sharp knife in each puff. Whip the cream until stiff, adding sugar to taste. Fill some of this into each of the puffs and place on a serving plate. Dust each puff generously with sifted icing sugar.

Smaller puffs can be made and filled as above and then piled in a heap in a glass bowl and served with a hot chocolate sauce.

PASSOVER BUNS or PUFFS

I am always being asked if we have some special pastries or cakes that can be eaten during the Passover, so I have here some Passover Buns. They taste and look like choux pastry but are not quite so light.

1 cup (1¼) water
½ cup (⅔) vegetable oil
¼ lb. (1 cup) matzo cake flour
¼ lb. (1 cup) matzo meal

1 tablespoon (1¼) sugar
6 eggs, separated
1 tablespoon (1¼) lemon juice

Combine the water and oil in a deep pan and bring to the boil. As soon as it boils take from the heat and at once mix in the flour, meal and sugar. Stir quickly and firmly until the mixture is smooth. Beat the egg yolks until they are creamy and stir these into the flour mixture, beating consistently until the eggs are well blended into the thick paste. This beating is important since the pastry is dependent on the air to help it rise. Add the lemon juice. Beat the egg whites until stiff but not dry. Fold these into the batter. Drop from a tablespoon on to a lightly oiled baking (cookie) sheet some 2 in. apart (the puffs will rise). Bake in the oven at 350°F. (175°C.) Mark 4 for 20 minutes or until they are puffed up and a light golden brown. Do not open the oven on any account during the first 10 minutes cooking or the puffs will collapse. Like ordinary choux pastry puffs, these Passover puffs should rise to twice their diameter and be quite hollow. Take from the oven, prick to let the steam out, and let them cool before filling them with a cream filling through a slit in the side or top.

CHOCOLATE ÉCLAIRS

choux pastry (page 170)
1 oz. (1 square) bitter chocolate, grated
1 tablespoon (1¼) water

4 oz. (¾ cup) icing (confectioner's) sugar
½ pint (1¼ cups) whipping cream
caster sugar

Make the choux pastry and pipe it on to the prepared baking (cookie) sheet in 3-in. lengths, i.e. long fat fingers. Bake in a hot oven, 400°F. (205°C.) Mark 6 until the pastry is a golden brown, crisp and firm to the touch. Take from the oven, prick to release the steam and leave to cool. Slit along one side.

While the éclairs are cooling, prepare the icing. Melt the chocolate in the water in a pan over a low heat. Add the icing sugar and mix well. Add 1–2 tablespoons (1¼–2½) of water to make a pouring consistency. Put aside until required. Whip the cream until stiff, adding sugar to taste. Pipe this mixture into the cooled éclairs, making quite sure they are filled. Heat the icing (frosting) to blood heat and spread swiftly over the top of the éclairs.

COFFEE ÉCLAIRS

These are made in the same manner as chocolate éclairs but with a coffee icing.

CHOCOLATE or COFFEE CREAM

2 egg yolks
2 oz. ($\frac{1}{4}$ cup) caster sugar
1 tablespoon ($1\frac{1}{4}$) plain flour
$\frac{1}{2}$ pint ($1\frac{1}{4}$ cups) milk

3 oz. (3 squares) chocolate or coffee essence
1 egg white

Beat the egg yolks with the sugar until smooth. Add the flour, mix well, then add enough of the milk to make a smooth paste. Break the chocolate into small pieces and put into a pan with the remaining milk. Stir over a low heat until the chocolate is melted, then bring to the boil. Stir this over the paste and stir until the mixture is thoroughly blended. Return the cream to the pan and continue cooking and stirring over a moderate heat until the cream thickens. Whip the egg white until stiff, pour a little of the hot cream into a bowl and fold in the egg white. Stir this back into the hot cream and stir carefully over a low heat for about 3 minutes. Turn the cream into a bowl to set. If a coffee flavouring is preferred, add about 1 tablespoon ($1\frac{1}{4}$) of coffee essence to the cream naturally omitting the chocolate.

CRÈME PATISSIÈRE

2 egg yolks
2 oz. ($\frac{1}{2}$ cup) icing (confectioner's) sugar
$\frac{3}{4}$ oz. (scant $\frac{1}{4}$ cup) plain flour

1 teaspoon ($1\frac{1}{4}$) cornflour (cornstarch)
$\frac{1}{2}$ pint ($1\frac{1}{4}$ cups) milk
1 egg white
vanilla flavouring

Beat the egg yolks with the sugar until the mixture is thick. Gradually add the flour with the cornflour and a little of the milk and beat the mixture to a thin paste. Heat the remainder of the milk, pour it on to the egg mixture, whisking briskly all the time. Return the mixture to the heat and continue cooking and stirring until the cream thickens. Whip the egg white until stiff. Pour about one-third of the cream into a bowl, fold in the egg white, mixing evenly. Add vanilla to flavour. Return this to the pan and continue to cook for about 3 minutes to 'set' the egg white, but stirring quickly all the time. Take the pan from the heat and let the cream cool before using.

OTHELLO or INDIANA

One of the best of pastries. I will give here the recipe but it is only for the very ambitious cook; it is quite a task to make these lovely-looking and delicious pastries. Even for my very able mother it was too big an effort, so she left it to the experts and bought hers from a pâtisserie. She ordered them specially for great occasions and she only liked the small ones. We agreed they looked very elegant but my brothers and I cared little about elegance – we liked the big ones filled with a lot of beautiful whipped cream, then so many years ago so much better than it is now. Can it be that I have a quite different appetite now? Never mind, it is still a lovely pastry and you just have it and I am sure you will enjoy it. When you make Indiana take a medium-strength flour. Here is the recipe:

6 eggs, separated **whipping cream**
3 oz. (full ⅓ cup) caster sugar **apricot jam**
3 oz. (¾ cup) plain flour **cochineal**
1 oz. (2 tablespoons) cornflour **rum**
  (cornstarch) **coffee**
a pinch of cream of tartar

Whisk the egg whites until stiff, add the sugar gradually and beat to a firm meringue. Beat the yolks thoroughly, then slowly and carefully fold in the flour. Add the cornflour with the cream of tartar. Finally add the meringue mixture. Be careful not to allow the meringue to stand too long or it will collapse. Put a sheet of greaseproof paper on a baking sheet; put the mixture into a piping bag with a plain ½-in. tube and pipe blobs of it on to the baking sheet. The oven should be heated to 400°–420°F. (205°–214°C.) Mark 6. Put the baking sheet in the oven but leave the door open a little otherwise the Indianas will collapse. After 5–6 minutes touch them to see if they are firm – it is difficult to tell the exact time. When the Indianas are firm, take from the oven and quickly and carefully remove the paper and slit the pastries across; trim the bottom so that they will stand firmly, and scoop out a little of the centre, leave to become cold and fill with whipped cream; be generous with the cream.

You can make three kinds of Indianas; for the first you put sweetened whipped cream; this one is the one which you put the top on and mask with a little boiling apricot jam; the second one you add a little cochineal to the whipped cream and flavour it with rum The third one has whipped cream flavoured with strong coffee. The white cream one should be covered with chocolate fondant; the rum and pink cream should be covered with coffee-flavoured fondant.

Very fussy people cover the whole Indiana with fondant and then make a little hole in the bottom of the cake and force the whipped cream into the middle with a piping bag.

STRUDEL (Austria)

In Hungary, you would not find a house, small or large, rich or poor, without *Strudel*, called *retes* in Hungary. It is a favourite with men and women because it is really not fattening. It is a little bit tricky to make but once you know the trick, it will become very easy and quick. It is no wonder that it is so well liked, as it is very light and very tasty, and there are so many kinds to choose from. The ingredients are very cheap and you can keep it for days and days. If you put it in a warm oven for a few minutes, it gives you a fresh sweet dish.

I once had a Greek chef who made a *Strudel* paste which he said he could stretch from London to Athens if he really wanted to, and he showed me his secret. He put an extra pinch of salt in the paste and it does not affect the flavour because when it is crisply baked you cannot taste the salt any more. I promise you he made wonderful *Strudel*.

1 lb. (4 cups) plain flour
1 egg
½ oz. (1 tablespoon) lard, oil,
    butter or margarine

1 teaspoon (1¼) vinegar
good pinch of salt

Work the ingredients well together, adding enough lukewarm water to make a soft dough. It is important to test how soft or hard it is. We have to learn this by experience. Knead the dough till absolutely smooth; this is very important. When the pastry is smooth and silky, divide into 2 balls and brush the tops with a little melted oil or butter. Leave it on the table and cover with a deep dish. The best is a china pudding dish. Leave it to rest for about 20 minutes.

Cover a large table, at least 6 – 7 ft. long, with a well-floured cloth. Put one of the pastry balls in the middle of the tablecloth. Brush it over with melted butter, oil or margarine and then flatten the pastry with a rolling pin till it is about ¼ in. thick. And now for the tricky part of the operation! Flour your hands and with the palms *underneath* the pastry, pull it towards the edge of the table all round. You will find that the pastry comes easily, shall I say happily, to your hand, and you can pull it and pull it, till it is as thin as paper and reaches the edge of the table and is overlapping it. The test is where the pastry is thin enough for you to be able to read a newspaper laid underneath. The edges will remain somewhat thick. These parts should not be used for the *Strudel* pastry. Now leave the pastry for 12–15 minutes to dry. This is important because if the pastry is not dry enough you will not be able to bake it properly and it will not become crisp. When it is dry enough first sprinkle it with melted butter and after that sprinkle on the filling. If it is apple, slice it thinly; sprinkle chopped almonds, walnuts, a very few breadcrumbs and as much sugar as you like on top. If the apples are sour add more sugar. If your filling is morello cherries, much more sugar is needed, but sprinkle it also with warm butter, almonds or walnuts. You can make *Strudel* filling with cottage or cream cheese mixed with 1 or 2 yolks of eggs and well washed sultanas; and spread this also on the dry *Strudel*. The rolling up is another art. You do it by lifting the tablecloth and rolling it away from yourself to the other end of the table. Cut it according to the size of your baking sheet, which should be well greased before you put the *Strudel* on it. Bake in the oven at 400°F. (205°C.) Mark 6 for 15–20 minutes. It is just as good hot or cold.

PETITS FOURS

Petits fours are known throughout the whole world, at least in those parts of the world where I have travelled; that is Europe, America and Africa. Everywhere petits fours play a big part in the entertaining world. They belong in the luxury food class.

On the Continent petits fours were called tea biscuits or tea pastries, because no tea party was considered complete without them.

There are two kinds of tea pastries, sweet and savoury. I came across a lot of petits fours in the Arab world. They were mostly made with almonds and were killingly sweet. They were served with a green, over-sweetened tea. Of course, we Europeans would not eat more than one or two and that only to be polite.

On the other hand, the best petits fours of all in our part of the world – that is to say Hungary, Austria, France and Germany – are made in Belgium; all very light, some very crispy, some deliciously fluffy. I am sure there are eighty or a hundred varieties, or rather there used to be when we had more leisure and when households and businesses could afford the time to make them. We still make a very good variety at my place. Our greatest enemy now is lack of time.

I personally serve petits fours after dinner parties, usually with the coffee, and they are always very well received.

The best restaurants in America and here serve *friandises* after dinner with the ice-cream or just on their own. *Friandises* are made from all kinds of fruit and from marzipan. They are very decorative. They look well on the table. If cleverly arranged in a silver platter, they can look like a little flower garden.

To make, have ready dates, stuffed with marzipan or with a blanched almond; dried prunes, from which you remove the stones and replace with any kind of nut you like. Also green almonds, marrons glacés, green and black grapes, stem ginger, glacé ginger and in season cherries on the stem. I think that nothing is more decorative than currants (red and black), Cape gooseberries and, if in season, our own big, sweet gooseberries, or stick three or four hazelnuts together with a little bit of caramel sugar and so on. When these are all prepared, then prepare a very thick syrup by boiling about 1 lb. lump sugar in ½ pint (1¼ cups) water. You have to test the syrup for thickness. I don't suggest for a minute that you must have a sugar thermometer, but you can test the syrup in the nice old way. To do this put ice-cold water in a big bowl near your syrup, be brave and put your two fingers and thumb in the water and then – in a very quick and neat movement – dip them into the boiling syrup and pull them out at once. Separate the two fingers from the thumb. If the syrup then forms a string between the two fingers and the thumb, then the thickness is the right one. It should not be *too* thick, because the result will not be nice if the sugar is too thick and too hard.

Tip all your fruit into the syrup quickly on a fork and then put them on an oiled tray.

Here I remember, when I was a very young girl, my mother took me out to the kitchen so that I should learn to cook from her and from our delightful fat cook. Both explained to me what to do and when I wanted to do it, my mother always told me: 'Oh, wait! Let me do it for you.' That's what I want to tell you too.

We make *friandises* on request; in season we dip strawberries in sugar or in fondant. I am, however, always nervous of serving them, especially in this country, because the humidity spoils them very easily. So I recommend petits fours at the end of dinner on most occasions.

The savoury petits fours – which are all made of puff pastry – are made in different shapes and can have a great variety of fillings – little 'horseshoes' filled with smoked salmon; small crescents stuffed with chopped ham mixed with a little cream; very small 'baskets' filled with cheese (Gruyère cheese is the best) or egg; little squares filled with chopped mushrooms; narrow strips rolled round anchovies; puff pastry rolled out very thin, and filled with chopped cabbage roasted in butter, salt and black pepper.

Roasted hazelnuts to my mind have the best flavour of all in making pastries and petits fours. Of course, it is important here as in everything else that the best raw material should be used. Hazelnuts can be so different, depending on where they come from; the same applies to almonds and walnuts. The best walnuts are French or Rumanian; the best almonds come from Avola in Italy and the best hazelnuts come from Piedmont.

In many of the following recipes finely ground nuts are used. In all cases, if the nuts are ground at home a better flavour will be obtained. Nuts are easily ground to the required fineness either in an electric grinder or in any type of nut-grinder. It may take a few moments longer to prepare one's cakes or biscuits (cookies) but at least one knows that it is ground almonds or hazelnuts on the table and not something quite different, often in disguise.

Vanilla sugar is used in a number of the following recipes, also vanilla beans or pods. Vanilla beans are easily available and can be kept quite a long time. When they are cooked in milk or cream, they should be taken out when the milk is ready then dried and stored. Vanilla sugar is easy to make. Simply fill up a large jam jar with caster sugar or icing (confectioner's) sugar and push in 1 vanilla bean broken into 3

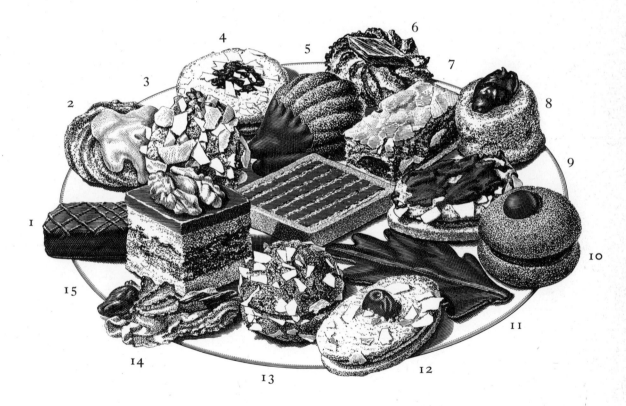

A selection of petits fours: 1. chocolate bar; 2. vanilla crescent (*see* recipe page 212); 3. Florentine (*see* recipe page 188); 4. cherry sandwich; 5. chocolate *beignet* (*see* recipe page 184); 6. chocolate petit four; 7. *restelt*; 8. almond cherry; 9. duchesse; 10. chocolate Nero; 11. chocolate leaf; 12. cherry *galette*; 13. hazelnut ball (*see* recipe page 185); 14. almond sticks (*see* recipe page 187); 15. walnut square pieces. Cover the jar tightly and leave for 3 months. As the sugar is used, replenish keeping the same pieces of vanilla in the jar. Small packets of vanilla sugar suitable for flavouring are available in a large number of grocery and delicatessen stores.

ICED PETITS FOURS

The best-known petits fours, also called mignons, are those made with a Genoese sponge mixture, cut into fancy shapes, decorated and coated with glacé icing.

Genoese sponge (page 121)   **apricot jam**

Make the Genoese sponge mixture and pour it into a greased and floured shallow baking pan. Bake at 375 °F. (191 °C.) Mark 5 for 25–30 minutes or until the sponge is firm to the touch and a pale golden colour. Turn out to cool on a wire rack. When quite cold, cut into fancy shapes, rounds, squares, rectangles, diamonds, triangles etc. Warm and pass through a sieve enough apricot jam to thickly coat each of the sponge pieces, top and sides. Prepare 2 or 3 or more glacé icings, if liked. Coat the sponge pieces top and sides with the icing and decorate. Usual decorations are glacé cherries, shelled walnuts, almonds or hazelnuts, crystallized violets or rose petals, chocolate vermicelli, thin slivers of angelica. Or a strip or layer of almond paste can be placed over the top of some of the pieces before the icing is added.

FROSTED FRUITS

fruit   **8 tablespoons (10) water**
8 oz. (1 cup) caster sugar   **caster sugar for coating**

The best fruits for this recipe are redcurrants, grapes and Cape gooseberries. Clean the fruits and leave in clusters – seedless grapes are the best but either black or white grapes may be used. Dissolve the sugar in the water and boil until it begins to caramelize. Dip the prepared fruit into this, then toss in caster sugar. Dry on a rack. To avoid burning the fingers, tie the fruit to a piece of strong thread. Remove this before serving the frosted fruit.

WALNUT PETITS FOURS (Hungarian)

4 oz. (½ cup) butter   **1 tablespoon (1¼) each rum and**
2 oz. (¼ cup) sugar   **cream**
2 eggs   **4 oz. (1 cup) coarsely chopped**
12 oz. (3 cups) plain flour   **walnuts**
                                             granulated sugar

French Wedding Cake (*profiteroles*)

Cream the butter and sugar until light and fluffy. Beat in 1 egg. Sieve the flour, add the rum and cream and, if necessary, a little water to make a firm dough. Leave for 1 hour. Roll out the dough on a floured board to about ½-in. thickness. Beat the remaining egg and with this brush the top of the dough. Sprinkle with a mixture of walnuts and granulated sugar. Press down lightly with the hand. Cut the dough into strips 2 × 1 in. with a sharp knife dipped in cold water. Place these on a buttered and floured baking (cookie) sheet and bake for about 25–30 minutes at 375°F. (191°C.) Mark 5 or until a light golden brown.

MERINGUE (Italian)

8 oz. (1⅓ cups) cube sugar
½ cup (⅔) water

4 egg whites
a pinch of salt and cream of tartar

Put the sugar with the water into a pan and cook quickly (about 260°F. – 126°C.) to the heavy thread stage. In the meantime beat the egg whites until very stiff. Add the salt and cream of tartar. Pour the syrup gradually over the egg whites, beating all the time, and continue to whisk briskly until the sugar has been absorbed and the mixture is cold. The mixture can be used to make the conventional meringues or meringue baskets, or for coating.

ALMOND AND DATE MERINGUES

4 egg whites
8 oz. (1 cup) caster sugar
1 cup (1¼) stoned dates, roughly
  chopped

4 oz. (scant 1 cup) blanched
  chopped almonds

Beat the egg whites until stiff but not dry. Add half the sugar gradually, a tablespoonful at a time, continuing to whisk until the mixture is so stiff it stands up in brittle peaks. Fold in the rest of the sugar with a metal spoon. Rub a board or baking (cookie) sheet with absolutely clean greaseproof paper and rub very lightly with oil. Gently fold the dates and almonds into the meringue mixture and spoon the mixture into small round blobs on the paper. Bake in the oven at 200°F. (94°C.) or the lowest gas setting until they are firm and crisp both on top and underneath. The meringues are not so much baked as dried in the oven. The time to cook them can take between 3 and 4 hours. Do not let them over-cook and become coloured or dry. To ensure the correct temperature, the door of the oven can be left ajar.

Making Strudel pastry

BEIGNETS

Beignets belong to the best of the petits fours and I am giving the *beignet* recipe because it is one of my favourite petits fours and I wish you to pass it on to your children or grandchildren.

½ lb. (1⅓ cups) ground almonds	carmine or green vegetable
½ lb. (1 cup) caster sugar	colouring
10 egg whites	finely chopped lemon or orange
1 whole egg	candied peel
grated lemon peel to taste	icing (confectioner's) sugar

Butter and lightly dust a large number of small petit four moulds of varying shapes. Mix together the ground almonds, caster sugar and 2 egg whites. Mix well and pound to a paste. Add the whole egg and again mix thoroughly, this time until the paste is softened. Add the grated lemon peel and the chosen colouring or the paste can be left *au naturel*. Mix well. Beat the remaining egg whites until stiff and fold these into the marzipan. Fill this mixture into the prepared moulds, decorate with the candied fruit, sprinkle with sifted icing sugar and bake in the oven at about 300°F. (146°C.) Mark 2 until the *beignets* are firm. Let them cool in the moulds before turning out.

Instead of candied peel, crystallized pineapple, cut into slivers, may be used as a flavouring, or vanilla. For chocolate *beignets*, after they have cooled dip one end into melted chocolate and leave until the chocolate dries. Instead of using petits fours moulds, small fancy biscuit moulds can be used.

BEAR'S PAWS

½ lb. marzipan	coarsely chopped almonds
2 oz. (4 tablespoons) caster sugar	icing (confectioner's) sugar
3 egg whites	chocolate butter cream

Soften the marzipan by beating it with a wooden spoon. Add half the sugar and 1 egg white. Continue beating until the mixture is light and smooth. Beat the remaining egg whites until stiff and dry, gradually add the rest of the sugar and continue beating until the mixture is stiff. Fold the beaten egg whites into the marzipan mixture. Line a baking sheet with greaseproof paper. Fill the marzipan mixture into a piping bag with a star-shaped nozzle and pipe the mixture on to the paper in the shape of a shell. Lightly decorate with almonds – the pieces should be the same size roughly as sugar nibs – and dust with sifted icing sugar. Bake in the oven at 380°F. (194°C.) Mark 5 for about 7–8 minutes. Leave until cool and then sandwich together with chocolate butter cream (see page 140).

HAZELNUT BALLS

2 eggs, separated
4 oz. (½ cup) butter
4 oz. (1⅓ cups) cake crumbs or soft breadcrumbs

4 oz. (⅔ cup) ground hazelnuts
2 oz. (¼ cup) sugar
2 oz. (½ cup) chopped hazelnuts

Beat the egg whites until stiff. Soften the butter and beat with the yolks until creamy. Combine the crumbs, ground hazelnuts and sugar, mix well. Add the creamed butter and eggs, again mix, then fold in the egg whites. Fill this mixture into a large forcing bag with a plain nozzle. Rub a baking (cookie) sheet with fat or line with rice paper. Pipe the hazelnut mixture into little bundles on to the paper or baking sheet. Sprinkle the tops with the chopped hazelnuts and bake in the oven at 300°F. (146°C.) Mark 2 until the balls are crisp and a pale golden colour.

ORANGE PETITS FOURS

2 egg whites
4 oz. (½ cup) sugar
2 oz. (¼ cup) butter

2 oz. (½ cup) plain flour
finely shredded orange peel

Whip the egg whites until stiff, add the sugar and mix well together. Warm the butter slightly, add it slowly to the mixture, then add the flour. Finally the orange peel. Butter liberally a large baking (cookie) sheet and using a teaspoon place little bundles on to the sheet in regular rows. When the sheet is full bang it once or twice to spread the mixture slightly. Bake for 6–7 minutes at a temperature of 400°F. (205°C.) Mark 6. When cooked remove the petits fours quickly from the sheet and roll each one round a thin rod such as a pencil or the handle of a wooden spoon or a steel rod made specially for the purpose. You must work very quickly.

This petit four is a very good standby and can be kept in an airtight tin.

HUSSAR'S KISSES (Hungary)

In Hungary, every girl (and whether she was a very modest little maid or the heiress of a castle their dreams were the same) wanted to have a Hussar, a soldier or an officer, if not as a partner for lifetime at least for the coming dance season. Perhaps a little pastrycook girl, in her dream, produced a petit four which she called 'Hussar's Kiss'. I give you the recipe.

4 oz. (½ cup) butter

6 oz. (1½ cups) plain flour

2 oz. (¼ cup) sugar

2 egg yolks

1 egg white

2 oz. (⅓ cup) blanched
   almonds, coarsely chopped

glacé cherries

Slightly soften the butter. Sieve the flour and sugar in a bowl, add the butter rubbing it in thoroughly. Add the egg yolks, one at a time, and mix to a dough, kneading well. Break off small pieces of the mixture and shape these into balls, about the size of a walnut. Place these on a greased baking (cookie) sheet. Press your thumb in the middle of each 'ball' to make a 'dimple'. Slightly beat the egg white. Brush the dimpled balls with egg white and scatter the chopped almonds over the top. Bake in the oven at 350°F. (175°C.) Mark 4 for 15–20 minutes or until the 'kisses' are a pale golden colour. Take from the oven and place in each dimple a piece of chopped glacé cherry.

HAZELNUT CRESCENTS (Hungary)

5 oz. (10 tablespoons) butter

8 oz. (2 cups) plain flour

2 oz. (2 squares) bitter chocolate,
  grated

4 oz. (⅔ cup) ground hazelnuts

1 oz. (1 tablespoon) vanilla sugar

1 egg yolk

melted chocolate for coating

Rub the butter into the flour until the mixture looks crumbly. Add the chocolate, hazelnuts and sugar. Mix well, add the egg yolk and enough cold water to make a dough. Knead well together and leave in the refrigerator for 1 hour. Roll out on a floured board and cut into crescents with a cutter. Place these on a lightly buttered baking (cookie) sheet and bake in the oven at 375°F. (191°C.) Mark 5 for 15–20 minutes. Take from the oven, turn out on to a rack and, when cold, spread with melted chocolate.

CHOCOLATE ROCKS

7 oz. (1 cup) chopped almonds

4 oz. (⅔ cup) raisins

1 lb. (16 squares) melted plain
  chocolate

Mix the almonds, raisins and chocolate. Using a teaspoon, place small amounts on to greaseproof paper and allow to harden. Some of the almond can be replaced by cornflakes if so desired. These are tasty and easy to make.

CAT'S TONGUE (*Langue de chat*)

4 oz. (½ cup) butter
4 oz. (½ cup) caster sugar
4 oz. (1 cup) plain flour

½ vanilla pod
3 egg whites

Butter and dust a baking (cookie) sheet with flour. Beat the butter until soft, add the sugar and continue beating until the mixture is creamy. Mix in the flour. Scrape out the centre of the vanilla pod, add it to the mixture. Slightly whisk the egg whites and gradually add these to the batter, beating thoroughly after each addition. Fill into a piping bag with a plain nozzle and pipe out on to the baking sheet in finger-lengths about as thick as a large pencil. Bake in the oven at 425°F. (216°C.) Mark 7 for about 5 minutes. As soon as the biscuits (cookies) are taken from the oven, slip them off the baking sheet to cool on a wire rack.

These *langues de chat* can either be eaten plain, with ice-cream or fruit salad, or two can be stuck together with praline butter cream. The latter make very good petits fours.

ALMOND or AVOLA STICKS

5 oz. (1¼ cups) plain flour
3½ oz. (⅔ cup) ground almonds
2 eggs

4 oz. (½ cup) sugar
3 oz. (6 tablespoons) butter

Mix all the ingredients to make a smooth soft dough. Leave for 1 hour in a cool place. Roll out on a floured board and cut into short sticks or fingers. Place these on a floured baking (cookie) sheet and bake at 300°F. (146°C.) Mark 2 for 25–30 minutes or until a pale golden colour. Leave until cold to serve. They will keep for quite a long time.

PEANUT BUTTER KISSES (U.S.A.)

In America I ate and liked several cakes and petits fours made with peanut butter.

This recipe comes from a very kind friend of mine; she wishes that I should use it in my book, so I do, and would be very happy if you like it.

4 oz. (½ cup) butter   approx. 4 oz. (1 cup) plain flour
4 oz. (½ cup) white sugar   1 egg
4 oz. (½ cup) brown sugar   vanilla essence to taste
6 oz. (½ cup) peanut butter   pinch bicarbonate soda

Beat the butter with a wooden spoon until it is creamy. Add both the sugars and, when well blended, slowly add the remaining ingredients to make a firm dough. A little more flour might be required. Butter and flour a baking (cookie) sheet and drop the peanut butter mixture on it in little heaps. Flatten with a fork and bake at 350°F. (175°C.) Mark 4 for 15–20 minutes or until they are lightly browned and set.

FLORENTINES

4 oz. (½ cup) butter   4 oz. (1 cup) candied orange peel,
4 oz. (½ cup) caster sugar   finely chopped
2 oz. (⅓ cup) glacé cherries   a little chopped angelica
4 oz. (1 cup) blanched almonds,   2 tablespoons (2½) whipping cream
   coarsely chopped   4 oz. (4 squares) bitter chocolate
2 oz. (½ cup) flaked almonds

Grease a baking (cookie) sheet with a little melted lard or butter. Melt the butter, add the sugar and, stirring it all the time, bring it slowly almost to the boil. Stir in the cherries, the chopped and flaked almonds, candied peel and angelica. Whip the cream until thick, fold it into the mixture, then take from the heat and leave until cold. Spoon the mixture in small heaps on to the baking sheet, leaving plenty of room for the florentines to spread during baking. Bake for 7–10 minutes in the oven at 375°F. (191°C.) Mark 5. Take from the oven and leave to set before removing them from the baking sheet with a palette knife. Melt the chocolate on a plate over hot water. Take it from the heat and let it cool until creamy, working it well with a palette knife. Spread the smooth side of the florentines with the chocolate just as it is on the point of setting. Make wavy lines across the chocolate, this is normally achieved with what is called a confectioner's comb but, failing this instrument, use a fork, or if you have a setting comb which is absolutely clean this could be used.

MADELEINES (France)

English madeleines are baked in dariole moulds and then coated with jam and desiccated coconut. In France the name is applied to little cakes of a sponge-cake texture, made in small fluted cake moulds, easily obtainable in specialist household stores.

4 oz. (1 cup) plain flour   **4 oz. ($\frac{1}{2}$ cup) caster sugar**
4 eggs   **4 oz. ($\frac{1}{2}$ cup) butter**

Sieve the flour. Beat the eggs with the sugar until the mixture is thick and mousse-like. Warm the butter to almost melting point. Add the butter to the eggs, mix thoroughly and then add the sifted flour. Fill the mixture into the lightly buttered madeleine moulds – this quantity makes about 24 – and bake in the oven at 375°F. (191°C.) Mark 5 for about 10 minutes. Serve quite plain.

CHESTNUT PURÉE RINGS (Hungary)

$\frac{3}{4}$ oz. (1 cake) yeast   chestnut filling:
$2\frac{1}{2}$ oz. (scant $\frac{1}{3}$ cup) sugar   **1 oz. (2 tablespoons) butter**
milk   **2 oz. ($\frac{1}{4}$ cup) sugar**
9 oz. ($2\frac{1}{4}$ cups) plain flour   **1 tablespoon ($1\frac{1}{4}$) each rum and**
9 oz. ($1\frac{1}{8}$ cups) butter   **cream**
1 egg yolk   **1 lb. sieved cooked chestnuts**
cream

Mix the yeast with a little sugar and very little warm milk and flour; let it rise in a warm place. When it has risen add the remaining flour, butter, sugar, egg yolk and as much cream as it takes to make a dough soft enough to manipulate easily. Mix well together till it becomes very smooth. Then put it on a pastry board and let it rest for 30 minutes or so. While you wait for the dough to rise, make the filling. Add the butter, sugar, rum and cream to the chestnuts. Mix all these well together. Now roll out the rested pastry as thin as a match. Cut out 3-in. squares and put down the middle of each a good tablespoonful of the chestnut cream, roll them up like a cigarette and make into rings. Arrange them on a greased and floured baking (cookie) sheet, wash over with milk or egg yolk and leave to rise again. Bake in the oven at 400°F. (205°C.) Mark 6 for 16 – 18 minutes.

VIENNESE CRESCENTS

This recipe comes from a friend in Chicago. I tasted it in her house, I like it, therefore, I pass it on to you.

8 oz. (1 cup) butter

1½ oz. (3 tablespoons)
   caster sugar

8 oz. (2 cups) plain flour

6 oz. (1 cup) ground almonds

vanilla essence to taste

Cream the butter, add the remaining ingredients and mix to a paste. Roll out ½-in. thick and cut into crescents. Place on a buttered baking (cookie) sheet in neat rows, well apart, and bake at 280°–300°F. (136°–146°C.) Mark 1–2 for about 30–35 minutes or until a golden brown. Take from the oven and dust with sifted icing (confectioner's) sugar.

RUM BABAS

This yeast pastry recipe has an old and romantic origin. It developed from *Gugelhupf*. A King of Poland, Stanislaus Leczinski, invented it in 1609. He sprinkled rum and syrup on a *Gugelhupf*. My husband invented several variations of this recipe; sponge cakes, rice *soufflets* and pancakes. Whatever he found to be very dry was not just sprinkled with liquid but he would pour on it wine or rum, liqueur or raspberry juice.

King Stanislaus gave to his favourite pastry – at least history claims – the name of the hero of his favourite story in *The Thousand and One Nights* – Ali Baba. Later on, at the beginning of the nineteenth century, it was a great success in Paris. It was then called simply Rum Baba.

1 oz. (¾ cake) yeast

1 tablespoon (1¼) sugar

4 eggs

1 lb. (4 cups) plain flour

1 tablespoon (1¼) currants

2 tablespoons (2½) sultanas (white
   raisins)

jam

whipped cream

sugar syrup:

1½ cups (2) water

2 cups (2½) sugar

rum

Mix the yeast in a bowl with a fork to crumble it, then add the sugar and mix to a wet paste. Beat in the eggs and mix thoroughly. Put aside. Sieve the flour into a large wooden bowl, make a well in the centre and pour in the yeast and egg mixture. Work it all to a dough and mix so thoroughly and vigorously that the sticky dough comes clean off the bowl and fingers. It should be punched and slapped until it is so elastic if pulled it will stretch at least 12 in. Shape the dough into a ball, cut across an inch deep on the top, sprinkle with flour and cover the bowl with a thick damp cloth. Let it rise in a warm place until it has doubled in bulk, about 2 hours. Take from the bowl, punch down, then add the currants and sultanas and mix well.

Butter the baba moulds (these are cylindrical, about 2 in. deep and the same in diameter, and the quantity makes about 20–24 babas). Break off pieces of the dough to fill one-third of each mould – about 1 heaped tablespoonful (1¼). Press the dough lightly into the bottom of the moulds and place them, uncovered, in a warm place to rise until the dough is about ¼ in. above the top of the moulds; this will take between 1 and 2 hours.

Make sure the oven is preheated for the dough must be baked as soon as it has risen above the top of the moulds, otherwise it will sink. Bake in the top part of the oven at 375°F. (191°C.) Mark 5 for about 15 minutes. By this time the dough will have slightly shrunk from the sides of the pan and be a golden colour. Turn out on to a wire rack to cool. At once begin to prepare the rum syrup. Cook the water and sugar until the sugar has dissolved and then bring to the boil. Boil for 2–3 minutes. Take from the heat and when the syrup is cooled to lukewarm, add the rum. Arrange the warm babas in a shallow dish, their puffed tops uppermost. Prick the tops in several places with a needle, pour the rum-syrup over them and leave to absorb the rum, basting from time to time as the rum runs out of the babas. They should absorb enough of the liquid until they become spongy and moist but still hold their shape. Return to the wire rack to drain for about 30 minutes. Brush over with warmed apricot jam (or other jam) and decorate (if liked) with whipped cream.

I can recommend this pastry; it is very useful. It can be made in several shapes, large or small, individual ones, or those for six, eight or ten people, baked in 'baba' pans.

BROWNIES (U.S.A.)

8 oz. (1 cup) butter	vanilla essence
1 lb. (2 cups) sugar	½ lb. chopped pecan nuts or walnuts
4 eggs	pinch of bicarbonate of soda
4 oz. (4 squares) bitter chocolate	raisins (optional)
4 oz. (1 cup) plain flour	

Melt the chocolate and butter in a double boiler. Beat eggs and sugar well together and then mix in the flour and soda. Blend well. Stir in the nuts (and raisins if you are using them) and finally the chocolate mixture and vanilla. Pour into a greased and floured oblong baking pan. Bake for 45 minutes at 275°F. (133°C.). When cooked remove from the oven and cut into rectangles. Cool on a wire rack. I saw these cakes being eaten many times by children in the U.S.A. They loved them and there were never any left on the plate at the end of tea.

CUPID CAKES

6 glacé cherries
1 large piece candied peel
3 oz. (full ⅓ cup) butter
3 oz. (full ⅓ cup) caster sugar
4 oz. (1 cup) plain flour
pinch of salt

¼ teaspoon (⅓) baking powder
1 egg, beaten
vanilla essence to taste
1 tablespoon (1¼) brandy (optional)
water icing

Chop the cherries and peel. Cream the butter and then beat in the sugar. Sieve the flour with the salt and baking powder, add to the creamed butter alternately with the egg. Add the peel, vanilla and brandy, and if required a little warm water to form a dough of stiff dropping consistency. Half-fill paper cases or greased patty pans and bake for 10–15 minutes at 400°F. (205°C.) Mark 6. When the cakes are baked and cooled, decorate with the cherries and cover with the water icing. To make the water icing, mix icing (confectioner's) sugar with a little water flavoured with vanilla, lemon or rum. Spoon this over the top of the cherries.

ISCHLER RINGS or BISCUITS

As a young girl I spent some years at school in Vienna. That was in the happy era of the Emperor Franz-Josef. For me Vienna was then the top of the world and I could not dream of anything better than to have lived in Vienna. I am sure that I was right. One saw and felt Vienna as a most cultured city, full of music. Every shop girl, any young hairdressers' assistant talked of music and literature.

From Vienna as a schoolgirl, I was taken on an outing to Ischl, a small summer resort in the mountains south of Salzburg, which became famous, because the Emperor Franz-Josef went there once a year.

In that very small Austrian town there was a small pastry shop which became world famous because Franz-Josef patronized it. I give you a very simple pastry recipe which is still fashionable and very much liked in eastern Europe. This is a little chocolate pastry, we could really call it a biscuit, known as *Ischler*. We, in my bakery, still make it and the public, even in England, still likes it. If you have the recipe it is very easy to make.

6 oz. (¾ cup) butter
6 oz. (1½ cups) plain flour
3 oz. (½ cup) grated almonds,
   walnuts ot hazelnuts
3 oz. (full ⅓ cup) caster sugar

pinch of cinnamon
a little vanilla
raspberry or redcurrant jam
8 – 10 oz. (8 – 10 squares) bitter
   chocolate

Rub the butter into the flour, add the almonds, sugar, cinnamon and vanilla and knead to a smooth dough. Success in making these little cakes depends on kneading thoroughly. Leave it for an hour to rest and then roll it out on a floured board to less than ¼-in. thickness. Cut with a 2½–3 in. cutter into rounds and place them on a buttered, lightly floured baking (cookie) sheet. Put into the oven at 375°F. (191°C.) Mark 5 and bake for 10–15 minutes or until they are firm and crisp. Take from the oven, turn on to a wire rack and let them cool. When cool, stick together in pairs with jam. Return to the wire rack. Melt the chocolate carefully until it is of pouring consistency. Pour a little of the chocolate over each pair of biscuits (cookies) and leave until the chocolate dries. *Ischlers* will keep for several days.

ALMOND CAKES

I was once invited to visit a very old lady, who insisted that I should come and have tea with her. I tried to persuade her to come to me instead, but she told me I had to come and taste her almond cake. I went, I found her charming and delightful. Her small tea table was beautifully laid, and her little almond cake, as she had suggested, was very good indeed.

What touched my heart most was that the recipe of the cake had already been written down on her very elegant writing-paper. I have to mention that the old lady was French. As my son George explained it to me just now, we don't fulfil our existence if we don't do something for humanity, so I hand over the French lady's recipe to you.

7 eggs
2 egg yolks
8 oz. (1 cup) sugar
6 oz. (1½ cups) flour, sifted
5 oz. (scant cup) ground almonds

½ teaspoon (⅔) vanilla essence
5 oz. (scant ⅔ cup) melted butter
2 oz. (⅓ cup) blanched
    almonds, chopped

Beat the eggs, including the yolks, add the sugar and continue beating until the mixture is smooth. Pour into a thick small pan and cook over a low heat, whisking all the time with a wire whisk. When the mixture begins to thicken, take it from the heat, stir in the flour, the ground almonds and vanilla. Add the butter. Rub some small moulds, like *brioche* moulds, and in the bottom put a few bits of chopped almonds. Fill the moulds two-thirds full and bake them in a cool oven for 45 minutes.

TALKELLI (Yeast or Puff Balls) (Hungary)

A very simple everyday little pastry, but when we were children, it was one of our favourites.

2 cubes sugar	pinch of salt
¾ oz. (1 cake) yeast	fat or oil
¾ cup (1) lukewarm milk	icing (confectioner's) sugar
10 oz. (2½ cups) plain flour	apricot jam
3 eggs	

Crush the sugar and put into a bowl with the yeast, crumbled, and one-third of the milk. Leave to rise. Sieve the flour into a bowl, make a well in the centre, add the eggs, the salt, yeast and finally the rest of the milk. Mix it all together to make a very soft dough. Cover the bowl with a cloth and leave to rise to double its bulk. Put 1 teaspoon (1¼) of fat in patty or bun pans and put into the oven to get hot. When the dough has risen, spoon a tablespoonful of it into each of the pans and bake in the oven at about 425°F. (216°C.) Mark 7 until they are a golden brown in colour, about 10–15 minutes. Take from the oven, sandwich the puff-balls together in pairs, dredge with icing sugar and serve hot with apricot jam or any other jam.

MACAROONS

rice paper	5 oz. (scant cup) ground almonds
2 egg whites	glacé cherries, halved
few drops almond essence	blanched almonds, halved
6 oz. (¾ cup) caster sugar	

Cover a baking (cookie) sheet with rice paper. Whip the egg whites until very stiff. Add the essence and then gradually the sugar, beating it in all the time. Fold in the ground almonds – a little more may be required if the egg whites are large. Roll the mixture lightly into balls and place them well spaced out on the rice paper. Put a cherry or almond on top of each ball. Bake in the middle of the oven at 375°F. (191°C.) Mark 5 for 20–25 minutes. Take from the oven and leave to cool on the pan. When almost cold, take from the pan, cutting or tearing round the rice paper.

CHOCOLATE MACAROONS

This is a very good macaroon which is useful after dinner, or with tea or coffee; again, good to have in reserve.

4 egg whites
5 oz. (scant ⅔ cup) caster sugar
1 tablespoon (1¼) ground rice
2 oz. (2 squares) bitter chocolate, grated

2 oz. (⅓ cup) ground hazelnuts or almonds
blanched halved almonds

Cover a baking (cookie) sheet with rice paper. Beat the egg whites until very stiff. Gradually add and beat in the sugar. Fold in the ground rice, grated chocolate and hazelnuts and gently blend. Break off small pieces, roll these into balls and place, well spaced apart, on to the baking sheet. Flatten them lightly with a knife and place an almond in the middle of each. Bake them at 375°F. (191°C.) Mark 5 for 20–25 minutes.

MARZIPAN DATES

1 stoned date for each petit four
marzipan

1 egg yolk
a few drops of caramel

Cover the dates thinly with marzipan and shape them to look like a torpedo. Take the egg yolk, add to the few drops of burnt sugar and wash over the marzipan dates. They should be the same colour and shape as the dates really are. Bake the marzipan dates for 10 minutes at 400°F. (205°C.) Mark 6.

COCONUT PYRAMIDS or KISSES

2 egg whites
5 oz. (scant ⅔ cup) caster sugar

5 oz. (1⅔ cups) desiccated coconut

Beat the egg whites until stiff, fold in the sugar and continue beating until the mixture is stiff and smooth. Fold in the coconut. Pile into small heaps on rice paper and shape the piles into small pyramids. Bake in the oven at 300°F. (146°C.) Mark 2 for 45 minutes or longer until the pyramids are a pale beige colour. The mixture may be lightly tinted pink or green before being baked.

PASTRY CRESCENTS

7 oz. (scant cup) sugar　　　　　**4 eggs**
10 oz. (1¼ cups) butter　　　　**14 oz. (3½ cups) plain flour**
half a vanilla pod　　　　　　　**lemon icing**

Beat the sugar and butter till very light. Scrape out the centre of the vanilla pod and mix it into the mixture. Then beat in the eggs one at a time. Finally fold in the flour and continue to stir till the flour is absorbed. Take a piping bag fitted with a small star tube and pipe small crescents on greaseproof paper placed on a baking tray. Bake in the oven at 400°F. (205°C.) Mark 6 for about 15 minutes. When cool brush with lemon icing.

COTTAGE CHEESE PETITS FOURS

3 oz. (6 tablespoons) butter　　**1 egg yolk, lightly beaten**
½ lb. (2 cups) plain flour　　　**pinch of salt**
5 oz. (¾ cup) cottage cheese　　**1 tablespoon (1¼) sour cream**

Mix the butter into the flour, then add the cheese, egg yolk, salt and cream, and mix thoroughly. Knead the dough and roll out thickly. Cut into fancy shapes with a cutter. Place on a lightly greased baking (cookie) sheet and cut a slit on the top of each. Bake in the oven at 375°F. (191°C.) Mark 5 for 10–12 minutes.

BISCUITS

Like wedding cakes, crumpets and muffins are very English, part of the English way of life. They were so foreign to me at first that I could not believe that I would ever make them myself. Making biscuits in England was even more alien to me. I think that nowhere in the world do people eat so many biscuits as in this country and I think that they are made better here than anywhere else.

Therefore I was very surprised, when I got orders from Fortnum and Mason for several kinds of biscuits. It was immediately after the war, or perhaps even during it, that we started to make and pack in Fortnum and Mason tins thousands and thousands of biscuits. Several of the biscuit recipes we got from Fortnum and Mason. We could never make enough. We would send one consignment and it would stay only a few hours in the shop before being sold.

ALMOND BISCUITS (Cookies)

4 oz. ($\frac{1}{2}$ cup) butter	2–3 egg yolks
$\frac{1}{2}$ lb. (2 cups) plain flour	1 tablespoon ($1\frac{1}{4}$) rum
$\frac{1}{2}$ lb. ($1\frac{1}{3}$ cups) ground almonds	1 extra egg yolk
$\frac{1}{2}$ lb. (1 cup) caster sugar	

Soften the butter, sieve the flour on to a large board. Make a well in the centre, add the almonds, sugar and butter. Break in 2 egg yolks and the rum and carefully mix everything together. It is important to make the mixture only moist enough to bind together – too much or too little liquid makes the dough difficult to handle. Knead to a paste. Should the consistency seem too stiff, add the third egg yolk. Roll out on on a floured board into 2 'sausages'. Slice these thinly and roll into balls. Place these on a buttered baking (cookie) sheet. Brush each ball twice with egg yolk and make a slit in each lightly with a knife. Bake for 20 minutes at 375°F. (191°C.) Mark 5.

ABERNETHY BISCUITS

½ lb. (2 cups) plain flour	caraway seeds to taste
a pinch of baking powder	1 beaten egg
3 oz. (full ⅓ cup) butter	1 tablespoon (1¼) milk
3 oz. (full ⅓ cup) caster sugar	

Sift the flour and baking powder together into a bowl and rub in the butter. Add the sugar, caraway seeds, egg and milk and stir to make a stiff dough. Roll out thinly and cut into rounds 3 in. in diameter. Prick the centres. Bake in the oven at 375°F. (191°C.) Mark 5 for 10–15 minutes, cool on a wire rack.

AMERICAN REFRIGERATOR COOKIES

6 oz. (¾ cup) butter	8 oz. (2 cups) plain flour
7 oz. (scant cup) caster sugar	1 teaspoon (1¼) baking powder
1 egg	salt
vanilla	5 oz. (scant cup) chopped walnuts

Cream the butter, add the sugar gradually beating until the mixture is light. Add the egg, beat again, then flavour with vanilla. Sieve half the flour with the baking powder and salt. Stir this into the creamed mixture. Add the nuts and remaining flour and mix thoroughly. Roll the paste into a large sausage, about 2-in. thick. Wrap the roll (or rolls) in greaseproof paper and keep in the refrigerator for 24 hours or until the paste is absolutely chilled. To use the paste, cut the rolls into the thinnest possible slices. Place these on a greased baking (cookie) sheet and bake at 400°F. (205°C.) Mark 6 for about 10 minutes or until the cookies are a pale honey colour. The paste may be kept in the refrigerator for some days as it is not necessarily intended to be all used up at the same time. The above quantity makes 40-odd cookies.

Gâteaux: Dobos Torte and friandises; Baumkuchen; Nougatine gâteau; coffee hazelnut gâteau; fruit flan; mignons; fruit gâteau

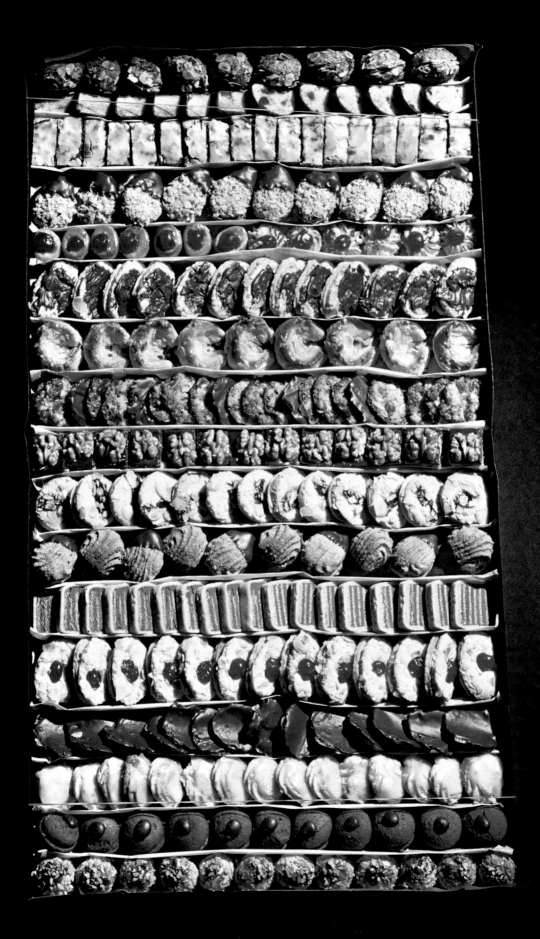

BRANDY RINGS

6 oz. (1½ cups) plain flour
3 oz. (⅓ cup) caster sugar
6 oz. (1 cup) ground almonds
6 oz. (¾ cup) butter
2 egg yolks

pinch ground cinnamon
2 teaspoons (2½) grated lemon rind
brandy
icing (confectioner's) sugar

Sieve the flour and sugar together in a mixing bowl. Add the almonds and mix well. Add the butter, cut into small pieces and rub it into the flour mixture until it is crumbly. Add the egg yolks, cinnamon and lemon rind and just enough brandy to make a firm dough. Knead until the dough is smooth, wrap in greaseproof paper and put into the refrigerator for about 30 minutes. Roll out the dough on a floured board about ¼-in. thick, cut into rings with 2 circular biscuit cutters of different sizes, and place these on a buttered and floured baking (cookie) sheet. Brush each ring with brandy and sprinkle fairly thickly with sifted icing sugar. Brush again with brandy so that the biscuits are covered with a thick moist layer of brandy and sugar. Bake in the oven at 375°F. (191°C.) Mark 5 until they are a deep golden brown.

BRANDY SNAPS

A very interesting sweet biscuit (cookie) which I first met in this country.

2 oz. (¼ cup) butter
2 oz. (¼ cup) sugar
2 tablespoons (2½) golden syrup
2 oz. (½ cup) plain flour

½ teaspoon (⅔) ground ginger
a few drops of brandy
whipped cream to fill

Put the butter, sugar and syrup into a pan and melt slowly. Take the pan from the heat. Let it cool slightly. Sieve the flour and the ginger together and mix into the cooled syrup mixture. Add the brandy, if using. Generously rub 2 or 3 baking (cookie) sheets with butter. Put teaspoonfuls of the mixture on them, spaced at least 3–4 in. apart, for the mixture spreads. Bake in the oven at 325°F. (162°C.) Mark 3 for 8–12 minutes. You can peek into the oven after about 5 minutes. They are ready to take out when they are a uniform golden brown and well spread. When opening the oven after 5 minutes to peek, put the second pan of brandy snaps into the oven, and the third after about 10 minutes, or when taking the first lot out. When the first batch of snaps come out do not touch them for 2 minutes as they will be too soft. Test after this time with a palette knife. If it can be slipped under the brandy snaps, they are ready. Rub the handle of a wooden spoon with butter and quickly roll a brandy snap

A selection of petits fours

round it; press it lightly and hold for a couple of seconds. Carefully slip off the handle and place on a wire tray to dry. Repeat this with the remaining brandy snaps, working as quickly as possible for once they begin to harden they cannot be removed from the pan. If this happens, return them to the oven to soften again. Just before serving, fill with whipped cream which can, if desired, be lightly flavoured with brandy. If not using the brandy snaps immediately, they can be stored but must be stored alone and in an airtight jar or tin.

CHOCOLATE BISCUITS (Cookies)

2 oz. (1¼ cup) margarine

1½ tablespoons (2) golden syrup

cocoa or drinking chocolate to
    taste

1 cup (1¼) plain flour

pinch of baking powder

2 oz. (¼ cup) caster sugar

Slightly melt the margarine and mix with the syrup. Pour into a bowl and add the remaining ingredients. Beat the mixture well – if it is too soft add more flour or flour and cocoa (or chocolate mixed.) Roll the dough out to about ¼-in. thick and cut into small rounds. Place on a greased and floured baking sheet and bake at 400 °F. (205 °C.) Mark 6 for 15–20 minutes or until firm and brown.

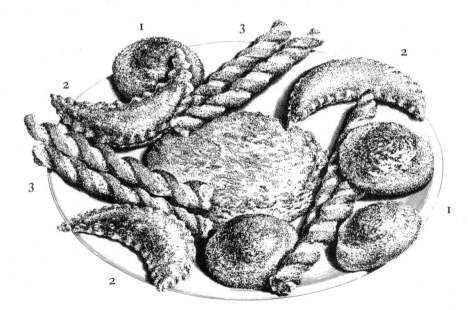

A selection of biscuits: 1. almond biscuits; 2. cheese crescents; 3. cheese straws; (*centre*) lemon biscuit

CINNAMON CIGARETTES

2 egg whites
4 oz. (½ cup) caster sugar
2 oz. (4 tablespoons) butter

4 tablespoons (5) plain flour
½ teaspoon (⅔) ground cinnamon

Beat the egg whites, gradually add the sugar and beat until the mixture is smooth. Melt the butter. Sieve the flour with the cinnamon. Add the butter and flour to the beaten egg whites. Pipe the mixture in finger shapes on to a greased and lightly floured baking (cookie) sheet spaced well apart as the mixture spreads. Bake for 5–10 minutes in the oven at 400°F. (205°C.) Mark 6. Take the biscuits out of the oven and leave for 2 minutes. Remove them from the baking sheet with a knife placing each one upside down on the table. Roll each one lightly round a small wooden spoon handle or thick pencil, holding it firmly with your hand. Slip off at once from the spoon and leave until cool. Store in an airtight tin.

FLAPJACKS

6 oz. (¾ cup) butter
6 oz. (1½ cups) demerara sugar

8 oz. (3 cups) quick cooking rolled oats

This is one of the quickest and easiest of cookies to make. It is not very elegant but homely and a great favourite with hungry boys when they come home from school. Melt the butter in a pan over a gentle heat. Combine the sugar and oats and stir them into the warmed butter. Turn the mixture on to a well-greased baking (cookie) sheet or shallow baking sheet and press it lightly. Smooth the top with a palette knife. Bake in the middle of the oven at 375°F. (191°C.) Mark 5 for about 35 minutes or until the flapjacks are a golden brown. Take from the oven, leave for a few minutes to cool and set, and then cut into squares or fingers. Let them remain in the pan until they are quite cold.

GINGER SNAPS or NUTS

8 oz. (2 cups) plain flour

2 teaspoons (2½) ground ginger

1 teaspoon (1¼) mixed spice

1 teaspoon (1¼) ground cinnamon

4 oz. (½ cup) butter

6 oz. (¾ cup) brown sugar

golden syrup

blanched and split almonds

Sieve the flour, ginger and spices into a mixing bowl. Beat the butter until soft, add the sugar and beat until creamy. Stir in the dry ingredients with the syrup – just enough of the latter to make a fairly stiff dough. (The syrup may be slightly warmed to make mixing easier.) Mix well and roll into balls, not too large for the mixture will spread while cooking. This recipe makes about 24–30 balls. (Flour the hands to prevent stickiness.) Place the balls well spaced apart on a greased baking (cookie) sheet and flatten each one slightly at the top. Lightly press a split almond into each ball and bake at 375°F. (191°C.) Mark 5 for 20–30 minutes or until the ginger snaps are brown and crisp. Leave on the baking sheet to cool before removing.

GYPSY SLICES

2 oz. (2 squares) dark chocolate

1 oz. (2 tablespoons) butter

4 eggs

4 oz. (½ cup) caster sugar

4 oz. (1 cup) plain flour

filling:

½ pint (1¼ cups) whipping cream

4 oz. (4 squares) chocolate, grated

First make the filling. This should be prepared before the cake is baked. Put the chocolate in the top a of a double boiler or in a bowl over hot water. Let it melt, add the cream and let the mixture come to the boil slowly, stirring all the time. Let the cream bubble up once, take from the pan and stir until the mixture is cold. Chill. Whisk lightly until it just begins to make peaks and chill again before using.

Break the chocolate into small pieces, mix with the butter and melt over a very low heat over hot water. Break the eggs into a bowl, lightly beat, add the sugar and continue whisking over hot water until they are thick and creamy. Take from the heat and continue whisking until the mixture is cool. Sift in the flour and gently fold it into the beaten eggs. Add the butter-chocolate mixture and mix well but lightly. Line a baking (cookie) sheet with greaseproof paper. Spread the chocolate mixture over it to about ½-in. thick. Bake in the oven at 410°F. (210°C.) Mark 6–7 for about 20 minutes. Take from the oven and turn out while still hot, pulling off the greaseproof paper. Cut into slices, cut through each slice and at once fill with the cream.

HAM AND CARAWAY SEED BISCUITS (Savoury Cookies)

10 oz. (2½ cups) plain flour
pinch of salt
6 oz. (¾ cup) butter
2-hard boiled eggs
milk

1 egg, lightly beaten
2–3 oz. finely chopped lean ham
coarse salt
caraway seeds to taste

Sieve the flour and salt into a mixing bowl. Rub in the butter. Separate the whites from the yolks of the eggs. Crumble the yolks into fine crumbs. Add to the flour. Mix well, add just enough milk to make a stiff dough. Knead the dough until smooth, pat into a round and chill for 1 hour. Roll out thinly on a floured board. Brush lightly with egg and sprinkle with ham. Fold sides to middle of the pastry and roll out again. Brush again with egg and sprinkle with ham, fold and roll a second time. Leave to rest for 30 minutes. Roll out thinly again, sprinkle with coarse salt and generously (if the flavour is liked) with caraway seeds. Cut into biscuit shapes and bake at 410°F. (210°C.) Mark 6–7 until they are a golden brown, 20–25 minutes.

HAZELNUT BISCUITS (Cookies)

6 glacé cherries
3 egg whites
6 oz. (¾ cup) caster sugar

¼ lb. (⅔ cup) ground hazelnuts
raspberry jam

Finely chop the cherries. Whisk the egg whites until stiff, gradually add half the sugar, whisking it in until the mixture is stiff. Fold in the remaining sugar alternately with the hazelnuts. Mix well but gently and add the cherries. Put the mixture into a forcing bag and pipe on to lightly greased and floured baking (cookie) sheets in small regular shapes. Bake in the oven at 200°F. (94°C.) Mark Low until the biscuits are just tinged with colour. Take from the oven, cool and then sandwich together with raspberry jam.

HONEY BISCUITS (Cookies)

4 oz. (1 cup) blanched almonds
½ lb. (¾ cup) honey
4 oz. (½ cup) sugar
2 eggs
12 oz. (3 cups) plain or wholemeal (graham) flour
1 tablespoon (1¼) kirsch or rum

1 tablespoon (1¼) grated lemon rind
a little ground cinnamon and cloves
a good pinch of nutmeg
3 oz. (scant cup) chopped candied peel

Coarsely chop the almonds. Gently heat the honey with half the sugar. Beat the eggs with the rest of the sugar until thick. Sift the flour into a mixing bowl, make a well in the middle, add the remaining ingredients, bring the flour from the sides of the bowl over the top and then work to a firm paste. Knead well and then roll out to about ¼-in. thick. Cut into biscuit shapes. Place them close together on a buttered and floured baking (cookie) sheet and leave until the next day in a cool place. Bake in the oven at 380°F. (194°C.) Mark 5 for 15–20 minutes.

LEMON BISCUITS (Cookies) (1)

6 oz. (1 cup) cube sugar
1 tablespoon (1¼) grated lemon rind
2 eggs

12 oz. (3 cups) plain flour
3 oz. (6 tablespoons) butter
juice ½ lemon

Pound the sugar until fairly fine with a mortar and pestle. Beat the eggs until smooth, add the lemon rind. Sift the flour into a mixing bowl, add the butter, cut into small pieces, and rub into the flour until the mixture is crumbly. Add the sugar and mix well, and then add the eggs and lemon juice and work to a dough. If necessary add cold water, the paste should be of a dropping consistency. Drop the mixture in teaspoonfuls on to a buttered baking (cookie) sheet and bake in the oven at 400°F. (205°C.) Mark 6 for 15–20 minutes or until the biscuits are a pale golden colour.

LEMON BISCUITS (Cookies) (2)

4 oz. (½ cup) butter
3 oz. (full ⅓ cup) caster sugar
6 oz. (1½ cups) plain flour

1 egg
grated rind 1 lemon
icing (confectioner's) sugar

Warm the mixing bowl slightly. Add the butter, beat this until soft, then beat in the sugar and continue beating until the mixture is creamy. Add the flour. Beat the egg until smooth, add this to the bowl, then the lemon rind. (If an orange flavour is preferred, use an equal quantity of orange rind.) Mix to a dough, adding a few drops of cold water if necessary. Leave to rest for 1 hour. Roll out thinly and cut into biscuit shapes. Place these on a buttered baking (cookie) sheet and bake in the oven at 375°F. (191°C.) Mark 5 until they are a golden brown, about 15–20 minutes. Take from the oven, turn out, dust with icing sugar and leave until cold.

ORANGE GINGER BISCUITS (Cookies)

¾ lb. (3 cups) plain flour
6 oz. (¾ cup) caster sugar
3 oz. (6 tablespoons) butter
pinch of soda and cream of tartar

1 teaspoon (1¼) ground ginger
grated rind 2 oranges
2 eggs
icing (confectioner's) sugar

Sift the flour and sugar together in a mixing bowl; rub in the butter, cut into small pieces until the mixture is crumbly. Add the soda, ginger and orange rind. Lightly beat the eggs, add to the flour etc. and mix to a stiff dough, adding a little milk or orange juice if it is too stiff. Place in neat small heaps on a greased baking (cookie) sheet. Bake in the oven at 400°F. (205°C.) Mark 6 for 25–30 minutes or when the biscuits are a pale golden colour. Take from the oven and sprinkle with sifted icing sugar, preferably orange-flavoured.

MELTING MOMENTS

6 oz. (¾ cup) butter
4 – 6 oz. (½ – ¾ cup) sifted icing
   (confectioner's) sugar
6 oz. (¾ cup) cornflour (cornstarch)

2 oz. (½ cup) plain flour
1 teaspoon (1¼) baking powder
1–2 beaten eggs

Beat the butter until soft, add the sugar and continue beating until the mixture is creamy. Sift the cornflour, flour and baking powder together, work this into the creamed butter. Mix well and then add enough beaten egg to make a dough soft enough to pipe through a forcing bag. Pipe neatly in small oblongs on a buttered baking (cookie) sheet and bake in the centre of the oven at 375°F. (191°C.) Mark 5 for about 15 minutes. Take from the oven and let the biscuits cool on the baking sheet. Sandwich in pairs with butter icing.

OATMEAL BISCUITS or OATCAKES

I like everything made with oatmeal. I wouldn't mind eating porridge every day; I like it for breakfast, I wouldn't mind it for lunch. I would be pleased to have it for my supper, but I never do! But I don't want to talk about myself I want to give you a good biscuit recipe.

½ lb. (3 cups) fine oatmeal	¼ teaspoon (⅓) cream of tartar
2 oz. (½ cup) plain flour	½ teaspoon (⅔) salt
sugar to taste	3 oz. (6 tablespoons) butter
½ teaspoon (⅔) baking soda	milk

Mix together the dry ingredients. Add the butter and rub it in until the mixture is crumbly. Add enough milk to mix to a stiff dough. Let it rest for 30 minutes and then roll out on a floured board to ¼-in. thickness. Cut into rounds or squares, rather larger than usually for biscuits, and bake in the oven at 375°F. (191°C.) Mark 5 for about 20 minutes. Oatcakes can be served with butter and honey or marmalade.

PARMESAN BISCUITS (Savoury Cookies)

You can never tell when people are coming in for a drink, or your husband or sons will bring some friends for a drink. It is always good to be prepared. I was once terribly embarrassed, when I took a friend to a family, where I had been invited and asked to bring this friend. At first we had difficulty in being admitted. The puzzled servants did not know what to do; at last our host came and showed us in. With a few embarrassed words he ushered us into a beautiful sitting room. A few minutes later the lady of the house appeared and tried to entertain us.

'I'm so sorry I have not a drink in the house', she said apologetically. 'I have nothing to offer you'.

We answered, though surprised: 'We only wanted to see you. We have only a minute. We are invited to dinner.' We made our stay as short as possible and left. I decided then never to be without something, however modest, to offer to unexpected guests. So I give you a very simple and inexpensive recipe for such occasions.

2 oz. (4 tablespoons) butter	2 oz. (⅔ cup) grated Parmesan
8 oz. (2 cups) plain flour	cheese
pinch of salt	milk
	1 well beaten egg yolk

Rub the butter into the flour, add the salt and cheese. Mix well, stir in enough milk to make a fairly soft dough. Knead it until soft and elastic. Turn on to a floured board and roll out as thinly as possible. Cut into shapes with a biscuit cutter and place on a buttered baking (cookie) sheet. Brush lightly with egg and bake in the oven at 400°F. (205°C.) Mark 6 for 8–10 minutes or until the biscuits are a golden brown. These biscuits can be served hot or cold. If they are rolled very thinly two can be sandwiched together with a savoury butter-cream and a Parmesan cheese filling.

PLAIN BISCUITS (Cookies)

Just something very easy to have at home in reserve when somebody drops in for tea. They can be kept in the larder in a tin. It's nothing but a little shortbread.

½ lb. (2 cups) plain flour	**6 oz. (¾ cup) butter**
pinch of salt	**1 egg yolk, beaten**
3 oz. (full ⅓ cup) sugar	

Mix the dry ingredients together and rub in the butter thoroughly. Mix well, then knead the mixture to a firm smooth dough, adding if necessary a little water. Roll out on a floured board and cut into neat rounds, crescents or any shapes you like but finger-shapes are more usual. Place on a greased and floured baking (cookie) sheet, prick well with a fork and brush with beaten egg. Bake in the oven at 350°F. (175°C.) Mark 4 for 15–20 minutes or until the biscuits are a pale golden colour.

RATAFIA BISCUITS (Cookies)

Once this biscuit was made by the industrious housewife; now it is usually made commercially, mainly in Holland. I include it because from time to time, some nice old lady asks for them and seems disappointed to learn that we don't make them, as she had hoped to get them from us. Thus I give you a recipe for this modest and very old-fashioned biscuit:

3 oz. (½ cup) ground almonds	**2 egg whites**
2 oz. (⅓ cup) bitter almonds, ground	**½ lb. (1 cup) sugar**
1 dessertspoon (1 tablespoon) brandy	

Pound both the ground almonds together adding the brandy. Beat the egg whites until stiff and add to the pounded almonds. Sift and add the sugar. Beat the mixture to a firm paste. Cover a baking (cookie) sheet with rice paper and bake 1 or 2 tiny rounds of the paste to test for lightness. If they seem too heavy, add another 1 or even

2 well-beaten egg whites. Place the mixture in thin flat rounds about 1 in. in diameter (even a trifle less) and bake in the oven at 380°F. (194°C.) Mark 5 for 10–12 minutes or until they are lightly browned. Let them become cold on the rice paper and then pull off. Ratafia biscuits will keep for weeks and weeks if stored in an airtight tin.

GROUND RICE BISCUITS (Cookies)

¼ lb. (1 cup) plain flour	4 oz. (½ cup) butter
pinch of salt and baking powder	lemon or vanilla essence to taste
4 oz. (⅔ cup) ground rice	1 egg, well beaten
3 oz. (full ⅓ cup) caster sugar	

Sieve the flour, salt and baking powder into a bowl. Add the ground rice and sugar. Mix well, rub in the butter. Add the flavouring, mix well, add the egg and work to a dough, adding if necessary a little milk. Knead the dough thoroughly and then roll out on a floured board about ⅛-in. thick. Cut into small rounds with a biscuit cutter and place on a greased baking (cookie) sheet. Bake in the oven at 400°F. (205°C.) Mark 6 for 10–15 minutes or until the biscuits are a pale golden colour. Serve plain or sandwiched in pairs with apricot or raspberry jam.

SHORTBREAD BISCUITS (Cookies) (1)

1 lb. (4 cups) plain flour	12 oz. (1½ cups) butter
4 oz. (½ cup) sugar	icing (confectioner's) sugar

Sieve the flour and sugar together in a mixing bowl. Rub in the butter with the fingers and gradually knead it all to a firm dough. Turn on to a floured board and roll or press out to the required thickness, ½–¾ in., and cut into rounds or squares, oblong or crescents. Prick with a fork. Bake in the oven at about 375°F. (191°C.) Mark 5 for about 1 hour or until a pale golden colour. Dust with sifted icing sugar when cool.

SHORTBREAD BISCUITS (Cookies) (2)

piece of vanilla pod	4 oz. (½ cup) butter
1 oz. (¼ cup) icing (confectioner's) sugar	4 oz. (1 cup) plain flour

Leave the vanilla in a jar with the icing sugar overnight. Cream the butter in a warm bowl, gradually beat in the icing sugar (sifted) and the flour. Beat until the mixture is soft and creamy. Pipe it through a forcing bag with a fluted nozzle straight on to a greased baking (cookie) sheet. The biscuits may be any size desired. Tiny ones are elegant for coffee parties, large for tea. Bake in the oven at 350°F. (175°C.) Mark 4 for 45–60 minutes or until a pale golden colour.

SPICE BISCUITS (Cookies)

2 oz. ($\frac{1}{4}$ cup) butter
2 oz. ($\frac{1}{4}$ cup) caster sugar
1 teaspoon ($1\frac{1}{4}$) treacle
4 oz. (1 cup) plain flour

pinch of baking powder
$\frac{1}{2}$ teaspoon ($\frac{2}{3}$) mixed spice
1 egg

Beat the butter and sugar to a cream. Warm the treacle and mix it into the butter. Sift the flour, baking powder and spice together and stir into the butter mixture alternately with the egg. Work to a firm dough and roll out on a floured board. Cut into thin rounds about $\frac{1}{4}$-in. thick. Bake in the oven at 350°F. (175°C.) Mark 4 for 25–30 minutes or until a pale golden colour.

TEA BISCUITS (Cookies)

6 oz. ($\frac{3}{4}$ cup) butter
1 lb. (2 cups) sugar
$\frac{1}{4}$ pint ($\frac{1}{3}$) milk
3 eggs

1 teaspoon ($1\frac{1}{4}$) vanilla essence
$1\frac{1}{4}$ lb. (5 cups) plain flour
$2\frac{1}{2}$ teaspoons (3) baking powder

Cream the butter with the sugar. Beat the milk into the eggs. Add the vanilla. Sift the flour and baking powder together. Add this alternating with the egg and milk mixture to the creamed fat. Work to a dough, knead thoroughly until smooth and pliable. Chill. Break off small portions of the dough and roll out on a floured board to about $\frac{1}{4}$-in. thick. Put the remaining dough into the refrigerator to keep it chilled. Cut the rolled-out dough into varying shapes with a biscuit cutter. Put the scraps into the refrigerator for the final rolling so that the dough does not become over-worked. Repeat until all the dough is rolled out and cut into shapes. Place these on a greased baking (cookie) sheet and bake at 375°F. (191°C.) Mark 5 for 15–20 minutes or until the biscuits are a golden colour. They must not however over-brown. Take from the oven and dust with sugar, preferably vanilla sugar. This recipe will produce about lb. of biscuits which can be stored in an airtight tin or jar.

WALNUT BISCUITS (Cookies)

12 oz. (3 cups) plain flour
6 oz. (¾ cup) butter
5 oz. (scant cup) ground walnuts
4 oz. (½ cup) sugar

juice and grated peel ½ lemon
1 tablespoon (1¼) rum
1 egg
coarse sugar

Sift the flour into a bowl, rub in the butter, add the walnuts and sugar and mix thoroughly. Add the lemon juice and rind, rum and egg. Work to a firm paste, if it seems to be too stiff or crumbly, add some milk to cream to loosen it. Roll out the paste on a floured board to ½-in. thick. Cut into fancy shapes. Sprinkle each one lightly with coarse sugar and place on a greased baking (cookie) sheet. Bake at 350°F. (175°C.) Mark 4 for 15–20 minutes or until the biscuits are a pale golden colour. Take from the oven and tumble on to a wire rack to cool.

WINE BISCUITS (Cookies)

1 lb. (4 cups) plain flour
4 oz. (½ cup) butter
3 tablespoons (3¾) icing
   (confectioner's) sugar

1 egg, well beaten
cream

Sift the flour twice, rub the butter into it, sift and add the sugar, mix well, add the egg and then as much cream as will make a stiff dough. Roll this out very thinly and stamp into rounds with the top of a wineglass. Bake in the oven at 400°F. (205°C.) Mark 6 until the biscuits are crisp and a golden brown, about 15 minutes. A few currants or caraway seeds may be added if liked. This is an old-fashioned recipe.

VANILLA CRESCENTS (Austria)

4 oz. (1 cup) plain flour
1½ oz. (3 tablespoons) caster sugar
2 oz. (⅓ cup) ground almonds

3 oz. (6 tablespoons) butter
vanilla sugar

For this recipe unblanched ground almonds are the best, but if these are not available, use blanched almonds. Sift the flour and sugar together. Add the almonds, mix well, cut the butter into small pieces and rub into the dry ingredients until the mixture is crumbly. Work to a stiff dough on a floured board. Break off small pieces of the paste and roll these with your fingers into crescents. Place on a buttered and floured baking (cookie) sheet and bake in the oven at 400°F. (205°C.) Mark 6 until the crescents are a strong golden brown. Roll in vanilla sugar while still hot.

CONFECTIONERY

Many years ago, the craft of the confectioner was distinct from that of the bread maker. It is still so today. There is evidence that the art of confectionery can be traced back to Egypt some 3,500 years ago and while this art was by no means primitive at that time, it was not until Greek and Roman influence became paramount that the confectioner took his place in the select band of skilled craftsmen.

At this time the basic raw material for the confectioner was honey. This was due to the fact that the process of sugar refining was not known. This process was first used in India and was basically the evaporation of the juice from sugar cane. This skill passed from India to China and thence to Persia where the first sugar refinery was started in the seventh century A.D.

The first mention of sugar in England was in 1319, when 100,000 pounds was imported by way of Venice from India. The price of sugar at that time was 1/9½d. per pound, in those days a very considerable sum. Sugar in fact was not sold at a reasonable price until the use of beet sugar became more common during the Napoleonic wars at the beginning of the nineteenth century. Beet sugar had been discovered by Margraff of Berlin in 1747 but was not developed until 1801 when a factory was established by Archard in France. This did not prosper, however, until the British Continental blockade made it impossible to obtain supplies of cane sugar from outside Europe, and so beet sugar manufacturer was quickly developed on the European continent.

This had the effect of putting much more sugar on the market and as a result sugar prices quickly dropped. Far more sugar and confectionery became generally available.

Confectioners in the past were much concerned with sugar and sugar-boiling. The modern confectioner has still to know a great deal about this subject.

Today sugar is cheap and very thoroughly refined, in fact it may be said that there are few purer foods available. Quite a large proportion of the sugar used in this country today is made from beet and the finished article is undectectable from that obtained from sugar cane.

As a food sugar is invaluable as a fuel, and so is a source of energy.

There is now hardly any demand for the elaborate and costly confections made from pulled and spun sugar, so typical of late Victorian and Edwardian cookery. The place of this type of sugar work is taken over by fondant. We colour the fondant, we flavour it, we use it a great deal for icings, fillings as well and the French use it even more than we do here; they like fondant more than chocolate and so do I. For sweet-making in France they use fresh fruit juices: we, in our sweet or cold chocolate kitchen, use only fresh fruit covered with a thin layer of chocolate. It is very convenient to have in your food cupboard a jar of both white and chocolate fondant. You can make chocolate fondant to add to the already prepared fondant. To make this, melt the fondant with the help of a little syrup, then add to it a little unsweetened and sweetened chocolate mixed. Of course all this is quite a lot of trouble – so if I may corrupt you try to be friendly with your local pâtisserie and ask them to sell you a pound or a half pound of fondant. It is no trouble to them; it has to be made anyway! It is a shame that you cannot buy ready-made fondant anywhere in the shops because it is such an effort and a lot of work for the housewife to make it. I have a few friends who became friends through being my customers and I let them have ready made fondant when they want to make their own Christmas cakes or any other cakes at home.

FONDANT

1 lb. cube sugar
1½ pints (2 pints) water

a pinch of cream of tartar
1 teaspoonful (1¼ teaspoonfuls) glucose

Put the sugar and water into a heavy, thick-bottomed saucepan. Allow to heat up slowly until the sugar is dissolved. Then add the cream of tartar dissolved in a spoonful of water. Mix these well together. Lower the heat under the syrup and allow to come to the boil. Add the glucose. Remove the lid and then place in your sugar thermometer (sacrometer). Let the sugar boil rapidly until it just reaches 240°F. (116°C.). Wash the sides of the pan with a soft wet brush from time to time. Stop the sugar boiling immediately when it reaches 240°F. (116°C.). The best way to do this is to stand the saucepan in cold water. When the syrup has cooled slightly pour it on a watered marble slab. Sprinkle the surface of the syrup slightly with cold water and allow to cool for a few minutes; then work it with a sugar scraper or a wooden spoon; do this without stopping until the fondant turns snow white. Then taking a little fondant at a time begin to knead it into a ball. Cover it with a damp cloth and let it mellow for an hour or two before using it.

It is possible by making even the slightest variations of recipes and cooking processes to produce a different creation. The most important thing to remember is to note the ingredients and the precise method of cooking adopted, so that should something different and pleasing materialize, it will be possible to reproduce it.

A good example of variation in ingredients and method giving different textures and tastes is apparent in the making of fudge.

A basic recipe is shown from which, with a little practice, a good, smooth and creamy fudge will be produced. If, however, the dextrose content is reduced by half, the finished texture will be much rougher and quite crumbly. If the dextrose content is doubled, the finished article will be very soft and could be used as a filling or a topping for a cake. By cooking the batch very slowly the sugars will have far more time to caramelize and a much more pronounced flavour will be noticed. With the addition of some plain chocolate or some coffee, different fudges will be produced. Similarly, chopped walnuts, ginger or seedless raisins will all give striking variations.

The important thing is to be willing to experiment and make careful notes and in this way you may well produce a sweetmeat that will be truly yours and one that cannot be readily copied.

Sweetmaking has become a highly technical and professional craft. However, there are many sweets which may be made at home. These are roughly divided into two classes, the cooked and the uncooked sweets. The uncooked are obviously easier and call for little instruction. Proper wrapping will help to give a professional air and will also improve storing. Cooked sweets require some specialized equipment for the most satisfactory results. A little knowledge of the nature and behaviour of sugar when heated will be helpful in achieving success.

Sugar melts at 320°F. (159–160°C.); if it is heated further it becomes honey coloured, then brown, dark caramel and lastly black. It is easily soluble in water. Cold water will dissolve double its weight of sugar. If sugar is boiled its characteristics will alter at different degrees and each of these degrees has its own name. Sugar is best boiled as a syrup, that is in a water solution. A practical guide is to allow $\frac{1}{2}$ pint ($1\frac{1}{4}$ cups) to 2 lb. sugar. Boiling the sugar will evaporate the water, and when the surface is covered with little bubbles, cooking has started and from then on it must be very carefully watched. The different degrees relevant to making simple confectionery are:

Large thread, 219°F. (104°C.), when threads form if a little sugar is pulled between finger and thumb.

Small ball, 220°F. (104–5°C.) a little sugar dropped into cold water will form a soft gluey ball. Also known as *soft ball*.

Large ball, 230°F. (106°C.) when sugar is dropped into water the ball will be harder and more resistant to the fingers.

Small crack, 264°F. (129°C.) when dipped in water and touched with a finger the sugar will break but will cling to the teeth. Also known as *first crack*.

Hard crack, 289°F. (143°C.) now the sugar will break like glass when dipped in water and will have become a rich brown. Any overcooking will caramelize the sugar which will taste burnt and be extremely hard.

These remarks and tests apply to toffee mixtures of all kinds as well as pure sugars. The addition of glucose will help prevent graining during boiling and will also give a glossy appearance to the sweets.

Utensils

To make confectionery at home, therefore, successfully, a proper sugar thermometer is essential, although with these guides to sugar degrees it makes it possible to make some confectionery with a reasonable chance of success. But wastage is avoided and results are much more certain with a thermometer. These are not very expensive and cover a very wide range of temperatures. A marble slab for cooling and pulling the confectionery and a large heavy pan are also very useful.

VANILLA FUDGE

¾ lb. (1½ cups) sugar
4 oz. (½ cup) brown sugar
1 cup (1¼) milk, fresh or
    evaporated

3 oz. (¾ cup) dextrose
1½ oz. (3 tablespoons) butter
3 oz. fondant
vanilla essence

Put the sugars, milk and dextrose into a pan and cook over a low heat until the sugar is dissolved, stirring all the time. Bring to the boil, stirring gently, until it reaches 238°F. (114°C.). Take from the heat, add the fondant (broken into small pieces) and essence, but do not stir them in. Leave undisturbed for 5–10 minutes, then stir in the butter, cut into pieces, until the fudge just begins to grain. Pour at once into a prepared pan and smooth over the top) This can be done with a slightly greased rubber scraper or with a cut lemon. Leave the fudge until it is cold, then cut into squares or other shapes and wrap in greaseproof paper. Fudge if kept too long becomes sugary and therefore should be eaten as soon as possible after it has been made.

GINGER FUDGE

To vanilla fudge add drained and chopped preserved ginger to taste but omit the vanilla.

WALNUT FUDGE

Add blanched and chopped walnuts to the mixture after it has rested for 10 minutes. Continue as for Vanilla Fudge.

Other flavours can be used. Orange or lemon rind, using 2 teaspoons (2½) of rind and juice instead of vanilla. For chocolate fudge, add 2 oz. (2 squares) of melted chocolate at the same time as the fondant and vanilla. For coffee fudge, add 2 tablespoons (2½) of coffee essence after the fudge has been removed from the heat. Add almond essence to taste instead of vanilla.

CARAMELS (Plain)

8 oz. (1 cup) granulated sugar	6 oz. (1½ cups) dextrose
4 oz. (½ cup) brown sugar	6 oz. (¾ cup) unsalted butter
½ cup (⅔) water	6 oz. (¾ cup) condensed milk

Place the sugars, water and dextrose in a pan, bring to the boil and cook until the temperature reaches 280°F. (136°C.). Remove from the heat and slowly add the butter and milk previously mixed and warmed. Stir thoroughly and continue cooking slowly till hard crack is reached. Pour on to a metal tray, lightly greased with butter. Allow to cool and harden, cut with a knife using light and very brisk strokes. ('Hard crack' means that on a trial the toffee will snap when a little is cooled in a cup of cold water.)

CHOCOLATE CARAMELS

6 oz. ($\frac{3}{4}$ cup) caster sugar
1 tablespoon ($1\frac{1}{4}$) drinking
   chocolate powder
$\frac{1}{4}$ lb. ($\frac{1}{2}$ cup) butter

1 tablespoon ($1\frac{1}{4}$) liquid glucose
5 tablespoons ($6\frac{1}{4}$) milk
vanilla essence to taste

Rub an 8-in. shallow baking pan lightly with butter. Put the sugar, chocolate powder, one-third of the butter and glucose into a pan and dissolve gently over a low heat, stirring all the time until blended. Bring to a quick boil still stirring to prevent burning and test with a thermometer. When it reaches 230°F. (110°C.) add another one-third of the butter, still stirring. Continue boiling at the same heat then take the pan from the heat and add the remaining butter, milk and vanilla, still stirring all the time. Do this quickly as the pan should not be too long off the heat. Return to the heat, bring again to a quick boil, stirring continuously. Pour into the prepared pan and leave until cold.

LEMON CARAMELS

A rather more unusual caramel with a refreshing flavour.

$\frac{1}{2}$ lb. (1 cup) soft light-brown sugar
2 tablespoons ($2\frac{1}{2}$) milk
juice $1\frac{1}{2}$ lemons

1 tablespoon ($1\frac{1}{4}$) liquid glucose
$\frac{1}{4}$ lb. ($\frac{1}{2}$ cup) butter
5 tablespoons ($6\frac{1}{4}$) cream

Rub a 7-in. shallow baking pan with butter. Put the sugar, milk, lemon juice, glucose and one-third of the butter into a small pan. Dissolve over a low heat, stirring all the time, then bring more quickly to the boil at 230°F. (110°C.), and add one-third more of the butter. Stir well, bring again to the boil, take the pan to one side, stir in the cream and the remaining butter. Stir well, return the pan to the heat and once more bring to the boil, this time to 245°F. (118°C.). Take at once from the heat and pour immediately into the prepared pan. Leave until it is quite cold and then cut into squares, diamonds or any similar shapes preferred and wrap in greaseproof paper. It is important that the bottom of the pan does not touch the heat and asbestos helps here. Stirring and care are important.

MAPLE CARAMELS (U.S.A.)

1 lb. (4 cups) brown sugar
16 oz. ($1\frac{1}{2}$ cups) maple syrup

$\frac{1}{2}$ cup ($\frac{2}{3}$) cream
1 tablespoon ($1\frac{1}{4}$) butter

Put the sugar, syrup and cream into a pan and cook over a low heat until the sugar is dissolved. Continue cooking until the mixture reaches the soft ball stage, 238°F. (114°C.). Add the butter. Pour the caramel into a buttered or oiled square pan and leave until it has almost set. Cut into squares, then leave until it hardens. Nuts may be added to the mixture while still in the pan or they may be sprinkled on the bottom of the pan before pouring in the caramel mixture.

CHOCOLATE TRUFFLES

8 oz. (8 squares) dark chocolate
2 tablespoons (2½) cream
black coffee or rum
2 well-beaten egg yolks

2 oz. (¼ cup) butter, cut
into small pieces
cocoa

Break the chocolate in a bowl, add the liquid and melt over boiling water (over a moderate heat), stirring all the time. Take the pan from the heat, beat the melted chocolate until creamy. Add the egg yolks, beating all the time, then add the butter. Continue beating until the mixture is smooth, about 3 minutes. Leave to cool and then chill for several hours, overnight if liked. Break off small pieces, roll these between the hands into round balls, roll in cocoa and put into small paper cases. Eat within 48 hours.

NOUGAT

4 oz. (1 cup) almonds
6 – 8 glacé cherries
1 oz. (3 tablespoons) pistachio nuts
6 oz. (1 full cup) icing
** (confectioner's) sugar**

2 teaspoons (2½) liquid glucose
4 oz. (½ cup) honey
2 egg whites

Blanch the almonds, coarsely chop and dry them in a warm oven until they begin to change colour. Slice the cherries and halve the pistachios. Completely line a tin roughly 6 × 4 in. top and bottom with rice paper. Put the sugar, glucose, honey and egg whites (unbeaten) in a pan. Cook over a low heat whisking or beating all the while until the mixture is thick and white. Test by dropping a little of the mixture into cold water. If it hardens immediately, it is ready. It will take about 20 minutes. Take at once from the heat and stir in the almonds, still warm, the cherries and the pistachio nuts. Turn on to a pastry board heavily dredged with icing sugar. Knead the nougat into a ball and press it into the prepared tin. Cover with a piece of wood and then put a weight on top. Leave for about 5 hours. Turn out and cut into squares or oblongs and wrap in fine wax paper.

MARZIPAN SWEETS

½ lb. (1 cup) sugar   6 oz. (1 cup) ground almonds
6 tablespoons (7½) water   1 egg white, unbeaten
1 teaspoon (1¼) glucose

Put the sugar and water into a small pan. Over a low heat dissolve the sugar. Add the glucose and boil the syrup until it reaches 240°F. (116°C.). Take from the heat and at once stir in all the ground almonds and the egg white. Return the pan to the heat and cook for 2–3 minutes over a low heat, stirring from time to time. (If the mixture seems too soft, cook it a minute or so longer.) Turn out on to a board and work with a wooden spoon until the mixture is stiff enough to be pinched into a thin sheet between the thumb and finger without it sticking. Turn it on to a board, dredge with sieved icing (confectioner's) sugar and knead to a smooth paste. Wrap in greaseproof paper and store in a tin until required.

Marzipan keeps for a long time in a cool dry place. If it gets a little dry on the outside, knead it lightly with a little egg white. This basic recipe can be flavoured and coloured to suit taste and need. For example, it will take about ¼ teaspoon (⅓) of almond, vanilla or ratafia essence, or 1 teaspoon (1¼) of strained lemon juice. If a brandy flavour is wished, use less water and substitute with brandy. If colouring the marzipan pink, use strawberry or raspberry essence for flavouring. Orange colour obviously takes orange or tangerine essence as its flavour. A pale delicate green shade can be matched with almond or ratafia, while pale mauve is best used with rum. Coffee essence will give both colour and flavour.

Marzipan sweets are usually made in the shape of potatoes, carrots, logs etc. To make marzipan potatoes, use plain marzipan, break off small pieces and roll between the hands into rounds or ovals. Mark 'eyes' with a skewer and roll the balls in powdered sweetened chocolate powder. To make carrots, add a little orange colouring to the marzipan when cooking. Break off small pieces and shape these into small 'carrots'. Put a tiny strip of angelica on the top of each one to resemble the stalk. Dust lightly in sieved icing sugar or chocolate powder. To make stuffed walnuts, either plain or differently coloured marzipan can be used. Break off small pieces and roll into perfect ovals. Press an unbroken half of a walnut on each side and toss at once into sifted granulated sugar.

For stuffed cherries, large glacé cherries are required and pink and plain marzipan. Cut the cherries neatly almost into halves. Roll the marzipan into small balls, pinching each one at one end. Push the pinched-in end of the marzipan into the cherries and toss at once into sieved granulated sugar.

And to make marzipan logs, divide the marzipan into two portions. Colour and flavour one half with melted dark chocolate. Make a roll some ¼-in. in diameter with the plain marzipan. Roll the chocolate marzipan as thinly as possible. Brush this with sieved apricot jam and wrap it neatly and firmly round the marzipan roll. With a fork mark the roll lengthwise to represent the bark, and then cut off lengths straight or diagonally and lightly toss in sieved icing sugar.

To make stuffed dates, use plain marzipan but when making add less water and about 1 tablespoon (1¼) of rum or brandy. Use good quality large dates. Slit them almost into halves, taking out the stone. Break off pieces of the marzipan to fit the dates, roll these into small date-like shapes and stuff each date. Close up the dates as tightly as possible and roll in caster sugar. Serve in paper cases.

MARRONS GLACÉS

2 lb. Italian chestnuts
1 oz. (¼ cup) plain flour

syrup:
3 lb. (6 cups) sugar
vanilla pod
pinch of cream of tartar
2 teaspoons (2½) glucose

Score the chestnuts, drop them into a pan of boiling water and boil for 5–10 minutes or until their outer skins will peel off easily. Peel and put them back into the pan, this time with cold water to cover and the flour (this cleans them). Bring to the boil and cook until the chestnuts are tender. Take care not to break them and peel off the brown inner skin. Dry them well. Pack them closely together in an earthenware vessel.

Make the syrup. Put 1 lb. (2 cups) of sugar into a pan with 1 cup (1¼) of water and the vanilla bean. Dissolve the sugar slowly over a low heat and then bring to the boil until it reaches 218°F. (103°C.). Pour this mixture over the chestnuts, cover and leave in a warm place for 2 days. On the third day drain off the syrup. Mix this with another 1 lb. of sugar and 1 cup (1¼) of water. Make this into a syrup, adding the cream of tartar. Bring this to the boil until it reaches 230°F. (110°C.) and let it boil for 5 minutes. Add the drained chestnuts and bring the syrup just to the boil. Drain off the chestnuts, place them on a wire rack to completely drain and then put into a warm place to dry. When the chestnuts are quite dry, prepare a third syrup, this time for the glacé cover. Put the remaining sugar into a pan with $\frac{1}{4}$ pint ($\frac{1}{3}$) of water and the glucose. Dissolve the sugar over a low heat and then bring the syrup to the boil until it reaches 225°F. (107°C.). Add the dried chestnuts and again bring the mixture to the boil. Lift out the chestnuts, drain them thoroughly and once more put them on the wire rack to dry in a warm place. When the marrons are quite dry, wrap each one separately in foil before storing.

ALMOND BARFI (India)

4 oz. ($\frac{1}{2}$ cup) caster sugar   **8 oz. ($1\frac{1}{3}$ cups) ground almonds**
2 oz. (4 tablespoons) butter

Put the sugar with 3 tablespoons ($3\frac{3}{4}$) of water into a pan, cook over a low heat until the sugar is dissolved and then bring to the boil and boil until it spins a thread. Take from the heat, at once stir in the butter and the almonds and pour on to a marble slab. Roll at once, working quickly, and cut into diamond shapes. The barfi should be rolled very thinly and, as it dries quickly, it must also be poured quickly from the pan.

PEPPERMINT CREAMS

8 oz. ($1\frac{1}{2}$ cups) icing   **$\frac{1}{2}$ teaspoon ($\frac{2}{3}$) peppermint oil or**
** (confectioner's) sugar**   ** essence**
pinch of tartaric acid   **1 egg white**

Sieve the sugar and tartaric acid, add the peppermint oil and enough of the egg white to make a moderately firm paste. Roll this out on a board, lightly sprinkled with sieved icing sugar to about a scant $\frac{1}{4}$-in. thick. Cut into rounds or ovals, place on greaseproof paper and leave overnight. Turn a couple or more times to allow the creams to dry on both sides. Other flavours can be used instead of the peppermint, and the fondant can be coloured. But peppermint creams are probably the most successful to make, also the most popular.

CREAM CANDY

1 lb. (2 cups) sugar   **2 oz. (4 tablespoons) butter**
$\frac{1}{4}$ lb. (1 cup) liquid glucose   **$\frac{3}{4}$ cup (1) cream**
1 cup ($1\frac{1}{4}$) water

Line a 6-in. shallow baking pan with greaseproof paper. Put the sugar with the glucose and water into a pan and over a low heat let it dissolve, stirring continuously. Bring to the boil until it reaches 250°F. (121°C.) and then slightly lower the heat and add the butter and cream. Return the pan to the heat and bring it again to the boil and, stirring continuously with a spatula, boil slowly for 8–10 minutes.

Remove the spatula and let the mixture boil quickly until it again reaches 240°F. (116°C.). (Still go on stirring but this time with the thermometer.) Take at once from the heat and stir with the spatula until the mixture seems to become cloudy, thick and creamy. Spread it at once into the prepared pan and let it set. Cut into squares and wrap in greaseproof paper.

GINGER CANDY

¾ lb. (1½ cups) sugar
¼ pint (⅓ cup) milk
1 teaspoon (1¼) liquid glucose

1 oz. (2 tablespoons) butter
4 oz. (½ cup) preserved ginger
ginger syrup to taste

Put the sugar with the milk into a pan and dissolve over a low heat. Add the glucose and butter, mix well and bring to the boil until it reaches 240°F. (116°C.). Add the preserved ginger and syrup, about 1 tablespoon (1¼) of the latter should be enough. Stir gently and bring once more to the boil, this time to 250°F. (121°C.). Pour this mixture into a bowl previously rinsed with cold water. Leave for 10 minutes. Beat with a wooden spoon until thick and creamy. Cover with greaseproof paper and a towel and leave for 20 minutes. Form into a cake about ½-in. thick and leave until quite cold, then cut into squares. For storing, wrap in greaseproof paper or put into a box lined with greaseproof paper.

COCONUT ICE

1 lb. (2 cups) granulated sugar
¼ pint (½ cup) water
a pinch of cream of tartar

6 oz. (2 cups) desiccated coconut
cochineal

Line an 8-in. shallow baking pan with greaseproof paper. Put the sugar and water into a pan and over a low heat dissolve the sugar. Add the cream of tartar. Bring to the boil slowly, stirring all the time until it reaches 240°F. (116°C.) or the firm ball stage. Take from the heat and stir in the coconut all at once. Pour half into the prepared pan and leave to set. With great care lightly colour this with cochineal and spread this over the white portion. Let it cool, cut into blocks and wrap in greaseproof paper.

TURKISH DELIGHT (*Lokum*)

1 lb. (2 cups) sugar
½ pint (1¼ cups) water
1 tablespoon (1¼) rosewater

3 oz. (scant ½ cup) cornflour
    (cornstarch)
almond or other sweet oil

Mix the sugar and water and cook this over a low heat until the sugar is dissolved. Bring to the boil and continue until it is a thick syrup. Stir frequently. Mix the rosewater with the cornflour and add enough water to make a thin paste. Stir this into the boiling syrup, stirring all the time until the mixture becomes very thick. It will look transparent. Take it from the pan and pour into a pan generously rubbed with almond oil, a shallow square cake pan will do. Leave to cool and then chill. Cut into squares and roll in icing (confectioner's) sugar. If a pink lokum is preferred, add a few drops of cochineal, not too much.

MARSHMALLOWS

2 tablespoons (2 envelopes)
   gelatine
1 cup (1¼) water
orange-flower water to taste

10 oz. (1¼ cups) sugar
1 dessertspoon (1 tablespoon)
liquid glucose
1 egg white
icing (confectioner's) sugar

Put the gelatine, half the water and the orange-flower water into a pan over a low heat. Stir well until the gelatine is dissolved and then put aside. In another pan put the remaining water, sugar and glucose and cook over a low heat, stirring frequently, until the sugar dissolves. Bring to the boil until it reaches 260°F. (125°C.). Bring the pan with the gelatine once more to the stove and gently re-heat. Pour the boiling sugar syrup over it, beating all the time with a whisk. Beat for 2 minutes, add the egg white and continue whisking until the mixture is white and stiff; this will take about 15 minutes. Leave the marshmallow in the pan for 30 minutes, loosen the mixture round the sides of the pan with a palette knife and turn out on to a large board sprinkled generously with sifted icing sugar. Leave on the board for 2 hours, rub icing sugar over the surface and then cut the marshmallows into cubes. Leave them in a warm room exposed to the air for 2 days, then store in a box lined with greaseproof paper. Other flavours instead of orange flower may be used: vanilla, raspberry or strawberry, coffee, even ground almonds, hazelnuts or rosewater.

ALMOND TOFFEE

4 oz. (1 cup) unblanched almonds
butter
1 lb. (2 cups) soft brown sugar
¾ cup (1) water
pinch of cream of tartar

1 tablespoon (1¼) golden syrup
1 tablespoon (1¼) treacle or
molasses
1 teaspoon (1¼) lemon juice

Blanch the almonds, cut into slivers and dry them in a cool oven. Rub a shallow baking tin approximately 8-in. square generously with butter. Spread this with the dried almonds. Put the sugar into a pan, add the water and stir over a low heat until the sugar is dissolved. Add the cream of tartar, golden syrup and treacle. Bring to a quick boil and boil rapidly until the toffee is a deep amber colour and when a little dropped into a saucer of cold water sets and does not stick to the teeth when tested. Add the lemon juice but do not stir. Pour the toffee at once over the almonds in the pan. When the toffee is beginning to set, mark it into small squares with a knife. Let it get quite cold, break off into squares and wrap in wax paper.

BUTTERSCOTCH

½ lb. (1 cup) sugar
½ lb. (1 cup) butter

½ lb. (2 cups) liquid glucose
½ pint (1¼ cups) cream

Rub a large square or rectangular shallow baking pan with butter. Put all the ingredients together into a pan and dissolve over a slow heat, stirring all the time to prevent burning. It is important the heat is very, very low otherwise the butterscotch will burn. When the mixture is completely dissolved, raise the heat and, stirring all the time, bring to the boil 280°F. (139°C.). Pour into the prepared pan and let it just begin to set. Mark it into squares with a knife and leave until cold. Break up into squares and wrap in greaseproof paper.

GOOSEBERRY CHIPS

1 lb. gooseberries

½ lb. (1½ cups) cube sugar

Put the gooseberries which should be unripe, green but fully grown, into a pan and boil until quite soft. Then slowly and gently add the sugar. Pour into saucers, and dry in the sun or in England where there is little sun, in front of the fire or in a low oven. When sufficiently dry cut into strips and twist into fanciful shapes. They keep well in tins packed between layers of paper.

BLACK TREACLE TOFFEE

¼ lb. (½ cup) butter
¼ lb. (½ cup) black treacle
6 oz. (¾ cup) soft brown sugar
2–3 tablespoons (2½ – 3¾) water

pinch of cream of tartar
2 oz. (⅓ cup) blanched and chopped
  almonds

Rub a square shallow baking pan generously with butter. Put the butter, treacle, sugar and water into a pan and over a moderate heat dissolve the sugar, stirring all the time. Bring to the boil, add the cream of tartar and let it boil for 5 minutes. Add the almonds. Pour into the prepared pan and when it is beginning to set, cut into small squares with a knife. Let the toffee get cold and harden, break up the squares and wrap in wax paper. Or, if preferred, the toffee can be allowed to set in one large sheet and then be smashed into irregular pieces with a kitchen hammer.

BARLEY SUGAR

1 lb. (2 cups) sugar
¼ lb. (1 cup) liquid glucose
½ cup (⅔) water

1 – 2 thin strips lemon rind
1 tablespoon (1¼) lemon juice
yellow colouring

To make barley sugar successfully a marble slab, generously oiled, is a help but if this is not available it can be set on a large porcelain or china platter. Mix the sugar, glucose and water in a large pan and cook over a low heat until the sugar is dissolved. Add the lemon rind and juice and raise the heat. When the syrup is at 200°F. (93°C.) take from the heat. Discard the lemon rind and add just enough yellow colouring to give a pale lemon colour. Pour the mixture on to the oiled slab or platter and fold the sides gently into the centre with an oiled palette knife. Leave to almost set and then cut into strips about 1 in. wide and twist each piece, like a screw. Leave to harden. Break into even lengths 3–4 in. long. As the barley sugar hardens quickly it is as well to have some assistance in the twisting of the strips. The barley sugar can be stored in airtight jars or polythene bags.

CONCLUSION

I feel that I cannot close this book without an account of the beginning of my little business, which first opened on January 4, 1939.

I left home very early indeed and walked to the nearest Underground station, where I bought a workman's ticket. I emerged from the station at Leicester Square and started to walk in the direction of Soho. It was quite dark and bitterly cold.

I felt frozen and my heart was an icy lump in my chest. I walked in the darkness. It seemed an endless journey, looking for the right turning. The streets were empty and I was lost. Suddenly I noticed a silhouette. I was pleased, stopped in the dark and asked the way. I could not see the face but a pleasant young voice said, 'I am sorry but I don't know the way. It is so dark and cold, wouldn't you like to come and have a cup of tea with me?' Suddenly I felt better, happy and cheerful. I answered the kind young man that I was in a hurry and couldn't stop but thanked him all the same. Then I went briskly on my way. It was a very long time since a strange man had invited me to tea. Suddenly the darkness lifted; in no time I found the right street and found myself in my own bakery. In a strong, cheerful voice I called for the lift. The lift came, I pressed the button, I entered and went up to the workroom. There I found my six bakers had already started work. That was the beginning of my first day. I was confident, I was self-assured, I knew that I would succeed.

I would like to leave you with a story from my youth. It is appropriate to a book on bread and bakery because it shows what a big part this plays in our lives. It happened to me in my courting days. One evening the man who wished to be my husband walked me home. We went on talking in the doorway of my house. He was standing with his back to the door, blocking my way. I wanted to go in, but he pleaded for yet one more minute and then one more again. His eyes were shining and my heart was beating, but in the end I was firm and said a quick goodnight and went indoors. It was pretty late and I went straight to my own room. I went to bed but could not sleep. I had a bad conscience about keeping him so long in suspense, I hated myself; I decided that I would tell him next day that I would marry him. I waited impatiently for the morning, for our next meeting. When he came at last, charming, pleasant, interesting, good humoured as always, my first question was, 'tell me how did you go home last night?' He answered with a big smile, 'I didn't walk, I ran all the way, I was suddenly so desperately hungry. I rushed to the kitchen, cut three or four slices of bread, toasted them quickly, spread them with butter and sat down and ate them there and then'. Was there ever such an anti-climax? But it all was right in the end for me as I hope you will find trying these recipes. Your success will be my reward.

Comparative Cookery Terms and Measures

BRITISH MEASURES	AMERICAN MEASURES	AMERICAN CUP EQUIVALENTS
	Liquid Measures	
1 teaspoon	1¼ teaspoons	
1 tablespoon	1¼ tablespoons	
1 fluid ounce	1 fluid ounce or 2 tablespoons	
2 fluid ounces	2 fluid ounces or 4 tablespoons	¼ cup
2⅔ fluid ounces	5⅓ tablespoons	⅓ cup
4 fluid ounces	8 tablespoons	½ cup
5⅓ fluid ounces	10⅔ tablespoons	⅔ cup
8 fluid ounces	8 fluid ounces or ½ U.S. pint	1 cup
10 fluid ounces or ½ Imperial pint	10 fluid ounces	1¼ cups
16 fluid ounces	1 U.S. pint	2 cups
20 fluid ounces or 1 Imperial pint	1¼ U.S. pints	2½ cups
1⅗ Imperial pints	2 U.S. pints or 1 U.S. quart	4 cups
2 Imperial pints or 1 Imperial quart	2½ U.S. pints	5 cups
6⅖ Imperial pints	8 U.S. pints or 1 U.S. gallon	16 cups
8 Imperial pints or 1 Imperial gallon	10 U.S. pints	20 cups

British and American Equivalent Ingredients

BRITISH	AMERICAN
Icing sugar	Confectioners sugar
Cornflour	Cornstarch
Sultanas	Raisins
Rusk	Zwiebach
Single cream	Light cream
Double cream	Heavy cream
Bicarbonate of soda	Baking soda
Scone	Biscuit
Soft brown sugar	Brown sugar
100 per cent wholemeal flour	Graham flour
Digestive biscuits	Graham crackers
Trex or Spry	Soft shortening
Butter or margarine	Shortening
1 oz. cooking chocolate	1 square chocolate
$\frac{2}{3}$ oz. bakers yeast, or	
3 level teaspoonfuls dried yeast	1 cake yeast
Okra	Gumbo
$\frac{1}{3}$ oz. powdered gelatine, or 1 level tablespoonful	1 envelope gelatine
Caster sugar	Granulated sugar
Biscuit	Cookie or Cracker
Minced meat	Ground meat
2 oz. egg (standard)	2 oz. egg (large)

Equivalent Gas and Electric Oven Temperatures

GAS	$\frac{1}{4}$	$\frac{1}{2}$	1	2	3	4	5	6	7	8	9
ELECTRICITY	240°	265°	290°	310°	335°	355°	380°	400°	425°	445°	470°

1 British fluid ounce is equal to 1 U.S. fluid ounce
British Standard Measuring Cup is equivalent to 10 fluid ounces
American Standard Measuring Cup is equivalent to 8 fluid ounces

In general British and American solid weights are equivalent

Throughout this book British measurements are given first : the American equivalents for both solids and liquids follow in brackets

Vintage Chart

YEAR	CLARET	BURGUNDY	WHITE BURGUNDY	SAUTERNES	RHONE	RHINE	MOSELLE	CHAMPAGNE	PORT	LOIRE
1945	7	6	—	6	7	—	—	5	7	—
1946	1	1	—	2	5	—	—	—	—	—
1947	5	6	—	6	6	—	—	6	7	—
1948	5	5	—	5	4	—	—	—	7	—
1949	6	5	—	5	7	—	—	6	—	—
1950	5	3	—	6	6	—	—	—	6	—
1951	0	1	—	2	4	—	—	—	—	—
1952	6	5	5	6	6	5	4	7	4	—
1953	6	5	4	5	6	7	6	6	—	—
1954	4	3	1	2	7	2	2	—	6	—
1955	6	5	4	6	6	5	4	6	7	—
1956	0	1	1	2	5	1	1	—	—	—
1957	5	5	5	4	7	4	4	—	5	—
1958	4	3	4	4	5	5	5	—	6	—
1959	6	7	6	6	6	7	7	7	—	6
1960	4	1	1	3	6	2	2	—	7	2
1961	7	7	7	5	7	5	4	7	—	5
1962	6	5	6	6	6	3	3	6	5	4
1963	1	4	3	2	5	3	2	—	7	1
1964	6	7	7	5	6	6	7	—	7	7
1965	0	1	2	2	5	1	1	—	4	1
1966	6	7	7	6	6	6	6	—	7	5
1967	5	5	7	5	6	5	4	—	6	6
1968	1	1	1	0	5	1	1	—	—	3

0 = No Good   7 = The Best

Fresh Food in its Best Season

	JANUARY	FEBRUARY	MARCH	APRIL	MAY	JUNE	JULY	AUGUST	SEPTEMBER	OCTOBER	NOVEMBER	DECEMBER
MEAT												
Beef	x	x	x	x	x	x	x	x	x	x	x	x
Veal		x	x	x	x	x						
Spring lamb					x	x	x	x	x			
Fed lamb	x	x	x	x						x	x	x
Pork	x	x	x	x	x	x				x	x	x
POULTRY												
Chicken	x	x	x	x	x	x	x	x	x	x	x	x
Duck	x	x	x	x	x	x	x	x	x	x	x	x
Turkey	x	x	x	x	x	x	x	x	x	x	x	x
FISH												
Bass	x	x	x	x	x	x	x	x	x	x	x	x
Carp	x	x	x	x	x	x	x	x	x	x	x	x
Cod	x	x	x	x	x	x	x	x	x	x	x	x
Dab	x	x	x	x	x	x	x	x	x	x	x	x
Eel	x	x	x	x	x	x	x	x	x	x	x	x
Flounder	x	x	x	x	x	x	x	x	x	x	x	x
(Grey) mullet	x	x	x	x	x	x	x	x	x	x	x	x
Haddock	x	x	x	x	x	x	x	x	x	x	x	x
Hake	x	x	x	x	x	x	x	x	x	x	x	x
Halibut	x	x	x	x	x	x	x	x	x	x	x	x
Herring	x	x	x	x	x	x	x	x	x	x	x	x
Lemon-sole	x	x	x	x				x	x	x	x	x
Mackerel				x	x	x	x	x	x	x	x	x
Pilchard	x	x	x	x	x	x	x	x	x	x	x	x
Salmon	x	x	x	x	x	x	x	x	x	x	x	x
Sardine				x	x	x	x	x	x	x	x	x
Sole	x	x	x	x	x	x	x	x	x	x	x	x
Trout	x	x	x	x	x	x	x	x	x	x	x	x
Whiting				x	x	x	x	x	x	x	x	

	JANUARY	FEBRUARY	MARCH	APRIL	MAY	JUNE	JULY	AUGUST	SEPTEMBER	OCTOBER	NOVEMBER	DECEMBER
CRUSTACEANS												
Crab	x	x	x	x	x	x	x	x	x	x	x	x
Lobster	x	x	x	x	x	x	x	x	x	x	x	x
Prawns – Shrimp	x	x	x	x	x	x	x	x	x	x	x	x
MOLLUSCS												
Mussel	x	x	x	x	x	x	x	x	x	x	x	x
Oyster	x	x	x	x					x	x	x	x
Scallop	x	x	x	x	x	x	x	x	x	x	x	x
Clams	x	x	x	x	x	x	x	x	x	x	x	x
FRUIT AND VEGETABLES												
Anise	x									x	x	x
Apples										x	x	x
Apricots						x	x					
Artichokes	x	x	x	x	x						x	x
Asparagus				x	x	x						
Avocados	x	x	x	x	x	x	x	x	x	x	x	x
Beans, Lima							x	x	x	x		
Beans, green			x	x	x	x	x	x				
Beets					x	x	x	x	x	x		
Blackberries						x						
Dewberries						x						
Loganberries						x						
Blueberries						x	x	x				
Huckleberries						x	x	x				
Broccoli	x	x	x							x	x	x
Brussels sprouts	x									x	x	x
Cabbage	x	x	x	x	x					x	x	x
Cantaloupes						x	x	x	x			
Carrots (home-grown)								x	x	x	x	
Cauliflower (home-grown)									x	x	x	x
Celery	x	x	x	x	x						x	x
Cherries					x	x	x					
Collards	x	x	x								x	x
Corn						x	x	x				
Cranberries										x	x	x
Cucumbers					x	x	x	x				
Currants							x					

FRUIT AND VEGETABLES (*continued*)	JANUARY	FEBRUARY	MARCH	APRIL	MAY	JUNE	JULY	AUGUST	SEPTEMBER	OCTOBER	NOVEMBER	DECEMBER
Eggplant							x	x	x	x		
Endive and Escarole								x	x	x		
Grapefruit (imported)	x	x	x	x						x	x	x
Grapes (home-grown)								x	x	x		
Kale					x	x			x	x		
Lettuce					x	x	x					
Melon (Cantaloupe)						x	x	x				
Mushrooms	x	x	x	x					x	x	x	x
Mustard Greens	x	x	x									
Okra							x	x	x	x		
Onions, dry	x	x	x						x	x	x	x
Onions, green				x	x	x	x	x				
Oranges	x	x	x	x	x							
Parsley	x	x	x	x	x	x	x	x	x	x	x	x
Parsnips	x	x	x							x	x	x
Peaches						x	x	x	x			
Pears								x	x	x	x	
Peas, green				x	x	x	x					
Peppers								x	x	x	x	
Persians								x	x	x		
Plums						x	x	x	x			
Potatoes	x	x	x	x	x	x	x	x	x	x	x	x
Sweet potatoes	x								x	x	x	x
Pumpkins										x		
Radishes			x	x	x	x	x					
Raspberries						x	x	x				
Rhubarb			x	x	x	x						
Shallots	x	x	x	x								x
Spinach			x	x	x	x						
Squash									x	x	x	x
Strawberries				x	x	x	x					
Tangerines	x										x	x
Tomatoes						x	x	x	x	x		
Turnips and Rutabagas	x	x	x							x	x	x
Watermelons						x	x	x				

INDEX

235